THE KEY

STUDENT STUDY GUIDE

THE KEY

THE KEY series of student study guides is specifically designed to assist students in preparing for unit tests, provincial achievement tests, and diploma examinations. Each **KEY** includes questions, answers, detailed solutions, and practice tests. The complete solutions show problem-solving methods, explain key concepts, and highlight potential errors.

TABLE OF CORRELATIONS

Castle Rock Research has designed **THE KEY** by correlating every question and its solution to Alberta Education's curriculum outcomes. Each unit of review begins with a Table of Correlations that lists the General and Specific Outcomes from the Alberta curriculum along with Related Questions that correspond to the outcomes. Usually the emphasis placed on outcomes, concepts, and skills within each unit varies. Students and teachers can quickly identify the relevant importance of each outcome and concept in the unit as determined by the number of related questions provided in **THE KEY**.

For grades 3, 6, 9, and 12, the weighting of each unit and concept is determined by analyzing the blueprint for the respective provincial achievement tests and diploma examinations. Based on this analysis, the Related Questions for outcomes and concepts are organized on a proportionate basis. For grades other than 3, 6, 9, and 12, the breakdown of each course is determined by consulting with experienced teachers and by reviewing curriculum guides and textbooks.

The Table of Correlations is a critical component of **THE KEY**. For students, it offers a visual cue for effectively organizing study time. For teachers, the Table of Correlations indicates the instructional focus for each content strand, serves as a curriculum checklist, and focuses on the outcomes and concepts that are the most important in the unit and the particular course of study. Students become "test wise" by becoming familiar with exam and question formats used most often in provincial examinations.

Canadian Cataloguing in Publication Data

Rao, Gautam, 1961 –
THE KEY – Math 9 AB   (2009 Edition)

    1.   Mathematics – Juvenile Literature. I. Title

Published by
Castle Rock Research Corp.
2340 Manulife Place
10180 – 101 Street
Edmonton, AB T5J 3S4

6 7 8 FP 08 07 06

Printed in Canada

Publisher
Gautam Rao

Contributor
Earl Wolff
Anthony Walsh

Dedicated to the memory of Dr. V. S. Rao

THE KEY – MATH 9

THE KEY for Math 9 is a resource designed specifically to conform to the Western Canadian Protocol and to supplement classroom instruction. It provides a collection of multiple-choice questions pertaining to the four sections defined in the Protocol: *Number Concepts*, *Patterns and Relations*, *Shape and Space*, and *Statistics and Probability*. The questions provide a complete set of illustrative examples of the general and specific outcomes for each unit. A **Table of Correlations** at the beginning of each chapter lists the learner expectations and related questions within the unit. Concepts are tested in a variety of ways, with the distribution of questions based on the weighting of each outcome.

To help students prepare for their final exam, two previously administered Provincial Achievement Tests are included. **Complete solutions** for all questions are provided to assist students in understanding the concepts and problem solving processes used to arrive at the correct answer.

THE KEY is organized into the following sections.

 I   ***KEY Factors Contributing to School Success*** provides students with examples of study and review strategies. Topics include information on learning styles, study schedules, and developing review notes.

 II ***Unit Review*** includes a section on each of the four areas of the Protocol. The questions in each unit provide students with an excellent source of course related material that can be used for review and to prepare for unit tests. Working through these exercises should help students reinforce the course material and identify those areas that may require more study. Questions range from fairly easy to more difficult, with the majority of questions being moderate. The more difficult questions are identified as *Challenger*. *Challenger* questions are intended to help students become familiar with the depth of knowledge required to achieve at the standard of excellence.

 III ***KEY Strategies for Success on Exams*** explores topics such as common exam question formats and strategies for responding, directing words most commonly used, how to begin the exam, and managing test anxiety.

 IV The ***Provincial Achievement Test*** section includes the 2000 and 2001 Provincial Achievement Tests. Students may use these as practice tests to become familiar with the format and rigor of the final exam. Answers and complete solutions are provided.

THE KEY Study Guides are available for Language Arts 9, Mathematics 9, Science 9, and Social Studies 9. A complete list of the **THE KEY** Study Guides available for grades 3 to 12 is included at the back of this book.

For information about any of our resources or services, please call Castle Rock Research at 780.448.9619 or visit our web site at http://www.castlerockresearch.com.

At Castle Rock Research, we strive to produce a resource that is error-free. If you should find an error, please contact us so that future editions can be corrected.

CONTENTS

KEY FACTORS CONTRIBUTING TO SCHOOL SUCCESS

UNIT REVIEW

ANSWERS AND SOLUTIONS

KEY STRATEGIES FOR SUCCESS ON EXAMS

PROVINCIAL ACHIEVEMENT TESTS

ANSWERS AND SOLUTIONS

APPENDICES

CREDITS

NOTES

KEY FACTORS CONTRIBUTING TO SCHOOL SUCCESS

NOTES

KEY FACTORS CONTRIBUTING TO SCHOOL SUCCESS

You want to do well in school. There are many factors that contribute to your success. While you may not have control over the number or types of assignments and tests that you need to complete, there are many factors that you can control to improve your academic success in any subject area. The following are examples of these factors.

- **REGULAR CLASS ATTENDANCE** – helps you to master the subject content, identify key concepts, take notes and receive important handouts, ask your teacher questions, clarify information, use school resources, and meet students with whom you can study

- **POSITIVE ATTITUDE AND PERSONAL DISCIPLINE** – helps you to come to classes on time, prepared to work and learn, complete all assignments to the best of your ability, and contribute to a positive learning environment

- **SELF-MOTIVATION AND PERSONAL DISCIPLINE** – helps you to set personal learning goals, take small steps continually moving toward achieving your goals, and to "stick it out when the going gets tough"

- **ACCESSING ASSISTANCE WHEN YOU NEED IT** – helps you to improve or clarify your understanding of the concept or new learning before moving on to the next phase

- **MANAGING YOUR TIME EFFICIENTLY** – helps you to reduce anxiety and focus your study and review efforts on the most important concepts

- **DEVELOPING 'TEST WISENESS'** – helps to increase your confidence in writing exams if you are familiar with the typical exam format, common errors to avoid, and know how the concepts in a subject area are usually tested

- **KNOWING YOUR PERSONAL LEARNING STYLE** – helps you to maximize your learning by using effective study techniques, developing meaningful study notes, and make the most efficient use of your study time

📖 KNOW YOUR LEARNING STYLE

You have a unique learning style. Knowing your learning style – how you learn best – can help you to maximize your time in class and during your exam preparation. There are seven common learning styles. Read the following descriptions to see which one most closely describes your learning preferences.

• **LINGUISTIC LEARNER** (sometimes referred to as an auditory learner) – learns best by saying, hearing and seeing words; is good at memorizing things such as dates, places, names and facts

• **LOGICAL/MATHEMATICAL LEARNER** – learns best by categorizing, classifying and working with abstract relationships; is good at mathematics, problem solving and reasoning

• **SPATIAL LEARNER** (sometimes referred to as a visual learner) – learns best by visualizing, seeing, working with pictures; is good at puzzles, imaging things, and reading maps and charts

• **MUSICAL LEARNER** – learns best by hearing, rhythm, melody, and music; is good at remembering tones, rhythms and melodies, picking up sounds

• **BODILY/KINAESTHETIC LEARNER** – learns best by touching, moving, and processing knowledge through bodily sensations; is good at physical activities

• **INTERPERSONAL LEARNER** – learns best by sharing, comparing, relating, cooperating; is good at organizing, communicating, leading, and understanding others

• **INTRAPERSONAL LEARNER** – learns best by working alone, individualized projects, and self-paced instruction

(Adapted from http://snow.utoronto.ca/Learn2/mod3/mistyles.html)

Your learning style may not fit "cleanly" into one specific category but may be a combination of two or more styles. Knowing your personal learning style allows you to organize your study notes in a manner that provides you with the most meaning. For example, if you are a spatial or visual learner, you may find mind mapping and webbing are effective ways to organize subject concepts, information, and study notes. If you are a linguistic learner, you may need to write and then "say out loud" the steps in a process, the formula, or actions that lead up to a significant event. If you are a kinaesthetic learner, you may need to use your finger to trace over a diagram to remember it or to "tap out" the steps in solving a problem or "feel" yourself writing or typing the formula.

📖 SCHEDULING STUDY TIME

Effective time management skills are an essential component to your academic success. The more effectively you manage your time the more likely you are to achieve your goals such as completing all of your assignments on time or finishing all of the questions on a unit test or year-end exam. Developing a study schedule helps to ensure you have adequate time to review the subject content and prepare for the exam.

You should review your class notes regularly to ensure you have a clear understanding of the new material. Reviewing your lessons on a regular basis helps you to learn and remember the ideas and concepts. It also reduces the quantity of material that you must study prior to a unit test or year-end exam. If this practice is not part of your study habits, establishing a study schedule will help you to make the best use of your time. The following are brief descriptions of three types of study schedules.

- **LONG-TERM STUDY SCHEDULE** – begins early in the school year or semester and well in advance of an exam; is the **most effective** manner for improving your understanding and retention of the concepts, and increasing self-confidence; involves regular, nightly review of class notes, handouts and text material

- **SHORT-TERM STUDY SCHEDULE** – begins **five to seven days prior to an exam**; must organize the volume of material to be covered beginning with the most difficult concepts; each study session starts with a brief review of what was studied the day before

- **CRAMMING** – occurs the night before an exam; is the **least effective** form of studying or exam preparation; focuses on memorizing and reviewing critical information such as facts, dates, formulas; do not introduce new material; has the potential to increase exam anxiety by discovering something you do not know

Regardless of the type of study schedule you use, you may want to consider the following to maximize your study time and effort:

- establish a regular time and place for doing your studying

- minimize distractions and interruptions during your study time

- plan a ten minute break for every hour that you study

- organize the material so you begin with the most challenging content first

- divide the subject content into smaller manageable "chunks" to review

- develop a marking system for your study notes to identify key and secondary concepts, concepts that you are confident about, those that require additional attention or about which you have questions

- reward yourself for sticking to your schedule and/or completing each review section

- alternate the subjects and type of study activities to maintain your interest and motivation

- make a daily task list with the headings "must do", "should do", and "could do"

- begin each session by quickly reviewing what you studied the day before

- maintain your usual routine of eating, sleeping, and exercising to help you concentrate for extended periods of time

KEY STRATEGIES FOR REVIEWING

Reviewing textbook material, class notes, and handouts should be an ongoing activity and becomes more critical in preparing for exams. You may find some of the following strategies useful in completing your review during your scheduled study time.

READING OR SKIMMING FOR KEY INFORMATION

- Before reading the chapter, preview it by noting headings, charts and graphs, chapter questions.

- Turn each heading and sub-heading into a question before you start to read.

- Read the complete introduction to identify the key information that is addressed in the chapter.

- Read the first sentence of the next paragraph for the main idea.

- Skim the paragraph noting key words, phrases, and information.

- Read the last sentence of the paragraph.

- Repeat the process for each paragraph and section until you have skimmed the entire chapter.

- Read the complete conclusion to summarize each chapter's contents.

- Answer the questions you created.

- Answer the chapter questions.

CREATING STUDY NOTES

Mind Mapping or Webbing

- Use the key words, ideas, or concepts from your reading or class notes to create a *mind map or web* (a diagram or visual representation of the information). A mind map or web is sometimes referred to as a knowledge map.

- Write the key word, concept, theory, or formula in the centre of your page.

- Write and link related facts, ideas, events, and information to the central concept using lines.

- Use coloured markers, underlining, or other symbols to emphasize things such as relationships, information of primary and secondary importance.

- The following example of a mind map or web illustrates how this technique can be used to develop an essay.

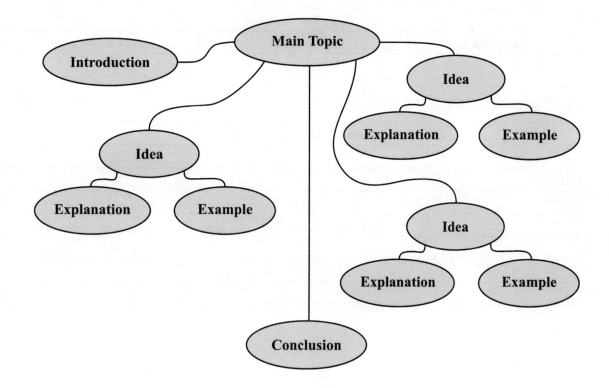

Charts

- ♦ Use charts to organize your information and relate theories, concepts, definitions, applications, and other important details.

- ♦ Collect and enter the information in key categories.

- ♦ Use the completed chart as a composite picture of the concept or information.

The following is an example of how a chart can be used to help you organize information when exploring an issue in subjects such as Social Studies, the Sciences, or Humanities.

Define Key Words		
1.		
2.		
3.		
Explore the Issue		
Yes to the Issue	**No** to the Issue	**Maybe** to the Issue
1.	1.	1.
2.	2.	2.
3.	3.	3.
Case Studies and **Examples**		
1.	1.	
2.	2.	
3.	3.	
Defense of Your Point of View		
1.		
2.		
3.		

Index Cards

♦ Write a key event, fact, concept, theory, word, or question on one side of the index card.

♦ On the reverse side, write the date, place, important actions and key individuals involved in the event, significance of the fact, salient features of the concept, essence, and application of the theory, definition of the word or answer to the question.

♦ Use the cards to quickly review important information.

International System of Units (SI)

International System of Units (SI)

SI base unit

Base quantity	Name	Symbol
length	metre	m
mass	kilogram	kg
time	second	s
amount of substance	mole	mol

SI Prefixes

Factor	Name	Symbol
10^6	mega	M
10^3	kilo	k
10^{-2}	centi	c
10^{-3}	milli	m
10^{-6}	micro	μ

Derived Measures

Measures	Unit	Symbol
volume	cubic metre	m^3

Symbols

♦ Develop your own symbols to use when reviewing your material to identify information you need in preparing for your exam. For example, an exclamation mark (!) may signify something that "must be learned well" because it is a key concept that is likely to appear on unit tests and the year-end exam. A question mark (?) may identify something you are unsure of while a star or asterisk (*) may identify important information for formulating an argument.

A check mark (✓) or an (✗) can be used to show that you agree or disagree with the statement, sentence, or paragraph.

Crib Notes

- Develop brief notes that are a critical summary of the essential concepts, dates, events, theories, formulas, supporting facts, or steps in a process that are most likely to be on the exam.

- Use your crib notes as your "last minute" review before you go in to write your exam. You can not take crib notes into an exam.

MEMORIZING

- **ASSOCIATION** relates the new learning to something you already know. For example, in distinguishing between the spelling of 'dessert' and 'desert', you know 'sand' has only one 's' and so should desert.

- **MNEMONIC DEVICES** are sentences you create to remember a list or group of items. For example, the first letters of the words in the sentence "**E**very **G**ood **B**oy **D**eserves **F**udge" helps you to remember the names of the lines on the treble clef staff (E, G, B, D, and F) in music.

- **ACRONYMS** are words formed from the first letters of the words in a group. For example, **HOMES** helps you to remember the names of the five Great Lakes (**H**uron, **O**ntario, **M**ichigan, **E**rie, and **S**uperior).

- **VISUALIZING** requires you to use your mind's eye to "see" the chart, list, map, diagram, or sentence as it exists in your textbook, notes, on the board, computer screen or in the display.

Number Concepts

Natural

Rational

Integers

Whole

NUMBER CONCEPTS

Table of Correlations		
General Outcome	**Specific Outcome**	**Questions**
Students are expected to:		
Explain and illustrate the structure and the interrelationship of the sets of numbers within the rational number system.	1. Give examples of numbers that satisfy the conditions of natural, whole, integral, and rational numbers, and show that these numbers comprise the rational number system.	1, 2, 4, 5, 8
	2. Describe, orally, and in writing, whether or not a number is rational.	6, 7, 9
	3. Give examples of situations where answers would involve the positive (principal) square root, or both positive and negative square roots of a number.	3, 11
Develop a number sense of powers with integral exponents and rational bases.	4. Illustrate power, base, coefficient, and exponent, using rational numbers or variables as bases or coefficients.	12, 14, 15, NR1, WR1
	5. Explain and apply the Exponent Laws for powers with integral exponents. $x^m \times x^n = x^{m+n}$ $x^m \div x^n = x^{m-n}$ $\left(x^m\right)^n = x^{mn}$ $\left(xy\right)^m = x^m y^m$ $\left(\dfrac{x}{y}\right)^n = \dfrac{x^n}{y^n}, \; y \neq 0$ $x^0 = 1, \; x \neq 0$ $x^{-n} = \dfrac{1}{x^n}, \; x \neq 0$	16, 17, 18, 19, 20, 21, NR2, 22, 23, NR11
	6. Determine the value of powers with integral exponents, using the Exponent Laws.	15, 37, 42, WR1
Use a scientific calculator or a computer to solve problems involving rational numbers.	7. Document and explain the calculator keying sequences used to perform calculations involving rational numbers.	10, 47, WR1
	8. Solve problems, using rational numbers, in meaningful contexts.	13, 24, 25, 26, 27, 28, NR3, 30, 31, NR4, NR5, 40, 41, NR6, WR2
Explain how exponents can be used to bring meaning to large and small numbers, and use calculators or computers to perform calculations involving these numbers.	9. Understand and use the Exponent Laws to simplify expressions with variable bases and evaluate expressions with numerical bases.	29, 32, 33, 34, 35, 36, 38, 39, 43, 44, NR7, NR8, 52
	10. Use calculators to perform calculations involving scientific notation and Exponent Laws.	NR9, 45, 46, NR10, 48, 49, 50, 51

In this unit, students are required to know the definitions of different sets of numbers. They are also required to explain and apply the exponent laws for powers. A brief overview is provided below.

DEFINITIONS

Natural Numbers (*N*)
  are counting numbers {1, 2, 3, ...}.
Whole Numbers (*W*)
  are all natural numbers and 0 {0, 1, 2, 3, ...}.
Integers (*I*)
  are all negative and positive numbers and 0 {..., –3, –2, –1, 0, 1, 2, 3 ...}.
Rational Numbers (*Q*)
  are all numbers that can be expressed in the form $\frac{a}{b}$, where *a* and *b* are integers and $b \neq 0$.
Irrational Numbers ($\overline{Q}$)
  are numbers that can only be represented by a non-repeating, non-terminating decimal.

EXPONENT LAWS FOR POWERS

$x^m \times x^n = x^{m+n} \rightarrow$ When powers with similar bases are multiplied, the exponents are added together.

$x^m \div x^n = x^{m-n} \rightarrow$ When powers with similar bases are divided, the exponents are subtracted.

$(x^m)^n = x^{mn} \rightarrow$ The exponents are multiplied.

$(xy)^m = x^m y^m \rightarrow$ The exponent is applied to each variable in the base.

$\left(\dfrac{x}{y}\right)^n = \dfrac{x^n}{y^n}; y \neq 0 \rightarrow$ The exponent is applied to the numerator and the denominator.

$x^0 = 1; x \neq 0 \rightarrow$ Any number raised to the exponent 0 is equal to 1.

$x^{-n} = \dfrac{1}{x^n}; x \neq 0 \rightarrow$ When a number is raised to a negative exponent, it can be represented as 1 over the number raised to a positive exponent.

1. Give examples of numbers that satisfy the conditions of natural, whole, integral, and rational numbers, and show that these numbers comprise the rational system.
2. Describe, orally and in writing, whether or not a number is rational.

The number systems are quite easy to remember once you understand how they are built.

First, we have the natural numbers. This is like counting on your fingers and toes, starting with one finger. So we have 1, 2, 3, 4, and so on.

| natural |

All of the natural numbers together are referred to as the set of natural numbers. We show the set of natural numbers using curly brackets. {1, 2, 3 ...} remember that '...' means the pattern continues on forever.

Next we have the set of whole numbers.

| whole |

The only difference is that we now include zero. So we have 0, 1, 2, 3, and so on. An easy way to remember this is that whole has an o which looks like a zero. Notice that all the natural numbers are also whole numbers.

We can show that by putting the natural

| whole |
| natural |

numbers box in the whole numbers box. We can also show the set of whole numbers {0, 1, 2 ...}.

Now we are showing that the set of whole numbers include all the natural numbers. The reason we use the box diagrams is that when we use set notation you can not tell that the natural numbers are part of the whole numbers as easily {0, 1, 2 ...}. We can say that the natural numbers are a subset of the whole numbers. Kind of like the natural numbers are submerged in the whole numbers.

If we include the negative counting numbers, we will end up with the set of integers.

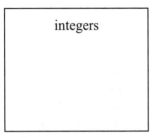

Integers include the whole numbers and the natural numbers. So now we have ... –3, –2, –1, 0, 1, 2, 3... Notice that the '...' is on both sides now. This means that it keeps going in both directions forever. In set notation we would write {...–3, –2, –1, 0, 1, 2, 3...}

As you might expect, we can show graphically that the natural numbers and the whole numbers are part of the integers.

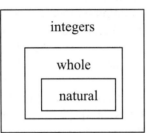

At this point, we need to remember that a fraction can also be written as a decimal number.

For instance, $\frac{1}{2}$ is 0.5 and $\frac{17}{5}$ is actually 3.4.

Also, $-\frac{1}{2}$ is –0.5 and $-\frac{17}{5}$ is actually –3.4.

So the set of rational numbers would include all positive and negative numbers including zero. The

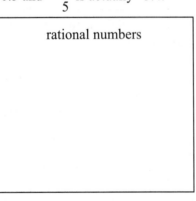

box graphic now shows its real usefulness. Think how difficult it is to show the set of rational numbers using set notation.

How would you ever show anything meaningful if you have to show all the positive and negative numbers no matter how small or how big?

Luckily using the box graphic we can show that the rational numbers contain all the integers, whole numbers and natural numbers. We can also say that each box inside another box is a subset.

The natural numbers are a subset of the whole numbers, but also of the integers and the rational numbers.

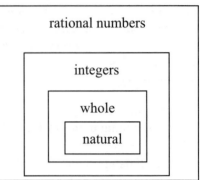

Related Questions: 1, 2, 4, 5, 6, 7, 8, 9

---

3. *Give examples of situations where answers would involve the positive (principal) square root, or both positive and negative square roots of a number.*

For this question we must be clear as to what a principal square root is. When we square a number, we multiply it by itself once.
$3^2 = 3 \times 3 = 9$

Square root is the opposite; we want to find what number multiplied against itself once will give us the original number. $\sqrt{9} = 3 \times 3$

Remember that any two negative numbers multiplied together equal a positive number. So, –3 × –3 = 9, in which case the opposite must be true. $\sqrt{9} = -3 \times -3$. The square root of 9 is 3, however, the square root of 9 is also –3. Usually, we are looking for the positive number when we find a square root. The positive square root is the principal square root. Unless the negative square root is actually asked for, always give just the positive (principal) square root as an answer.

Related Questions: 3, 11

---

4. *Illustrate power, base, coefficient and exponent, using rational numbers or variables as bases or coefficients.*

5. *Determine the value of powers with integral exponents using the exponent laws.*

$4x^2$ is a power. A power is a shorthand way of showing a certain type of multiplication that has to have a base and an exponent.

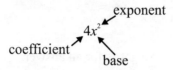

The letter x is a variable that is a base. This means that it can represent any number, so the value of x varies. We can say $x = 3$ or $x = 6$ or whatever we want. In this case, x is the base that the exponent acts on.

The exponent is 2. The exponent tells us how often the base is multiplied against itself. In the power $4x^2$, the exponent 2 means that x is multiplied against itself so that you see two x's. $x \times x$.

4 is called the coefficient. This means that after you find out what x^2 equals, you then multiply the result by 4.

If $x = 3$, then the power $4x^2$ would be calculated as:

$4x^2$; $x = 3$	Read as 4 times x exponent 2 when x is equal to 3
4×3^2	Substitute 3 for x
$4 \times 3 \times 3$	This shows how the exponent affects the base
4×9	Multiply using the coefficient
36	Answer

You can also divide by the coefficient. $\dfrac{x^2}{4}$

Let's see what happens when $x = 8$

$\dfrac{x^2}{4}$; $x = 8$	Read as x exponent 2 divided by 4 when x is equal to 8
$\dfrac{8^2}{4}$	Substitute 8 for x
$\dfrac{8 \times 8}{4}$	This shows how the exponent affects the base
$\dfrac{64}{4}$	Divide using the coefficient
16	Answer

Powers do not have to have variables. In the power 6^2, 6 is the base, 2 is the exponent, and the power 6^2 means 6×6.

In front of any single variable is a coefficient of 1 or –1.

In the power x^3, x is the base and 3 is the exponent and the coefficient is 1.
$x^3 = \times 1 \times x \times x \times x$.

In the power $-x^3$, x is the base and 3 is the exponent; however, there is a coefficient, which is 1.
$-x^3 = -1 \times x \times x \times x$

Be careful of brackets with exponents. For example, if we have $(-x)^4$ when $x = 3$, we would get:

$(-x)^4$; $x = 3$	Read as negative x exponent 2 when x is equal to 3
$(-3)^4$	Substitute 3 for x
$-3 \times -3 \times -3 \times -3$	This shows how the exponent affects the base
81	Answer

However, if the negative sign is outside the brackets like this $-(x^4)$, then we have

$-(x^4); x = 3$	Read as negative result of x exponent 2 when x is equal to 3
$-(3^4)$	Substitute 3 for x
$-(3 \times 3 \times 3 \times 3)$	This shows how the exponent affects the base
$-(81)$	Now we remove the brackets
-81	Answer

Related Questions: 12, 14, 15, NR1, 16, 37, NR6

---

6. *Explain and apply the exponent laws for powers with integral exponents.*
7. *Understand and use the exponent laws to simplify expressions with variable bases and evaluate expressions with numerical base.*
8. *Use a calculator to perform calculations involving scientific notation and exponent laws.*

The power laws allow us to deal with exponents in operations using powers.

It helps to understand the power laws if we use values for the exponents m and n. If $m = 5$ and $n = 3$, then we would have:

$x^m \times x^n = x^{mn}$; $m = 5$, $n = 3$
$x^5 \times x^3 = (x \times x \times x \times x \times x) \times (x \times x \times x)$
$\qquad = x \times x \times x \times x \times x \times x \times x \times x$
$\qquad = x^8$
or
$x^5 \times x^3 = x^{5+3} = x^8$

Notice that the base of the two powers being multiplied together must be the same.

$x^m \div x^n = x^{m-n}$; $m = 5$, $n = 3$
$x^5 \div x^3 = (x \times x \times x \times x \times x) \div (x \times x \times x)$
$\qquad = x^2$
or
$\dfrac{x^5}{x^3} = \dfrac{x \times x \times x \times x \times x}{x \times x \times x} = x^2$

Either way, we get x^2 for an answer. The exponent law tells us
$x^m \div x^n = x^{m-n}$; $m=5$, $n=3$
x^{5-3}
x^2

$(x^m)^n = x^{mn}$; $m=5$, $n=3$

$(x^5)^3 = (x^5) \times (x^5) \times (x^5)$
$\qquad = (x \times x \times x \times x \times x) \times (x \times x \times x \times x \times x)$
$\qquad\quad \times (x \times x \times x \times x \times x)$
$\qquad = x \times x \times x \times x \times x \times x \times x \times x \times x \times x$
$\qquad\quad \times x \times x \times x \times x \times x$
$\qquad = x^{15}$

or we can use the exponent law to say

$(x^m)^n = x^{mn} = x^{5 \times 3} = x^{15}$

Both ways, what we are doing is saying that we are multiplying x^5 against itself 3 times.

$(xy)^m = x^m y^m$, this law says that all bases in a set of brackets are equally affected by an exponent. Notice that the result is two different powers; remember that the bases must be the same to combine powers.

$\left(\dfrac{x}{y}\right)^n = \dfrac{x^n}{y^n}$; $y \neq 0$, this law also says that all bases in a set of brackets are equally affected by an exponent.

Notice that the result is two different powers; but this time it is division (a fraction line is a division line) and the denominator cannot equal 0 in a fraction; this is another way of saying you cannot divide by 0.

Both of the next laws can be explained using the same explanation.

$$x^0 = 1; \, x \neq 0$$

$$x^{-n} = \frac{1}{x^n}; \, x \neq 0$$

Notice the following pattern:

$$2^3 = 8$$
$$2^2 = 4$$
$$2^1 = 2$$
$$2^0 = 1$$
$$2^{-1} = \frac{1}{2}$$
$$2^{-2} = \frac{1}{4}$$
$$2^{-3} = \frac{1}{8}$$

Any power with a 0 exponent is equal to 1.

$$7^0 = 1, \qquad -5^0 = 1, \qquad 35^0 = 1$$

A negative power indicates that the number moves from one part of the fraction line to the other.

$$3^{-3} = \frac{1}{3^3} = \frac{1}{27}$$

$$2^{-3} = \frac{1}{2^3} = \frac{1}{8}$$

$$5^{-2} = \frac{1}{5^2} = \frac{1}{25}$$

Scientists have developed a short method to express very large or very small numbers. This method is called **scientific notation**. Scientific notation is based on powers of the base number 10.

The number 123 000 000 000 in scientific notation is written as

$$1.23 \times 10^{11}$$

The first number must have only a **single digit** before the decimal place. The digit before the decimal place must be greater than or equal to 1 and less than 10.

The second number must always be 10 in scientific notation. The base number 10 is always written in exponent form.

In the number 1.23×10^{11}, the number 11 is the exponent, 10 is the base, and 1.23 is the coefficient.

Scientific notation can also be used for very small numbers.

The number 0.000 000 000 234 in scientific notation is written as

$$2.34 \times 10^{-10}$$

To figure out the exponent to use, simply count the number of times you move the decimal point either right or left.

Related Questions: 10, 13, 17–21, NR2, 22, 23, 29, 32–36, 38, 39, 43, 44, NR7–9, 46, NR10, NR11, 48–52

---

1. What kind of number is $\frac{3}{7}$?

    A. An irrational number

    B. A non-repeating decimal

    C. A repeating decimal

    D. An integer

*Use the following information to answer
the next question.*

i. The set of whole numbers is a subset of the set of natural numbers.

ii. The set of integers is a subset of the set of rational numbers.

iii. The set of rational numbers is a subset of the set of irrational numbers.

2. Which of the following statements about the information above is correct?

    A. Statements **i** and **ii** are both true.

    B. Only statement **ii** is true.

    C. Statements **ii** and **iii** are both false.

    D. Only statement **iii** is false.

*Use the following information to answer
the next question.*

The Pyramids are ancient Egyptian tombs built by the pharaohs 4 000 years ago. The pharaohs built these tombs to protect their bodies as they prepared for the afterlife.  The pyramids were built with amazing precision. Their bases were **perfect squares**, and the limestone blocks that made up many pyramids fit so well that in many places you cannot slide a piece of paper between them.

3. If the base of a pyramid covers an area on the ground of 10 000 m² the length of one side of the pyramid, x, is

    A. 500 m   B. 400 m

    C. 250 m   D. 100 m

4. Which of the following numbers is **not** rational?

    A. $\sqrt{15-6}$

    B. $\sqrt{3.9}$

    C. $\frac{5}{11}$

    D. $-\sqrt{25}$

5. In the number system, the number $\frac{1}{2}$ is

    A. integral and rational

    B. natural and rational

    C. rational

    D. irrational

CHALLENGER QUESTION

6. In circle geometry, the number π is

    A. rational, since it can be expressed as 3.14

    B. either rational or irrational, depending on the dimensions of the circle

    C. rational, since $\pi = \frac{c}{d}$, where c is the circumference and d is the diameter

    D. irrational, since π is a non-repeating, non-terminating decimal

---

7. Which of the following numbers is irrational?

   A. $-\sqrt{80}$

   B. $\sqrt{25}$

   C. $\sqrt{\dfrac{16}{4}}$

   D. $-\sqrt{81}$

8. Which of the following diagrams represents the number system?

   A.

   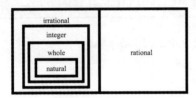

   B.

   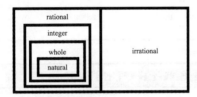

   C.

   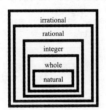

   D.

   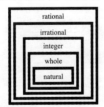

9. Which of the following statements defines a rational number?

   A. Any number that is a non-repeating, non-terminating decimal.

   B. Any number that can be expressed as a finite decimal.

   C. Any number that can be expressed as $\dfrac{a}{b}$, where a and b are integers and $b \neq 0$

   D. Any number that can be expressed as $\dfrac{a}{b}$, where a and b are natural numbers.

Use the following information to answer the next question.

$$99 \times (36 + 76) \div ((150 - 75) \div 32) =$$

10. Given the calculator keystroke sequence above, what was the original expression being solved?

   A. $\dfrac{(99 \times 36) + 76}{(150 - 75) \div 32}$

   B. $\dfrac{99 \times (36 + 76)}{150 - 75 \div 32}$

   C. $\dfrac{99 \times 36 + 76}{(150 - 75) \div 32}$

   D. $\dfrac{99 \times (36 + 76)}{(150 - 75) \div 32}$

11. The number of solutions for the equation $x^2 = 12$ is

   A. zero

   B. one

   C. two

   D. four

12. The coefficient of the term $\dfrac{-3x^5}{8}$ is

   A. -3

   B. 3

   C. $-\dfrac{3}{8}$

   D. $\dfrac{3}{8}$

Use the following information to answer the next question.

Renu, Jason, and Michelle are working on a group project at school. The students' assignment is to design a computer program to keep track of rentals and sales at a video store. Renu can complete the given assignment by herself in 9 h. It will take Jason 12 h and Michelle 18 h to finish the assignment if they work independently.

CHALLENGER QUESTION

13. How long will it take to complete the assignment if the three students work together?

   A. 2 h

   B. 3.5 h

   C. 4 h

   D. 7 h

14. Which of the following statements about the expression $\dfrac{-3x^2}{5}$ is **not** correct?

   A. The base of the expression is x.

   B. The coefficient of the expression is $\dfrac{-3}{5}$.

   C. The exponent of the expression is 2.

   D. The value of the expression is positive.

15. In the expression $2\left(\dfrac{x}{y}\right)^m$, the base is

   A. $2x$ B. x

   C. $2\left(\dfrac{x}{y}\right)$ D. $\left(\dfrac{x}{y}\right)$

Numerical Response

1. The value of the coefficient of $(2x)^3$ correct to the nearest whole number, is _____ .

16. Which of the following expressions is equivalent to $(6 \times 10^{11}) + (2.3 \times 10^{12})$?

   A. 1.34×10^{24}

   B. 8.3×10^{11}

   C. 8.3×10^{12}

   D. 29×10^{11}

CHALLENGER QUESTION

17. The value of $(-a^2)^{-3}$ is

   A. a^{-6}

   B. $-3a^2$

   C. $-a^{-6}$

   D. $-a^{-1}$

CHALLENGER QUESTION

18. When simplified, which of the following expressions equals $-\dfrac{1}{16}$?

   A. $\left(\dfrac{1}{2}\right)^{-4}$ B. $(-2)^{-4}$

   C. -2^{-4} D. 2^{-4}

19. In its simplest form, the expression

$$\frac{\left(2x^2y^3\right)\left(\dfrac{1}{2x^2y^3}\right)}{\left(\left(3x\cdot y^6\right)\left(4x^4y^{-1}\right)\right)^0\left(xy\right)^0} \text{ is}$$

A. $\dfrac{1}{3xy^6}$ **B.** $\dfrac{1}{12x^5y^5}$

C. undefined   **D.** 1

20. The expression $\dfrac{\left(4x^3y^2\right)\left(4x^5y^6\right)}{2x^3y^4}$ in its simplest form is

A. $8x^8y^3$ **B.** $8x^5y^4$

C. $6x^5y^8$ **D.** $4x^5y^4$

21. What is the value of b if $\dfrac{\left(2b^3\right)}{2^{-3}\left(b^2\right)} = 80$?

A. 1

B. 5

C. 20

D. 320

Numerical Response

2. If $n^2n^{-3} = 5$ then the value of n, rounded to the nearest tenth, is _____.

22. The equivalent of $4x^3y^2 \div 3xy^4$ is

A. $\dfrac{4}{3}x^2y^6$ **B.** $\dfrac{4}{3}x^2y^{-2}$

C. $12x^4y^6$ **D.** $\dfrac{4}{3}x^3y^8$

23. Which of the following statements is **not** correct?

A. $15^{11} \times 15^{21} = 15^{32}$

B. $202^{18} \times 202^{-70} = 202^{-52}$

C. $1500^3 \times 1500^0 = 0$

D. $142^0 \times 142^0 = 1$

24. The school fundraising committee sold 3 different sizes of chocolate bars last year. The sizes, the price, and the number of bars sold are shown below.

Size	Price	Number Sold
500 g	$2.50	140
300 g	$1.75	190
200 g	$1.25	?

If the total revenue from chocolate bar sales was $1 037.56, how many 200 g bars were sold?

A. 284   **B.** 332

C. 350   **D.** 355

Use the following information to answer the next question.

A college offers three different diplomas in the field of Information Technology (I.T.): computer programming, networking, and business applications. For either the programming or networking diploma, students must complete 1 160 hours of course work. The business diploma only requires 640 hours. At graduation, it is noted that the I.T. graduating class has completed a total of 164 800 hours of course work.

25. If a total of 120 students in the graduating class took the computing and networking courses, then how many students took the business course?

A. 394   **B.** 22

C. 160   **D.** 40

*Use the following information to answer
the next two questions.*

A local power company
charges customers $8.30
per month plus $0.07 for
each kilowatt hour
(kWh) used. A tax of
7% is then added to the
total bill.

26. Which of the following formulas can
customers use to calculate their monthly
power bill, *t*?

   A. $t = (8.30 + 1.07 \times kWh) \times 1.07$

   B. $t = (8.30 + 0.07 \times kWh) + 0.07$

   C. $t = (8.30 + 0.07 \times kWh) \times 1.07$

   D. $t = (8.37 \times kWh) \times 1.07$

27. If a customer receives a bill of $40.34 for a
particular month, how many kilowatt hours
of power were used during the month?

   A. 27 kWh   B. 420 kWh

   C. 457 kWh   D. 530 kWh

28. Mia works as a sales clerk at a clothing
store. She makes $5.50 per hour for a
7 hour workday, plus a 5 % commission on
what she sells. How much money will she
earn before tax if she sells $350.00 worth of
clothes per day over 10 days of work?

   A. $194.25

   B. $385.00

   C. $402.50

   D. $560.00

29. Which of the following expressions is equal
to $a^b \div a^c$

   A. a^{b-c}

   B. $a\dfrac{b}{c}$

   C. a^{-bc}

   D. $1\dfrac{b}{c}$

Numerical Response

3. The formula for the volume of a sphere is
$V = \dfrac{4}{3}\pi r^3$. If the volume of a ball is
36π cm^2, what is r^3?

*Use the following information to answer
the next two questions.*

Jean wants to purchase a custom-made tuxedo
for $1 500. He puts down a payment of $700.
He will pay the balance in one year.

30. If he pays interest of $\dfrac{1}{2}$ of 1 percent per
month on the outstanding balance, what is
the total amount paid by Jean after one year
(12 months)?

   A. $ 1 048

   B. $ 1 542

   C. $ 1 548

   D. $ 1 590

31. If Jean owes a total of $844 at the end of one
year, the annual interest rate that he would
have been charged on the outstanding
balance is

   A. 4.4 %

   B. 5.5 %

   C. 6.0 %

   D. 8.0 %

Numerical Response

4. The formula for the volume of a cylinder is $V = \pi r^2 h$ A roll of paper has a height, h, of 2.13 m and a radius, r, of 1.52 m. If the radius of the cardboard tube in the centre is 0.13 m, what is the volume of the paper roll, in m^3? _____

(Round to the nearest tenth.)

CHALLENGER QUESTION

32. The equation $\dfrac{4^4}{2^6} \div \dfrac{\left(3^4\right)\left(27^2\right)}{\left(9^2\right)^2}$ is equal to

A. 108	**B.** 36
C. 12	**D.** $\dfrac{4}{9}$

33. In simplest form, the expression $\sqrt{c^4 \div c^2}$ equals

A. c^3

B. c^2

C. c

D. $\dfrac{1}{c^2}$

Use the following information to answer the next question.

Rate of acceleration, a, can be calculated using the formula $a = \dfrac{v_f - v_i}{t}$, where v_f is the final velocity, v_i is the initial velocity, and t is the time taken to reach the final velocity.

Numerical Response

5. How many seconds does it take a car to go from a standing start ($v_i = 0$) to a final velocity of 2.67 m/s (v_f), if it accelerates uniformly at a rate of 5.56 m/s^2? _____
(Round to one decimal place.)

CHALLENGER QUESTION

34. In its simplest form, $\dfrac{\left(3x^3t^5\right)\left(4x^2t^7\right)^2}{\left(8x^2t^7\right)\left(x^3t^{-8}\right)}$ is

A. $6x^2t^{20}$

B. $\dfrac{6x^{12}t^{70}}{x^6t^{-56}}$

C. $6x^6t^{126}$

D. $\dfrac{3x^2t^{20}}{2}$

35. If only positive exponents are used, then the expression $\dfrac{\left(x^{-8}\right) \div \left(x^5\right)}{\left(x^2\right)^3\left(x^0\right)}$, when simplified, equals

A. $\dfrac{1}{x^7}$	**B.** $\dfrac{1}{x^9}$
C. $\dfrac{1}{x^{13}}$	**D.** $\dfrac{1}{x^{19}}$

36. The expression $\dfrac{\left(6^2\right)^2 \times 3^{-3}}{10^4 \div 5^4}$ is equal to

A. 3

B. 0.375

C. 0.218 7

D. 0.076 8

CHALLENGER QUESTION

37. The expression $\dfrac{\left(\frac{1}{2}\right)^3 \left(\frac{1}{2}\right)^{-2}}{\left(\frac{1}{3}\right)^{-2} \left(\frac{1}{4}\right)^2}$ can be

reduced to

A. 72

B. $\dfrac{8}{9}$

C. $\dfrac{4}{9}$

D. $\dfrac{1}{36}$

38. If $x = -3$ and $y = -2$, then $\dfrac{\left(x^3\right)^2 \left(y^{-2}\right)^3}{y^{-7}}$ is

equal to

A. 1 458

B. 486

C. −364.5

D. −1 458

39. The expression $\dfrac{7^2}{3^2}$ is equivalent to

A. $\left(\dfrac{7}{3}\right)^0$

B. $\left(\dfrac{7}{3}\right)^2$

C. $\left(\dfrac{7}{3}\right)^4$

D. 4^2

CHALLENGER QUESTION

40. Jake can paint a house in 4 h using a spray gun. Using just a roller, Susan will need 5 h to paint the same house. Ted requires 20 h to paint the same house using only a paint brush. If they all decide to work together, how long will it take to paint the house?

A. 30 min

B. 1 h 40 min

C. 2 h

D. 2 h 20 min

Use the following information to answer the next question.

	Games Played	Points Scored
Player A	68	85
Player B	68	?

41. If the average points per game for both players is 2.25, then how many points did player **B** score?

A. 238

B. 221

C. 153

D. 68

CHALLENGER QUESTION

42. Miro purchases hockey cards when visiting card shows. To track the total number of cards purchased, c, he uses the equation $c = 2^n - 1$ where n is the number of shows attended. What is the total number of cards purchased after 6 card shows?

A. 11

B. 31

C. 32

D. 63

Numerical Response

6. Miro stores his cards in a case that can hold up to 50 cards. How many cases would he need to store all of his cards after attending 9 card shows?

_____

(Round to the nearest whole number.)

---

43. When expanded, which of the following powers has 43 as the last two digits?

A. 5^{831}

B. 6^{831}

C. 7^{831}

D. 8^{831}

44. If $x = 6.3 \times 10^9$ and $y = 9.0 \times 10^{-3}$ then x divided by $10y$ is

A. 7.0×10^9

B. 7.0×10^{10}

C. 7.0×10^{11}

D. 7.0×10^{12}

Numerical Response

7. What is the value of the expression

$$\frac{\left(x^{-2}\right)^4 \div y^{14}}{3x} \times \frac{\left(x^2\right)^6 \left(y^2\right)^8}{5y}, \text{ if } x = 3 \text{ and}$$

$y = 5$? _____

8. The value of

$$\frac{\left(4^{-2}\right)^2 \times 5^3}{5\left(6^{-4} \div 6^{-2} \times 4^{-3}\right)} \text{ is } \underline{\hspace{2cm}}.$$

9. If $n = 4.0 \times 10^{-206}$ and $m = 1.6 \times 10^{-206}$ how many times larger is n than m? _____
(Round to one decimal place.)

---

45. If the mass of a bacterium is 1×10^{-5} g then how many bacteria would have a total mass of 50 kg?

A. 5×10^9

B. 5×10^6

C. 2×10^{-7}

D. 2×10^{-10}

Use the following information to answer the next question.

The volume of Earth is approximately 1.08×10^{12} km³ A particular asteroid is found to have a volume that is $\frac{1}{9}$ the total volume of Earth.

46. What is the volume of the asteroid?

A. 8.33×10^{-12} km³

B. 1.08×10^3 km³

C. 1.20×10^{11} km³

D. 9.72×10^{12} km³

Numerical Response

10. When x is divided by y, the quotient can be expressed in scientific notation in the form $Q \times 10^w$. What is the value of Q, if $x = 9.84 \times 10^{-23}$ and $y = 4.10 \times 10^{-28}$?
_____ (Round to one decimal place.)

Numerical Response

11 The value of $(b^0)(c)^{-1}$ when $b = -2$ and $c = \dfrac{1}{3}$, is _____.

Use the following information to answer the next question.

Dillon attempts to solve the expression
$$\frac{12.2 - 6.6}{2} + \frac{14.9 + 3.1}{3}$$
by using the following 2 keystroke sequences on a scientific calculator.

Sequence A:
$12.2 - 6.6 \div 2 + (14.9 + 3.1) \div 3 =$

Sequence B:
$(12.2 - 6.6 \div 2) + (14.9 + 3.1 \div 3) =$

47. Which of the following observations about the keystrokes above is correct?

   A. Sequence A uses fewer keystrokes and results in the correct answer.

   B. Sequence B uses fewer keystrokes and results in the correct answer.

   C. Sequence A uses fewer keystrokes but results in an incorrect answer.

   D. Sequence B uses more keystrokes but results in the correct answer.

The following two questions are about the solar system.

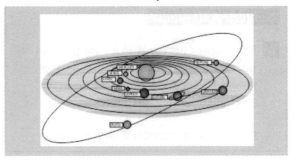

48. Our solar system is centred around the sun, which is just one star of billions in the galaxy. It is estimated that there are about 10^{11} stars in a typical galaxy and about 10^{11} galaxies in the universe. If this is accurate, approximately how many stars are there in the universe?

   A. 2×10^{11} **B.** 10^{12}

   C. 10^{22} **D.** 10^{121}

49. The mass of Earth is estimated to be 6×10^{24} kg, whereas the mass of the sun is about 2×10^{30} kg. What fraction of the sun's mass is Earth's mass ?

   A. 4×10^{6} **B.** 3.33×10^{6}

   C. $\dfrac{4}{5}$ **D.** 3×10^{-6}

Use the following information to answer the next question.

The distance from Earth to the farthest visible galaxy is approximately 10^{25} m The distance from Edmonton to Red Deer is approximately 10^5 m

50. If it takes 1 h to get to Red Deer from Edmonton, how many hours would it take to get to the farthest visible galaxy if the speed is the same?

   A. 10^5 **B.** 10^{20}

   C. 10^{30} **D.** 10^{125}

Use the following information to answer the next question.

Earth is gradually slowing down as it rotates on its axis, resulting in slightly longer days as time goes by. In the early days of the dinosaurs, about 2.5×10^8 years ago, 1 full day was only 22 hours long. By the end of the dinosaur era, about 7.5×10^7 years ago, 1 day had stretched to 23.4 hours.

51. The time it took for 1 day to increase by 1.4 hours was

    A. 1.75×10^7 years

    B. 5×10^7 years

    C. 1.75×10^8 years

    D. 5×10^8 years

Use the following information to answer the next question.

The town council has decided to buy a new water filtration system for the town swimming pool. The system is capable of filtering 1 150 000 L of water every 3 h.

52. The quantity of swimming pool water (in litres) that can be filtered in 24 h, expressed in scientific notation, is

    A. 1.15×10^5 L

    B. 1.15×10^6 L

    C. 9.2×10^6 L

    D. 9.2×10^7 L

Written Response

Use the table on the following page to answer the next question.

The following table of information compares certain physical properties of the 9 planets in our solar system. Except for the number of known satellites, the values have been given in terms of Earth units to make the comparisons easier to interpret.

For example, the distance from the sun to Earth is one astronomical unit, so the table shows that Mars is about one and a half (1.52) times farther from the sun than Earth is from the sun.

1. The masses of the planets vary widely. What is the ratio of the mass of the largest planet to that of the smallest planet, correct to the nearest power of 10?

    (2 marks)

2. How many revolutions of the sun will Mercury make in the time it takes Pluto to go around the sun once? (Correct to the nearest whole number.)

    (2 marks)

3. How many planets have a smaller diameter than Earth?

    (1 marks)

4. Modern theories on the formation of stars and solar systems suggest that along with the forces of gravitation, a large gas cloud or *nebula* created the sun and planets. These theories are often studied and explored with computer simulations of solar-system models having many thousands of particles. If each simulated particle will require one millisecond (10^{-3} seconds) of computer time to process, and if a simulation program will be run for 25 hours, then how many particles can be included in the model?

    (2 marks)

Planet	Distance from the Sun	Revolution Period (years)	Radius	Density	Mass	Number of Known Satellites
Mercury	0.39	0.24	0.38	0.98	0.06	0
Venus	0.72	0.62	0.95	0.96	0.82	0
Earth	1.00	1.00	1.00	1.00	1.00	1
Mars	1.52	1.88	0.53	0.71	0.11	2
Jupiter	5.20	11.86	11.2	0.24	317.8	16
Saturn	9.54	29.46	9.42	0.13	95.1	20+
Uranus	19.18	84.01	4.10	0.22	14.5	15
Neptune	30.06	164.79	3.88	0.31	17.2	8
Pluto	39.44	247.7	0.18	0.36	0.004	1

CHALLENGER QUESTION

2. At a grain storage facility, 2 loaders are used. The largest loader can completely fill a grain silo in 60 min, whereas the smaller loader can fill the same silo in 90 min. If both loaders are used at the same time, how long will it take to fill the silo?

(3 marks)

UNIT TEST 1 – NUMBER CONCEPTS

1. The best classification for the number 6 is

   A. natural, whole, integer, rational

   B. natural, whole, integer

   C. whole, integer, rational

   D. rational

2. The best classification for the number −3.2 is

   A. N, Q   B. I, Q

   C. W, I, Q   D. Q

Use the following number line to answer the next question.

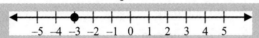

3. Looking at the number line above, the best classification of the number identified with the dot is

   A. N, I, Q

   B. N, Q

   C. N, W, I, Q

   D. I, Q

4. Which of the following is **not** a rational number?

   A. $\dfrac{9}{7}$ B. $\dfrac{3}{4}$

   C. $\dfrac{3}{0}$ D. $-\dfrac{4}{7}$

5. In $\sqrt{25} = 5$, 5 is the

   A. dividend

   B. principal square root

   C. addend

   D. quotient

6. Consider 6^2. In this expression, 6 is the

   A. exponent   B. base

   C. coefficient   D. power

7. In expanded form, $\left(2x^2\right)^4$ is

   A. $2x^2 \times 2x^2 \times 2x^2 \times 2x^2$

   B. $16x^8$

   C. $8x^8$

   D. $8x^2$

8. The coefficient in $4x^3$ is

   A. x B. 4

   C. 3   D. $4x$

9. $\left(-2x^3\right)\left(-2x^3\right)\left(-2x^3\right)$ is the expanded form of

   A. $-2x^3$ B. $-\left(2x^3\right)$

   C. $-\left(2x\right)^3$ D. $\left(-2x^3\right)^3$

Use the following information to answer the next question.

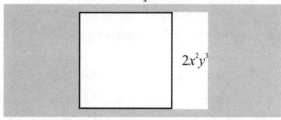

10. A simplified mathematical expression for the area of the square would be

   A. $2x^2y^3$

   B. $4x^4y^4$

   C. $2x^4y^6$

   D. $4x^4y^6$

11. The simplified form of $4(x^0)(3x^0)$ would be

    A. 4   B. 7
    C. $12x$ D. 12

12. The simplified form of $\dfrac{25x^4 y^6}{15x^2 y^8}$ would be

    A. $\dfrac{5x^2}{3y^2}$ B. $\dfrac{5x}{3y}$

    C. $\dfrac{15x^2}{y^2}$ D. $15x^2 y^2$

Use the following information to answer the next question.

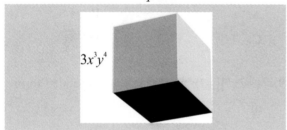

$3x^3 y^4$

13. A simplified expression for the volume of the given cube would be

    A. $9x^9 y^{12}$ B. $9x^6 y^{12}$
    C. $27x^{27} y^{64}$ D. $27x^9 y^{12}$

14. Simplify $3^0 - 2^{-3}$ to standard form

    A. $\dfrac{7}{8}$ B. $\dfrac{1}{4}$

    C. 8   D. $\dfrac{1}{8}$

15. Write $0.000\,000\,005\,67$ in scientific notation

    A. 56.7×10^{-10} B. 5.67×10^{10}
    C. 5.67×10^{-11} D. 5.67×10^{-9}

16. Which restriction would be placed on $\dfrac{3x^2 z^4}{2y^3}$?

    A. $\dfrac{3x^2 z^4}{2y^3} \neq 0$ B. $y \neq 0$

    C. $z \neq 0$ D. $x^2 \neq 0$

17. Which of the following is $\dfrac{1}{2 \times 2 \times 2 \times 2}$ written correctly in exponential form?

    A. 16^0 B. 16^{-2}
    C. 2^{-4} D. -16

18. Written in expanded form, 2×10^8 would be

    A. 200 000 000
    B. 20 000 000
    C. 2 000 000 000
    D. 0.000 000 02

19. Simplified, $(3 \times 10^{15}) \times (3 \times 10^9)$ would be

    A. (3×10^{24})

    B. (3×10^{135})

    C. (9×10^{24})

    D. (9×10^{135})

20. The answer to $(4 \times 10^{-19}) \times (2 \times 10^{22})$ in standard form would be

    A. 8×10^3
    B. 0.008
    C. 600
    D. 8 000

21. Which of the following is
$(-2)(-2)(-2)(-2)(-2)$ in exponential
form?

A. $(-2)^{-5}$ B. $(2)^{-5}$

C. $(-2)^{5}$ D. $-(-2)^{5}$

22. Written in scientific notation,
$0.000\,000\,000\,024 \times 500\,000\,000$ would be

A. 12×10^{-3} B. 1.2×10^{-2}

C. 1.2×10^{-3} D. 1.2×10^{3}

23. Evaluate $\dfrac{x^{5}y^{6}}{x^{3}y^{3}}$ for $x = 3$ and $y = -2$.

A. 72   B. -72

C. 24   D. -24

24. Simplify $\left(\dfrac{2x^{2}}{3y^{3}}\right)^{3}$.

A. $\dfrac{5x^{5}}{6y^{6}}$

B. $\dfrac{5x^{6}}{6y^{9}}$

C. $\dfrac{8x^{5}}{27y^{6}}$

D. $\dfrac{8x^{6}}{27y^{9}}$

25. Simplify $-\left(-2x^{3}\right)^{4}$.

A. $8x^{12}$

B. $-8x^{12}$

C. $16x^{12}$

D. $-16x^{12}$

26. If we simplify $\left(\dfrac{4x^{3}y^{8}}{2x^{5}y^{6}}\right)^{3}$, the correct answer
in exponential form without negative
exponents would be

A. $\dfrac{8y^{6}}{x^{6}}$

B. $\dfrac{16x^{9}}{y^{9}}$

C. $\dfrac{8x^{9}}{y^{9}}$

D. $8x^{6}y^{6}$

Written Response

1. Harold earned $275.23 in the first month of
his job. If Harold makes the same amount
for the rest of the year, how much money in
total will Harold make for the year?

2. The distance from planet Faraway to planet
Distant is 198 000 000 000 km. Calculate
the speed of a ship that is capable of
covering this distance in 8 000 hours.
Write your answer in scientific notation.

$$\text{Speed} = \frac{\text{Distance}}{\text{Time}}$$

3. If you started with a penny and doubled its
value every day, how much money would
you have at the end of a 31-day long month?

NOTES

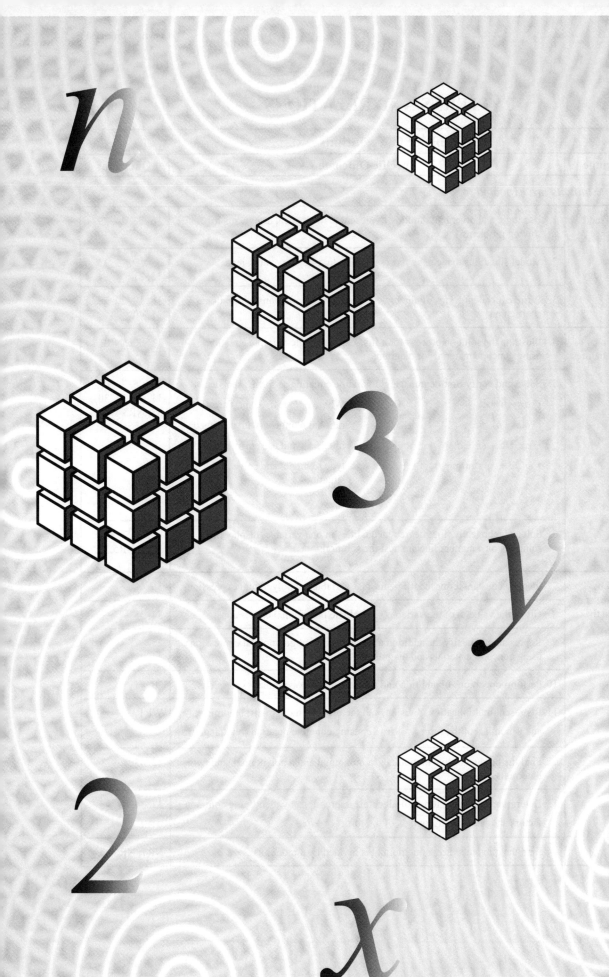

PATTERNS AND RELATIONS

Table of Correlations		
General Outcome	**Specific Outcome**	**Questions**
	Students are expected to:	
Generalize, design, and justify mathematical procedures, using appropriate patterns, models, and technology.	1. Use logic and divergent thinking to present mathematical arguments in solving problems.	16, 23, 24, 29
	2. Model situations that can be represented by first-degree expressions.	3, 4, 9, 12, 13, 15, 21
	3. Write equivalent forms of algebraic expressions or equations with rational coefficients.	18, 19, 20, 28, 31, 40
Solve and verify linear equations and inequalities in one variable.	4. Illustrate the solution process for a first-degree, single-variable equation, using concrete materials or diagrams.	1, NR1, NR2
	5. Solve and verify first-degree, single-variable equation of forms, such as: • $ax = b + cx$ • $a(x + b) = c$ • $ax + b = cx + d$ • $a(bx + c) = d(ex + f)$ • $\dfrac{a}{x} = b$ Where *a, b, c, d, e,* and *f* are all rational numbers (with a focus on integers), and use equations of this type to model and solve problem situations.	2, 5, 6, 7, 10, 11, 17, 22, 30, 33, NR3
	6. Solve algebraically, first-degree inequalities in one variable, display the solutions on a number line and test the solutions.	8, 26, 27, 35, NR4, NR5, NR6
Generalize arithmetic operations from the set of rational numbers to the set of polynomials.	7. Identify constant terms, coefficients, and variables in polynomial expressions.	36
	8. Given the value(s) of the variable(s), evaluate polynomial expressions.	37, 38
	9. Represent and justify the addition and subtraction of polynomial expressions using concrete materials and diagrams.	25
	10. Perform operations of addition and subtraction on polynomial expressions.	39, 41
	11. Represent multiplication, division, and factoring of monomials, binomials, and trinomials of the form $x^2 + bx + c$, using concrete materials and diagrams.	WR1
	12. Find the product of two monomials, a monomial and a polynomial, and two binomials.	42, 43
	13. Determine equivalent forms of algebraic expressions by identifying common factors and factoring trinomials of the form $x^2 + bx + c$.	32, 34, 44, 45
	14. Find the quotient when a polynomial is divided by a monomial.	NR7, NR8

1. *Use logic and divergent thinking to present mathematical arguments in solving problems.*

When you are given a problem, there are steps you can take to solve it. Logic problems require you to use your deductive reasoning powers.

1) The first step is to read the question carefully and list information that you are given.
2) Then write down exactly what is you are being asked to find.
3) Separate out any information that is not useful in your task.
4) Often the use of a table helps with logic problems.
5) Check that your answer agrees with the given facts.

Hao, Jessica and Emily attend the same school. One is in grade 7, one is in grade 9 and one in is grade 8. Use the clues to find which grade each is in.

Hao and the grade 7 student study with Emily.

Hao is not in grade 8.

Make a table using the information you know and then find the answer by putting x's where each person cannot be.

Name	Clues	Grade 7	Grade 8	Grade 9
Hao	Is not in grade 8	x	x	
Jessica				
Emily	Studies with Hao and grade 7 student	x		

For instance we know that Hao cannot be in grade 8 so we put an x in grade 8 for Hao. We know that neither Hao nor Emily is the grade 7 student because of the first clue where they are studying with the grade 7 student. Therefore, we put an x for Grade 7 for Hao and Emily. This means Hao must be the grade 9 student!

Name	Clues	Grade 7	Grade 8	Grade 9
Hao	Is not in grade 8	x	x	yes
Jessica		yes		
Emily	Studies with Hao and grade 7 student	x	yes	x

If Hao is the grade 9 student, then Emily can not be the grade 9 student and we can add an x for Emily for grade 9. This means that Emily must be the grade 8 student and by the process of elimination, Jessica is the grade 7 student. When we take our information back to the question, the answers match the clues.

Related Questions: 16, 23, 24, 29

2. *Model situations that can be represented by first-degree equations.*

The highest exponent of any term in a first-degree equation is one. The standard form for a first-degree equation is: $ax + b = c$, where $a, b,$ and c are constants and x is a variable.

A constant is a number that does not change in the equation.

A variable is a letter or symbol whose value can change.

A number that is multiplied against the variable is called the coefficient.

For example, in the equation $-2x + \dfrac{3}{4} = 7$ the numbers $\dfrac{3}{4}$ and 7 are constants, x is a variable, and -2 is a coefficient

If we have $3x + 2 = 8$, then 2 and 8 are constants; x is a variable and 3 is a coefficient. When a number is written right beside a variable it means multiplication. $3x$ means 3 times x.

Real life situations can be modeled using first–degree equations.

Sarah has a cell phone and she gets a bill each month. She is charged a flat rate of $20 each month as well as 10 cents for every text message. An equation that represents Sarah's cell phone bill is $C = 0.10x + 20$.

C represents the amount owing to the cell phone company. The 0.10 is the cost per text message and x represents the number of text messages sent in a month. The 20 is the flat rate amount.

If Sarah sent 4 text messages last month, her bill would come to:

$C = 0.10(4) + 20$
$= 0.40 + 20$
$= \$20.40$

Related Questions: 3, 4, 9, 12, 13, 15, 21

3. *Write equivalent forms of algebraic expressions, or equations, with rational coefficients.*
4. *Illustrate the solution process for a first degree, single variable equation using concrete materials or diagrams.*

$3x + 4$ is an **algebraic expression**.

$3x + 4 = 12$ is an **algebraic equation**.

An *equation* has an *equal* (=) sign in it.

A rational coefficient means that the coefficient is a fraction or a number with a repeating and terminating decimal.

It is often desirable to work with equations that do not contain fractions. Equations can be manipulated such that the fractions are eliminated as shown:

$$\frac{2x}{3} + \frac{4}{3} = 2$$
$$\left(\frac{2x}{3} + \frac{4}{3}\right)(3) = 2(3)$$
$$2x + 4 = 6$$

Recall: Whatever is done to one side of an equation must also be done to the other side.

To write an equivalent expression or equation, simply multiply both sides by a number that will remove the denominator of all fractions when multiplied through. In this case, multiplying both sides of the equation by 3 removes the denominator 3 and results in an equivalent algebraic equation that contains no fractions.

The value of a variable can also be determined when given an equation. Consider $x + 4 = 6$.

The expression $x + 4$ is represented on the left side of the equation using algebra tiles. On the right side 6 is represented.

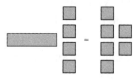

By adding negative 4 to each side, we can isolate the x because $x + 4 - 4 = 6 - 4$ leaves $x = 2$.

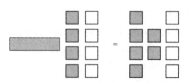

Or,

Related Questions: 1, 18 – 20, 28, 31, 40, NR1, NR2

5. *Solve and verify first-degree, single variable equations of forms, such as:*

    - $ax = b + cx$
    - $a(x+b) = c$
    - $ax + b = cx + d$
    - $a(bx+c) = d(ex+f)$
    - $\dfrac{a}{x} = b$

    where a, b, c, d, e, and f are all rational numbers (with a focus on integers), and use equations of this type to model and solve problem situations.

When solving equations, there are a few guiding rules that will help if followed.

1) Remember that the objective is to solve for x or whatever variable may be in the equation.

2) Whatever operation we do to one side of an equation we must do to the other side.

3) Follow a plan. A logical one is:

    i.   *Remove any denominators.*

    ii. *Complete any operations in the equation.*

    iii. *Move all the variables to the side of the equation whose variable has the largest positive coefficient and complete any possible operations.*

    iv. *Move all the constants to the other side of the equation and complete any possible operations.*

    v.   *Isolate the variable by moving any coefficient to the constant side of the equation.*

4) Some last suggestions are to be neat, keep the equal signs lined up as you do the equation, show all steps as you complete the equation, check your answer.

An example of how to solve
$ax = b + cx$

$$2x = 6 + 8x$$
$${-2x}{-2x}$$
$$0 = 6 + 6x$$
$${-6}{-6}$$
$$-6 = 6x$$
$$\frac{-6}{6} = \frac{6x}{6}$$
$$-1 = x$$

Check

$$2x = 6 + 8x; \; x = -1$$
$$2(-1) = 6 + 8(-1)$$
$$-2 = 6 - 8$$
$$-2 = -2$$

An example of how to solve
$a(x + b) = c$

$$4(x+2) = 16$$
$$4x + 8 = 16$$
$${-8}{-8}$$
$$4x = 8$$
$$\frac{4x}{4} = \frac{8}{4}$$
$$x = 2$$

Check

$$4(x+2) = 16; \; x = 2$$
$$4(2+2) = 16$$
$$4(4) = 16$$
$$16 = 16$$

An example of how to solve
$ax + b = cx + d$

$$3x + 13 = 4x + 8$$
$${-3x}{-3x}$$
$$13 = x + 8$$
$${-8}{-8}$$
$$5 = x$$

Check

$$3x + 13 = 4x + 8; \; x = 5$$
$$(3)(5) + 13 = (4)(5) + 8$$
$$15 + 13 = 20 + 8$$
$$28 = 28$$

An example of how to solve
$a(bx + c) = d(ex + f)$

$$3(4x + 7) = 3(5x + 5)$$

$$\underset{-12x}{12x + 21} = \underset{-12x}{15x + 15}$$

$$\underset{-15}{21} = \underset{-15}{3x + 15}$$

$$6 = 3x$$

$$\frac{6}{3} = \frac{3x}{3}$$

$$2 = x$$

Check

$$3(4x + 7) = 3(5x + 5); x = 2$$

$$3\big[(4)(2) + 7\big] = 3\big[(5)(2) + 5\big]$$

$$3(8 + 7) = 3(10 + 5)$$

$$3(15) = 3(15)$$

$$45 = 45$$

An example of how to solve $\dfrac{a}{x} = b$

$$\frac{16}{x} = 4$$

$$(x)\left(\frac{16}{x}\right) = (x)(4)$$

$$16 = 4x$$

$$\frac{16}{4} = \frac{4x}{4}$$

$$4 = x$$

Check

$$\frac{16}{x} = 4; x = 4$$

$$\frac{16}{4} = 4$$

$$4 = 4$$

Related Questions: 2, 5, 6, 7, 10, 11, 17, 22, 30, 33, NR3

---

6. *Solve algebraically, first-degree inequalities in one variable, display the solutions on a number line and test the solutions.*

An inequality is a relation that uses a greater than or a less than sign where the equal sign usually is. There may also be an equal sign with an inequality.

Left < Right	Left side is less than Right side (Or, Right side is greater than Left side)
Left > Right	Left side is greater than Right side (Or, Right side is less than Left side)
Left ≥ Right	Left side is greater than or equal to Right side (Or Right side is less than or equal to Left side)
Left ≤ Right	Left side is less than or equal to Right side (Or, Right side is greater than or equal to left side)

We solve inequalities in nearly the same way as we solve equations. The only difference is if you multiply or divide both sides of an **inequality** by a **negative** number, the direction of the inequality sign is **reversed**.

Example using only positive numbers:

$$\underset{-4}{3x + 4} > \underset{-4}{5}$$

$$3x > 1$$

$$\frac{3x}{3} > \frac{1}{3}$$

$$x > \frac{1}{3}$$

Considering the original inequality $3x + 4 > 5$, an answer of $x > \dfrac{1}{3}$ means that if any number greater than one third is substituted into the original equation, the left side will result in a number larger than 5.

Example using a negative number:

$$-3n + 6 \geq 9$$
$$ -6 \quad -6$$
$$-3n \geq 3$$

Notice that here the inequality is greater than or equal to
But now, after dividing by -3, the inequality is less than or equal to

$$\frac{-3n}{-3} \leq \frac{3}{-3}$$
$$n \leq -1$$

We can show the solution to an inequality on a number line. If the circle we start with is solid then the answer includes the number we are at (in other words if the inequality includes an equal sign such as $\leq$ or $\geq$ a solid circle is used). For instance, for the answer to the last equation we would draw

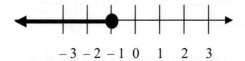

This shows that all values from -1 to the left are solutions to the inequality $-3n + 6 \geq 9$ **including** -1.

If the answer had been $n < -1$ instead of $n \leq 1$ the number line representation of the solution would have been

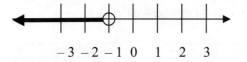

The open circle shows that -1 is not part of the answer set for the inequality.

To test an inequality, simply try substituting in an answer that should **not** work as well as the smallest answer that should.

$$-3n + 6 \geq 9; n \leq -1;$$
$$(-3)(2) + 6 \geq 9$$
$$-6 + 6 \geq 9$$
$$0 \geq 9$$

0 is not greater than or equal to 9

As we saw from above, the answer was not correct when 2 was used in place of n. This further confirms that the inequality is correct only when $n \leq -1$.

$$-3n + 6 \geq 9; n \leq -1$$
$$(-3)(-1) + 6 \geq 9$$
$$4 + 6 \geq 9$$
$$10 \geq 9$$

Related Questions: 8, 26, 27, 35, NR4, NR5, NR6

---

7. *Identify constant terms, coefficients, and variables in polynomial expressions.*
8. *Given the value(s) of the variable(s), evaluate polynomial expressions.*
9. *Perform operations of addition and subtraction on polynomial expressions.*

A polynomial is an algebraic expression that consists of one or more terms. A term is part of an expression separated from others by the operations of addition or subtraction.

For example, in the polynomial $5x^2 + 4x + 6$, there are three terms: $5x^2$, $4x$, and 6. In the polynomial, x is a variable (it is a letter or symbol used to represent the actual value), 6 is a constant (the value of a constant does not change), and 4 and 5 are numerical coefficient (these are numbers multiplied or divided against a variable).

To find the value of a polynomial we simply substitute the given values for the variables.

What is the value of $3x^2 + 2y^2 + 4x + 5$ when $x = 2$ and $y = 3$?

Replacing n with 2 should yield an untrue result because 2 is not less than or equal to 1.

$$3x^2 + 2y^2 + 4x + 5; x = 2, y = 3$$
$$3(2^2) + 2(3^2) + 4(2) + 5$$
$$3(4) + 2(9) + 8 + 5$$
$$12 + 18 + 13$$
$$43$$

To add or subtract polynomials, we simply gather like terms. Like terms are terms that have the exact same variables in the term. $2x^2$ and $5x^2$ are like terms because they both have x^2 as a variable.

$$2x^2 + 5x^2 = 7x^2$$

But $2x$ and $5x^2$ are not like terms. Neither are $2y$ and $2x$. Remember, the variables must be **exactly** the same (including the same exponent).

To add polynomials, just gather like terms.

$$(3x^2 = 5x = 5) = (4x^2 - 2x = 4y - 11)$$
$$3x^2 + 5x + 5 + 4x^2 - 2x + 4y - 11$$
$$7x^2 + 3x + 4y - 6$$

When subtracting polynomials, you must change every sign inside any polynomial that has a subtraction sign in front of it.

$$(2y^3 + 3x^2 + 4y - 12) - (5y^3 + 2x^2 + 2x + 4y - 5)$$
$$= 2y^3 + 3x^2 + 4y - 12 - 5y^3 - 2x^2 - 2x - 4y + 5$$
$$= -3y^3 + x^2 - 2x - 7$$

Related Questions: 36, 37, 38, 25

10. *Represent and justify the addition and subtraction of polynomial expressions using concrete materials and diagrams.*

11. *Represent multiplication, division, and factoring of monomials, binomials, and trinomials of the form $x^2 + bx + c$, using concrete materials and diagrams.*

These two outcomes usually refer to the use of algebra tiles. When you use actual algebra tiles the colours are green for positive x and x^2, red for positive constants and white for all negative numbers. In books that are not in colour, the positive x^2, x and constants are shaded and the negative x^2, x and constants are white.

The following shows
$(2x^2 - 3x + 4) + (x^2 + 5x - 6)$

A positive tile cancels out a negative tile of the same size.

The answer is $3x^2 + 2x - 2$

The following shows
$(2x^2 - 3x + 4) - (x^2 + 5x - 6)$

Remember when subtracting polynomials the sign of all terms in the second polynomial will change. When using algebra tiles, remember to flip the tiles of the second polynomial to the opposite colour.

The answer is $x^2 - 8x + 10$

To represent the product of $2x$ $(x + 3)$ we make a rectangle that is $2x$ tiles wide and $x + 3$ tiles long and then we fill in the square.

> We can see that the answer will be $2x^2 + 6x$

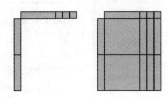

If negatives are involved, remember that a negative multiplied against a positive is a negative and a negative multiplied against a negative is a positive.

For instance, when representing the product of $2x + 2$ and $x - 3$, $(2x + 2)(x + 3)$, we would start by setting up the outside and then fill in the square again.

> We can see that the answer will be $2x^2 - 4x - 6$

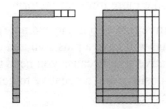

To factor a polynomial, we add the algebra tiles to the outside of a given figure. If we have the figure given below, we can see that it represents $x^2 + 5x + 6$.

We then add the algebra tiles to the outside and we can see that the factors are $(x + 2)(x + 3)$.

To show division of a polynomial, we would use the algebra tiles to represent the equation we are given and find the answer by completing the outside of the figure.

This figure shows $x^2 - 2x - 8 \div x - 4$. To find the answer we simply add the algebra tiles to the other side of the template. We figure out which are positive or negative by remembering again that negative multiplied against a positive is a negative and a negative multiplied against a negative is a positive

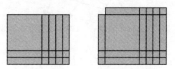

Related Questions: 39, 41, WR1

12. *Find the product of two monomials, a monomial and a polynomial, and two binomials.*

13. *Determine equivalent forms of algebraic expressions by identifying common factors and factoring trinomials of the form $x^2 + bx + c$.*

14. *Find the quotient when a polynomial is divided by a monomial.*

A monomial is a polynomial with a single term. A binomial is a polynomial with two terms and a trinomial is a polynomial with three terms. When we multiply terms together that have numerical and literal coefficients (the literal coefficient is the variable) we must make sure that the numerical coefficient from one term is multiplied against the numerical coefficient of the other term and the same for the literal coefficients (variables). Remember that when variables are multiplied together that the exponents are added together.

Monomial multiplied by a monomial:

$$(4x^2)(-3x)$$

$$-12x^3$$

When we multiply a monomial against a polynomial, we must ensure that the monomial is multiplied against each term in the polynomial.

Monomial multiplied against a polynomial:

$$(3y^2)(2y^2 + 3y - 4)$$

$$6y^4 + 9y^3 - 12y^2$$

When we multiply two binomials together, we must ensure that we multiply every term in one binomial against every term in the other binomial. To help with this we use FOIL. FOIL is a mnemonic device used to help remember how to multiply two binomials. F means the first two terms (multiply those together), O is the outside two terms (multiply those together), I is the inside two terms (multiply those together) and L are the last two terms (multiply those together). After we multiply the terms together, we must gather like terms. Remember that like terms are terms that have the exact same variables.

Binomial multiplied against a binomial:

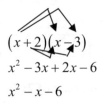

$$(x + 2)(x - 3)$$

$$x^2 - 3x + 2x - 6$$

$$x^2 - x - 6$$

Factoring is just identifying what the polynomials are that are multiplied together to create a different polynomial. To do this we identify the common factors in the terms of the polynomial, remove them and leave them multiplied against each other.

Factoring a binomial:

$$6x^2 + 8x$$

$$(2x)(3x + 4)$$

2 and x are common to both $6x^2$ and $8x$. When $2x$ is removed from the binomial, $3x$ and 4 are all that are left.

Factoring a trinomial is a little trickier. Luckily there is a process we can use to help us factor the trinomial. The factors of a trinomial will be two binomials. When we look at

$x^2 - x - 6$, notice that $-1x$ is the sum of $-3x$ and $2x$ and -6 is the product of -3 and 2. So when we factor a trinomial of the form $x^2 + bx + c$, we need to find two numbers that add to b and multiply to give c.

$$x^2 - x - 6$$

$$(x + \_)(x - \_)$$

$$(x + 2)(x - 3)$$

Here are some more hints for factoring:

If c is negative (like -6 in the example), then one binomial will have a plus sign and one will have a negative sign because you need to multiply a positive and a negative to get a negative answer.

If b is negative then the binomial with the larger constant will be negative. This is because when two numbers are added to give b, the only way for b to be negative is if the larger constant is negative.

If b is negative but c is positive, then both the binomials will have positive constants.

For example:

$$x^2 - 7x + 12$$
$$(x - \_)(x - \_)$$
$$(x - 4)(x - 3)$$

Factoring trinomials is a skill that takes a great deal of practice. Following the same steps each time will help make the process easier and faster with time.

When a polynomial is divided by a monomial, we use long division.

$$
\begin{array}{r}
x - 4 \\
x - 3 \overline{) x^2 - 7x + 12} \\
x^2 - 3x \\
\rightarrow -4x + 12 \\
\rightarrow 4x + 12
\end{array}
$$

> Remember to change the signs before subtraction! The $-3x$ will become $+3x$ because of the subtraction that occurs in long division

---

Related Questions: 32, 34, 42 – 45, NR7, NR8

---

1. Which of the following arrangements of algebra tiles does **not** represent the equation $-4x + 6 = 2x - 12$

   A.

   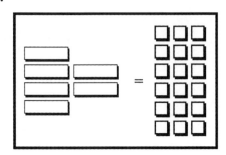

   B.

   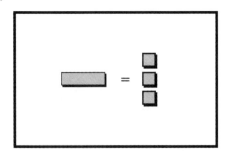

   C.

   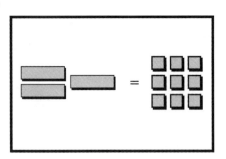

   D.

   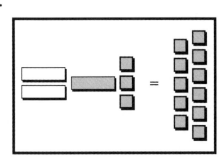

Use the following information to answer the next question.

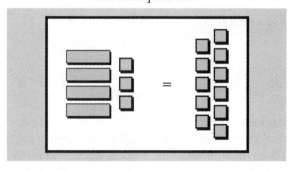

Numerical Response

1. In the equation represented by the algebra tiles above, what is the value of x ?

Use the following information to answer the next question.

Partially shaded algebra tiles can be used to represent fractional equivalents of x.

For example, $\frac{1}{3}x$ can be represented by ▭.

2. What is the value of x in the following arrangement?
(Correct to one decimal place.)

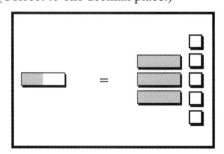

2. In the equation $2(3x + 5) = 5(x - 7)$, x equals

   A. -2

   B. -17

   C. -25

   D. -45

Use the following information to answer the next question.

Maggie wants to buy 3 CDs and 6 tapes. The price of a CD is $7.00 more than the price of a tape.

3. If the price of one CD is x, which of the following formulas can be used to find the total purchase price, P?

    A. $P = 9x - 42$

    B. $P = 9x + 42$

    C. $P = 9x + 21$

    D. $P = 3x + 13$

Use the following information to answer the next two questions.

A computer software store sells Sega game systems for $300.00. Customers who pay 20% of the purchase price at the time of sale can pay the balance in 3 equal payments.

4. If x represents the amount of one payment, which of the following equations can be used to find the amount of each payment?

    A. $x = \dfrac{300 - 20}{20}$

    B. $300 = 0.2(300) - 3x$

    C. $3x + 20 = 300$

    D. $300 = 0.2(300) + 3x$

Numerical Response

3. If a customer puts down an initial deposit of 40% of the total purchase price and pays the balance over 3 equal payments, what is the amount of each of the remaining payments?

5. Which of the following equations is equivalent to $3x = 4 - 2x$?

    A. $x = 4$ **B.** $6x = 4$

    C. $5x = 4$ **D.** $0 = 4 + x$

6. If $0.25x - 15.3 = 0.75x + 12.5$, then x equals

    A. -5.6 **B.** -13.9

    C. -27.8 **D.** -55.6

7. Which of the following expressions is **not** equivalent to $7(3x - 2) = -4(6 - 5x)$?

    A. $x - 10 = 0$

    B. $21x - 14 = -24 + 20x$

    C. $x = -10$

    D. $21x - 20x = 14 - 24$

Use the following information to answer the next question.

Molly is saving for a new mountain bike that costs $460.00, including taxes. She has $238.00 saved and can save an additional $3.70 for every hour that she works.

8. If Molly uses the inequality $238 + 3.70x \geq 460$ where x is the number of hours she works, then the number of hours of work that it will take for her to reach her goal is

    A. $x \geq 60$ **B.** $x \geq 65$

    C. $x \geq 125$ **D.** $x \leq 60$

Use the following information to answer the next question.

It costs $195.00 to rent a car for a week from a car rental company. After 100 km, there is an additional charge of 25¢/km.

9. Which of the following equations defines the cost, c, of renting a car if x is the number of kilometres over 100 km?

   A. $c = 195 + 100(0.25x)$

   B. $c = 195 + 0.25(x - 100)$

   C. $c = 195 + 0.25x - 100$

   D. $c = 195 + 0.25x$

10. A clothing store buys a tuxedo from a supplier for $569. The store charges $109 per day to rent the tuxedo. Each time the tuxedo is rented, the store must pay $10 for dry cleaning. In order to earn back the purchase price, how many times must the tuxedo be rented?

   A. 4   B. 5

   C. 6   D. 7

Numerical Response

4. Enrico needs an 80% average over five subjects in order to qualify for a scholarship. His marks for the first four subjects are 79%, 86%, 83%, and 77%. What mark must he get in the fifth subject to earn the scholarship?_____
(Correct to the nearest whole number)

Use the following information to answer the next question.

The owners of a hotel decide to renovate. The hotel has 198 rooms for guests to stay in, of which 9 are specialty suites.

11. If $7 000 000 was spent on refurbishing the rooms and twice as much was spent on each specialty suite as was on each regular suite then, rounded to the nearest dollar, how much was spent to refurbish each specialty suite? (Assume that an equal amount was spent on each specialty suite and an equal amount was spent on each regular suite).

   A. $33 817   B. $67 633

   C. $69 815   D. $135 266

Use the following information to answer the next question.

Amber wants to connect her home computer to the Internet. An Internet provider will supply the connection for $30.00 per month plus an additional 75 cents for each hour after the first 20 hours of online time.

12. Which of the following equations can Amber use to estimate her monthly Internet bill if t is the total cost and x is the number of on-line hours after the first 20 hours?

   A. $t = 30 + 20x + 0.75$

   B. $t = 30 + 0.75x$

   C. $t = 30 + 20x(0.75)$

   D. $t = 30 + x$

13. Every year Leah and Lin sell chocolate-covered almonds for their school fund raiser at $2.00 per box. If they each sell 5 boxes to their own families, which of the following equations can be used to calculate the total amount of money that they will collect? (t = total dollars, x = number of boxes sold outside of their families)

A. $t = 2.00x = 10.00$

B. $t = 2.00x - 10.00$

C. $t = 10.00x + 2.00$

D. $t = 2.00x + 20.00$

Use the following information to answer the next question.

"Invaders!" is an arcade game that costs 50¢ to play. Once a player is eliminated, the player must insert another 25¢ within 10 s to continue at the same level.

14. If c is the number of times a player chooses to continue, then which of the following equations can be used to determine t, the total cost of playing the game?

A. $t = 0.50 + 0.25c$ **B.** $t = 0.50c + 0.25$

C. $t = 0.50 - 0.25c$ **D.** $t = 0.50(0.25c)$

Numerical Response

5. If $x = 2$ and $y = 3$ then $2x^4y^3 - 9x^3y^0$ is equal to _____ .

Use the following information to answer the next question.

During the 1976 Olympic Games in Montreal, Nadia Comaneci of Romania became the first gymnast to score a perfect 10.0 on a routine. Gymnasts start with a score of 10.0 and points are deducted for every error made during the routine. By the end of the competition, she had received a perfect score seven different times.

15. If 0.1 is deducted for each error, which of the following equations represents the score (s) for a performance, given the number of mistakes (m) that the athlete made?

A. $s = 10(0.1m)$ **B.** $s = 10 - 0.1m$

C. $s = 10 + 0.1m$ **D.** $s = \dfrac{10}{0.1m}$

Use the following information to answer the next two questions.

16. The time differences between the successive clocks above form a sequence. By what factor has each time difference been multiplied to get the next?

A. 2   **B.** 4   **C.** 10   **D.** 20

17. In the sequence above, what time would the next clock in the above sequence read?

A. 1:40   **B.** 2:20

C. 2:40   **D.** 4:00

18. Given that the area of a triangle is $A = \frac{1}{2}bh,$ which of the following statements is **not** true?

A. Two times the area is equal to the base multiplied by the height.

B. Two times the area divided by the base equals the height.

C. The area divided by the height is equal to half the base.

D. One half the area equals the base multiplied by the height.

19. Which of the following equations is equivalent to $\frac{9x+15}{3} = 18?$

A. $3x = 13$

B. $3x + 3 = 18$

C. $9x + 15 = 6$

D. $9x + 15 = 56$

20. Which of the following equations is equivalent to $\frac{9x}{2} + \frac{3}{5} = \frac{1}{5}$

A. $45x + 4 = 0$

B. $\frac{9x+6}{10} = \frac{1}{5}$

C. $\frac{9x+6}{5} = \frac{1}{5}$

D. $45x + 6 = 50$

Use the following information to answer the next two questions.

Recently, an airplane called the Enviroplane established a world record for altitude for solar-powered aircraft. Temperatures at higher altitudes tend to be lower. There is about a 1°C decrease in temperature for every 1 000 m increase in altitude.

21. If it is 32°C at sea level when the plane takes off, which equation can be used to estimate the air temperature as the plane gains altitude? (Let t be the temperature and a be the altitude.)

A. $t = 32 + 1\,000a$

B. $t = 32 + \frac{a}{1\,000}$

C. $t = 32 - \frac{a}{1\,000}$

D. $t = 32 - \frac{1}{1\,000a}$

22. What would you expect the temperature to be at 50 000 m?

A. −18°C

B. 0°C

C. 18°C

D. 27°C

Use the following information to answer the next two questions.

Steel is often used in construction because it is lighter and more durable than iron. A form of carbon called graphite has begun to replace steel in many engineering applications. Graphite is used extensively in aircraft such as the Stealth Bomber since the tensile strength of graphite is even higher than that of steel. Tensile strength, which is the amount of pressure a substance is able to withstand, is measured in pounds per square inch (psi) or newtons per metre squared ($\frac{N}{m^2}$)

23. If the tensile strength of steel is approximately $500 \times 10^6 \frac{N}{m^2}$, and that of graphite is $770 \times 10^6 \frac{N}{m^2}$, how many times stronger is graphite than steel?

   A. 0.65

   B. 1.54

   C. 1.54×10^6

   D. 270×10^6

CHALLENGER QUESTION

24. An additional advantage of graphite over steel is its "lightness" (it is less dense than steel). If the density of steel is $20 \times \left(\frac{3}{4}\right)^4 \frac{g}{cm^3}$ and the density of graphite is $20 \times \left(\frac{1}{2}\right)^4 \frac{g}{cm^3}$ then how many times denser is steel than graphite?

   A. $\left(\frac{3}{2}\right)^4$ **B.** $\left(\frac{3}{8}\right)^3$

   C. $\left(\frac{3}{8}\right)$ **D.** $\left(\frac{3}{2}\right)$

Use the following information to answer the next question.

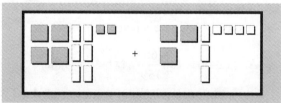

25. Which of the following algebraic expressions is represented by the algebra tiles above?

   A. $7x^2 - 8x + 2$

   B. $7x^2 + 8x + 6$

   C. $7x^2 - 4x + 2$

   D. $7x^2 - 8x - 2$

Use the following information to answer the next two questions.

In 1998, Mark McGwire of the St Louis Cardinals and Sammy Sosa of the Chicago Cubs broke the long-standing major league baseball record for most home runs in a single season. McGwire hit 70 home runs in 155 games while Sosa hit 66 home runs in 159 games.

Numerical Response

6. What was McGwire's season average for home runs per game?_____
(Correct to two decimal places)

26. If Sosa had maintained his regular season pace, which of the following inequalities can be used to calculate the additional number of games Sosa would have needed to exceed McGwire's home run total?

A. $x + 66 > 70\left(\dfrac{66}{159}\right)$, where x is the additional number of games needed to exceed McGwire's total.

B. $x + 70 > 66\left(\dfrac{66}{159}\right)$, where x is the number of home runs needed to exceed McGwire's total.

C. $66 + x\left(\dfrac{66}{159}\right) > 70$, where x is the number of additional games needed to exceed McGwire's total.

D. $66 + x\left(\dfrac{66}{159}\right) > 70$, where x is the number of home runs needed to exceed McGwire's total.

CHALLENGER QUESTION

Numerical Response

7. If $\dfrac{2y}{3} + 2y > 5 - \dfrac{4y}{3}$, then y is greater than _____.

(Correct to two decimal places)

---

27. Which of the following number lines displays all of the solutions to the expression $3m - 1 > -4$?

A.

B.

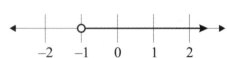

C.

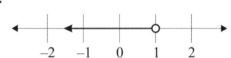

D.

Use the following information to answer the next question.

During the 1996 Summer Olympics in Atlanta, Donovan Bailey of Canada set a world record of 9.84 seconds for the 100 m sprint. During a race, Donovan reached a peak speed of about $(2.1)^5$ km/h. Canadian race car driver Jacques Villeneuve, the 1997 Formula 1 driver of the year, can drive his race car at speeds reaching $(2.1)^8$ km/h.

28. How many times faster is the race-car than the sprinter?

    A. 9.3

    B. 6.3

    C. 3.0

    D. 0.11

CHALLENGER QUESTION

29. Mr. Bueller, a math teacher, tells one of his students that he will be absent the following day. The student tells 2 friends that there will be a substitute teacher, and each of them then tells 2 friends, and so on. If each student who hears the news takes 10 seconds to tell two other students and no one hears the news more than once, how much time from the time that the first student hears the news will it take before the entire class of 31 students learns that a substitute is coming?

    A. 30 s

    B. 40 s

    C. 50 s

    D. 60 s

30. Jill works in a shoe store where she makes $6.25/h plus $3 in commission for each pair of shoes that she sells. Which of the following expressions represents her earnings, a, for an 8 hour day, where n is the number of pairs of shoes that she sells?

    A. $a = 6.25(8 + 3n)$

    B. $a = 8(6.25+ + 3n)$

    C. $a = 8(6.25) + 3n$

    D. $a = 8 + 6.25 + 3n$

31. The equation $\dfrac{4}{x} + \dfrac{3}{5} = \dfrac{1}{5}$ is equivalent to

    A. $\dfrac{20 + 3x}{5x} = x$

    B. $\dfrac{3}{5} = \dfrac{1}{5} + \dfrac{4}{x}$

    C. $\dfrac{20 + 3x}{5x} = \dfrac{1}{5}$

    D. $\dfrac{3}{5} + \dfrac{1}{5} = \dfrac{4}{x}$

32. The factor that is common to both $20x^2 - 125$ and $15x^2 + 5x^2 + 5x - 70$ is

    A. $2x + 5$

    B. $10x + 25$

    C. $x - 2$

    D. 5

Use the following information to answer the next question.

The half-life of a radioactive element is the amount of time required for half of its mass to decay. Carbon-14 has a half-life of 5 730 years and is commonly used for dating organic materials.

33. A wood sample, believed to be about 17 000 years (3 half-lives) old, is to be analyzed with carbon-14 dating. If the age estimate is correct, what fraction of the original mass of carbon-14 should be present in the sample?

    A. 0

    B. $\dfrac{1}{3}$

    C. $\dfrac{1}{8}$

    D. $\dfrac{1}{256}$

34. The expression $4x^2 + 4x - 10 + 4x - 2x^2$ when completely factored, equals

   A. $2(x - 1)(x + 5)$

   B. $2(x + 1)(x - 5)$

   C. $2(2x^2 + 4x - 5)$

   D. $2(x - 1)(x + 4)$

Numerical Response

8. When the expression $9n^4 + 36n^3 + 15n^2$ is divided by $3n$, what is the numerical coefficient of the n^2 term in the quotient?_____.

35. Which of the following number lines represents the solution to the inequality $5x + 5 < 3(2x + 2)$?

   A.

   B.

   C.

   D.

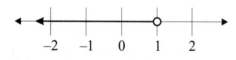

36. The numerical coefficient of $\dfrac{3x^4 y^5}{4}$ is

   A. 5   **B.** 4

   C. 3   **D.** $\dfrac{3}{4}$

37. What is the value of the expression $3x^3 + \dfrac{1}{2}x^4 - 2x + 2$, when $x = 2$?

   A. -10

   B. 14

   C. 30

   D. 106

38. What is the value of the expression $3p^3 + 14q^2 + r^3 - 2p^3$, when and $p = 1$, $q = -2$, and $r = -3$?

   A. 88

   B. 34

   C. 30

   D. -82

39. When simplified, $(6x^2 + 4x - 7) + (2x^2 - 4x - 3)$ equals

   A. $8x^2 + 8x - 10$

   B. $8x^2 + 8x - 4$

   C. $8x^2 - 10$

   D. $8x^2 - 4$

In 1687, Isaac Newton derived the Law of Universal Gravitation in order to understand the motion of the planets. The equation he discovered was

$$F = G\frac{m_1 m_2}{d^2},$$ where:

F = gravitational force,
G = a constant,
m_1 = mass of one planet,
m_2 = mass of another planet, and
d^2 = the square of the distance between them

40. If m_1 is the mass of Earth and m_2 is the mass of the moon, which of the following equations could be used to calculate Earth's mass?

A. $m_1 = \dfrac{Fm_2}{Gd^2}$

B. $m_1 = \dfrac{Fd^2}{Gm_2}$

C. $m_1 = \dfrac{Gd^2}{Fm_2}$

D. $m_1 = \dfrac{Gm_2}{Fd^2}$

41. Which of the following expressions is equal to $(4x^2 + 3x - 9) + (2x + 2 + 6x^2)$

A. $10x^2 + 5x - 7$

B. $6x^2 + 5x - 7$

C. $10x^2 + 5x - 11$

D. $24x^2 + 6x - 18$

Numerical Response

9. When $x = 2.3$, the value of $(5x^3 - 2x + 8x - 1) - (-2x^2 + 5x^3 - 4 + 8x)$ is

_____ .

CHALLENGER QUESTION

Numerical Response

10. If $2x + 3$ is multiplied by $3x + 4$, what is the least number of algebra tiles that would be needed to display the product?

_____

42. Multiplying $5x^2 + 3x + 14$ by $7x$ equals

A. $35x^3 + 21x^2 + 98x$

B. $35x^2 + 21x + 14$

C. $5x^2 + 10x + 14$

D. $35x^2 + 119x$

43. The expression $(8g^2 + 11g - 3)(6h^3 t^5)$ is equal to

A. $(8g^2 + 11g - 18h^3 t^5)$

B. $48g^2 h^3 t^5 + 66gh^3 t^5 - 18h^3 t^5)$

C. $96g^2 h^3 t^5 g$

D. $114g^2 h^3 t^5 - 18h^3 t^5$

44. Which of the following values is **not** a factor of $3n^2 + 9n - 84$

A. 3

B. $n + 7$

C. $n - 4$

D. $n + 4$

45. Which of the following factors is common to both $x^2 + 2x - 15$ and $x^2 + x - 20$?

    A. $x - 5$

    B. $x + 5$

    C. $x - 4$

    D. $x - 3$

Numerical Response

When $11p^5 + 12p^4 + 6p + 2$ is multiplied by $7q^2r^3$, the degree of the resulting polynomial is _____ .

Written Response

1. Multiply each of the following polynomials. Show your work for all steps.

$(7x^3y^2 - 4z)(x^2 - 5z^3)$ **(2 marks)**

$(2x + 3y)(3x - 4y)$ **(2 marks)**

$x(x + 1)(x - 1)$ **(3 marks)**

UNIT TEST 2 – PATTERNS AND RELATIONS

1. If $x = 2$ and $y = -5$, what is the value of the expression $3x^2 + 2y + 4$ equal to?

   A. 6

   B. 14

   C. 18

   D. 26

2. The expression $(5x^2)(3y)(2xy)$ is equal to

   A. $10x^3y^2$

   B. $10x^3 + 6y^2$

   C. $30x^3y^2$

   D. $30(x^2 + y^3)$

3. What is the quotient for $\dfrac{-7a^2bc^3}{21a^3b^2c}$?

   A. $\dfrac{-3c^2}{ab}$

   B. $\dfrac{-c^2}{3ab}$

   C. $\dfrac{-c^2}{3a^{-1}b^{-1}}$

   D. $\dfrac{c^{-2}}{3ab}$

4. Simplified, the expression
   $(-3e^2 + 4ef - 6f^3) + (e^2 - 2ef + 2f^3)$ is

   A. $4e^2 - 6ef + 4f^3$

   B. $-4e^2 + 6ef - 4f^3$

   C. $2e^2 - 2ef + 4f^3$

   D. $2e^2 + 2ef - 4f^3$

5. Which expression is the width of the following rectangle whose $P = 16r^2 + 2r - 2$?

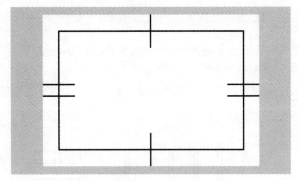

$$7r^2 + 3r - 4$$

   A. $r^2 - 2r + 3$

   B. $2r^2 - 4r + 6$

   C. $5r^2 + 7r - 10$

   D. $6r^2 + 5r - 7$

6. In the sequence, 81, 27, 9, 3, 1 …, what is the next number?

   A. -3

   B. $\dfrac{1}{3}$

   C. $-\dfrac{1}{3}$

   D. $-\dfrac{1}{6}$

7. Janice has a jar full of quarters and wants to put them in money rollers. Each complete roll has a value of $10.00. Which expression will help her make complete rolls?

   A. $4n = \$10.00$

   B. $4n = 100$

   C. $.25n = 100$

   D. $.25n = \$10.00$

8. The value of m in the equation $7m - 10 + 3m = 60$ is

A. 6

B. 7

C. 8

D. 9

9. Which diagram represents the following expression?

$$3x^2 + 2x - 4$$

A.

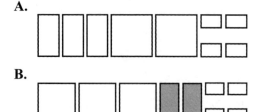

B.

C.

D.

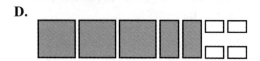

10. In the equation $\dfrac{x}{7} + 5 = 3$, the value of x is

A. −14

B. −12

C. −10

D. −8

11. In the equation $3x + 9 = 7x - 19$, the value of x is

A. −1

B. 1

C. 4

D. 7

12. In the equation $\dfrac{y+1}{7} = \dfrac{12}{21}$, the value of y is

A. 2

B. 3

C. 4

D. 5

13. If $e = 7$, $f = 3$ and $g = -5$, what is the value of $ef - fg + g$

A. 1

B. 11

C. 31

D. 41

14. In the polynomial expression, $4xy^3z + 7x^2yz + 3x^3y^2z$, the degree is

A. 4

B. 5

C. 6

D. 7

15. What is the greatest common factor (GCF) of $3m^2np^3$, $15m^3n^3p^4$ and $36m^2n^2p^3$?

A. $m^2n^2p^2$

B. m^2np^3

C. $3m^3n^3p^4$

D. $3m^2np^3$

16. The expression, $4a(2a + 3) - 2a(a + 2)$ in its simplified form is

A. $6a^2 - 10a$

B. $6a^2 + 10a$

C. $6a^2 - 8a$

D. $6a^2 + 8a$

17. The expression $\dfrac{12a^2b + 15ab^2 - 18a^2b^2}{-3ab}$ in its simplified form is

   A. $4a + 5b + 6ab$

   B. $-4a^2 - 5b^2 - 6ab$

   C. $-4a - 5b + 6ab$

   D. $4a^2 + 5ab + 6a^2b^2$

18. Factoring the following polynomial $4e^2f^2 + 16e^2f - 28efg$ gives

   A. $4ef(ef + 4e - 7g)$

   B. $4ef(e^2f^2 + 4e^2f - 7efg)$

   C. $e^2f^2g(4 + 16 - 28)$

   D. $4(e^2f^2 + 4e^2f - 7efg)$

19. As a trinomial, the expression $(-y + 2)(2y - 5)$, is

   A. $-y^2 - 7y = +3$

   B. $-2y^2 + 9y - 10$

   C. $2y^2 + 7y - 3$

   D. $2y^2 + 9y - 10$

20. Factoring the expression $m^2 - 2m - 15$ gives

   A. $(m + 3)(m - 5)$

   B. $(m - 3)(m - 5)$

   C. $(m - 2)(m - 15)$

   D. $(m + 2)(m - 5)$

21. Factoring the expression $(x^2 - 81)$ gives

   A. $(x + 9)(x + 9)$

   B. $(x - 9)(x - 9)$

   C. $(x + 9)(x - 9)$

   D. Not possible to factor

22. The product of $(3e - 5f)^2$ is

   A. $9e^2 - 25f^2$

   B. $9e^2 + 25f^2$

   C. $9e^2 + 30ef + 25f^2$

   D. $9e^2 - 30ef + 25f^2$

23. What is the product of $\dfrac{15m^2n^2}{2mn^2} \times \dfrac{2m^3n}{3m^2n^2}$

   A. $\dfrac{m}{5n}$ where $n \neq 0$

   B. $\dfrac{5m}{n}$ where $m \neq 0$

   C. $\dfrac{5m^2}{n}$ where $n \neq 0$

   D. $\dfrac{m^2}{5n}$ where $m \neq 0$

24. 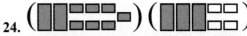 is equal to

   A. $6x^2 + 13x - 28$

   B. $5x^2 + 7x - 4$

   C. $6x^2 + 21x + 3$

   D. $5x^2 + 13x + 3$

25. The expression $(3x - 2)(x + 5)$ is represented by

A.

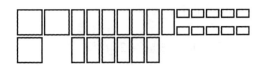

B.

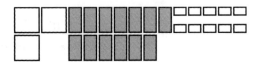

C.

D.

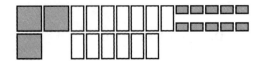

26. Expanding the expression $(x - 3)(x^2 + 2x - 4)$ gives

A. $x^3 + x^2 - 10x + 7$

B. $x^3 - x^2 - 12$

C. $x^3 + 5x^2 + 10x - 7$

D. $x^3 - 5x^2 + 10x - 12$

27. Simplifying the expression $\dfrac{x + 3}{4} + \dfrac{x - 2}{2}$ gives

A. $\dfrac{2x - 1}{6}$

B. $\dfrac{3x - 1}{4}$

C. $\dfrac{4x - 2}{4}$

D. $6x + 2$

28. The expression $4(x + 2) - 3(2x + 5)$ is equal to

A. $10x + 7$

B. $-2x + 23$

C. $2x - 7$

D. $-2x - 7$

29. In its factored form, $4x^2 - 16x - 48$ is equivalent to

A. $4(x + 6)(x - 2)$

B. $2(x - 6)(x + 2)$

C. $4(x + 6)(x + 2)$

D. $4(x - 6)(x - 2)$

30. The coefficient for $-\dfrac{3}{7}xy^4$ is

A. -3

B. 7

C. $-\dfrac{3}{7}$

D. 4

Numerical Response

1. What is the area of the shaded area if
$a = 1$ cm and $b = 2$ cm

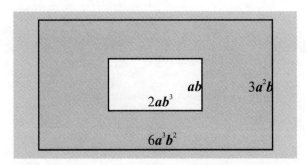

2. State the degree for the polynomials after they have been simplified in the following expression.

$$3e^2 + 5ef^3 - 2e^4g - 3ef^3 + 6fg$$

3. What number belongs in the shaded cell?

2	4	6	8	
5	7	9	11	
10	28	54	88	
5	21	45	77	

NOTES

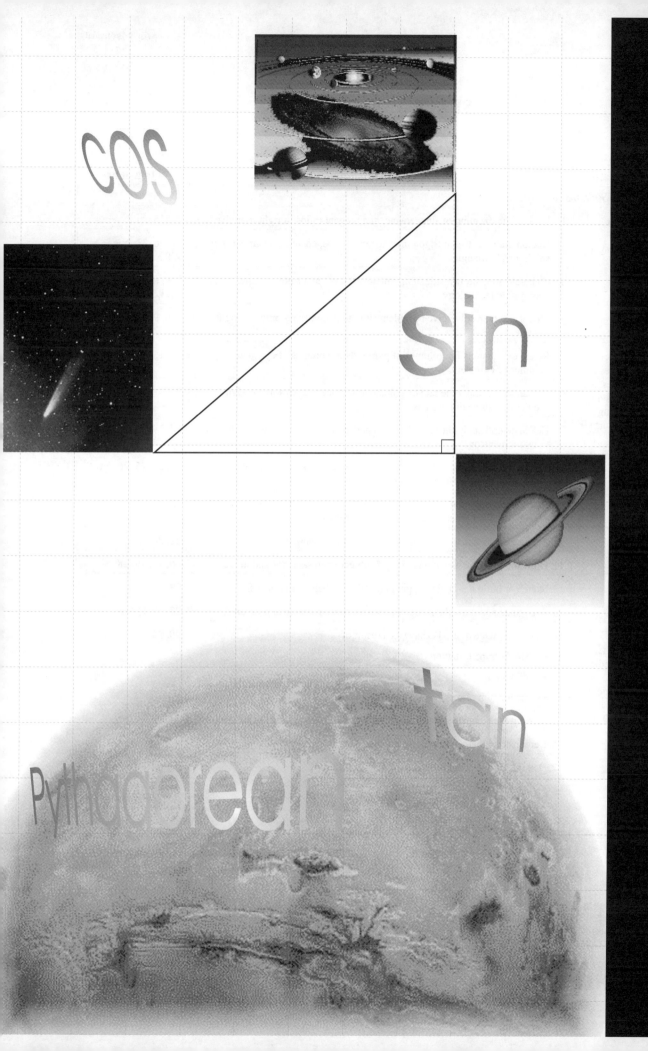

COS

Sin

tan

Pythagorean

SHAPE AND SPACE

Table of Correlations		
General Outcome	**Specific Outcome**	**Questions**
	Students are expected to:	
Use trigonometric ratios to solve problems involving a right triangle.	1. Explain the meaning of sine, cosine, and tangent ratios in right triangles.	2, 3, 5
	2. Demonstrate the use of trigonometric ratios (sine, cosine, and tangent) in solving right triangles.	11, 36, 37, NR7, WR1
	3. Calculate an unknown side or an unknown angle in a right triangle, using appropriate technology.	1, 4, 6, 10, 13, 14, NR3, NR4, NR10
	4. Model and then solve given problem situations involving only one right triangle.	7, 8, 9, NR9, NR11
Describe the effects of dimension changes in related 2-D shapes and 3-D objects in solving problems involving area, perimeter, surface area and volume.	5. Relate expressions for volumes of pyramids to volumes of cones to volumes of cylinders.	14, 15, 20, NR5
	6. Calculate and apply the rate of volume to surface area to solve design problems in three dimensions.	21
	7. Calculate and apply the rate of area to perimeter to solve design problems in two dimensions.	NR2, NR12
	8. Recognize when, and explain why two triangles are similar, and use the properties of similar triangles to solve problems.	18, 23, 25, 26, NR8
	9. Recognize when, and explain why two triangles are congruent, and use the properties of congruent triangles to solve problems.	12
	10. Relate congruence to similarity in the context of triangles.	22, 24
	11. Draw the plan and elevations of a 3-D object from sketches and models.	16, 17, 19, 28
	12. Sketch or build a 3-D object, given the plan and elevation views.	29
	13. Recognize and draw the locus of points in solving practical problems.	27, NR1, N6
Apply coordinate geometry and pattern recognition to predict the effects of translations, rotations, reflections and dilatations on 1-D lines and 2-D shapes.	14. Draw the image of a 2-D shape as a result of • a single transformation • a dilatation • combination of translations and/or reflections	30, 35
	15. Identify the single transformation that connects a shape with its image.	31, 32
	16. Demonstrate that a triangle and its dilatation image are similar.	
	17. Demonstrate the congruence of a triangle with its • translation image • rotation image • reflection image	33, 34

1. *Recognize when, and explain why two triangles are congruent, and use the properties of congruent triangles to solve problems.*

2. *Recognize when, and explain why two triangles are similar, and use the properties of similar triangles to solve problems.*

3. *Relate congruency to similarity in the context of triangles.*

Two triangles are **congruent** if all pairs of corresponding sides and angles are equal. That means the triangles are exactly the same size, but may have a different orientation (in other words, one triangle may be upside down or turned). The sign for congruent is $\cong$. There are three ways to check for congruency:

1. If all three sides of one triangle are equal to the corresponding sides of the other triangle (known as *SSS*).

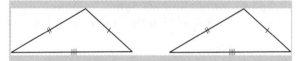

2. If any two sides and the angle contained within them is equal to the corresponding sides and contained angle of the other triangle (known as *SAS*).

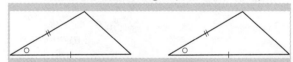

3. If any two angles and the side contained within them is equal to the corresponding angles and contained side of the other triangle (known as *ASA*).

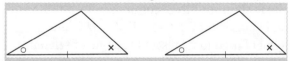

Example

Prove triangle $ABC \cong$ to triangle EFG.

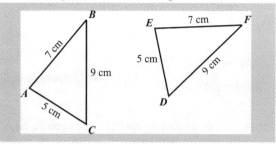

Therefore $\triangle ABC \cong \triangle DEF$ because of SSS.

Similar triangles have the same shape, but not necessarily the same size. We test to see if two triangles are similar by seeing if the measures of the corresponding angles are equal or if the ratios of the corresponding sides are equal. The symbol for similar is ~.

For these two triangles to be similar (~) you need to prove either

$$\angle A \cong \angle D \text{ and } \angle B \cong \angle E \text{ and } \angle E \cong \angle F$$

OR

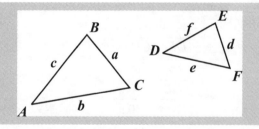

$$\frac{c}{f} = \frac{b}{e} \quad \text{or} \quad \frac{b}{e} = \frac{a}{d} \quad \text{or} \quad \frac{c}{f} = \frac{a}{d}$$

The diagram below shows how two triangles can be used to find the width of a river. Use the triangles to calculate the length of the river at $\overline{DE}$.

$\angle ABC = \angle CED = 90°$

$\angle ACB = \angle ECD$ 　　Opposite angles are equal

If two sets of angles in two triangles are equal,

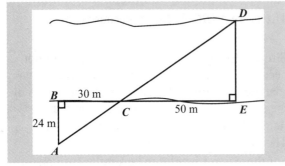

then the third set must be equal also.

Therefore, all corresponding angles are equal so $\triangle ABC \sim \triangle DEF$

This means that the ratio of the corresponding sides must be equal.

$$\frac{\overline{DE}}{\overline{AB}} = \frac{\overline{CE}}{\overline{CB}}$$

$$\frac{\overline{DE}}{24\,\text{m}} = \frac{50\,\text{m}}{30\,\text{m}}$$

$$\overline{DE} = \frac{(24\,\text{m})(50\,\text{m})}{30\,\text{m}}$$

$$\overline{DE} = \frac{1200\,\text{m}}{30\,\text{m}}$$

$$\overline{DE} = 40\,\text{m}$$

The width of the river at $\left(\overline{DE}\right)$ is 40 m.

Related Questions: 12, 18, 22 – 26, NR8

4. *Explain the meaning of sine, cosine, and tangent ratios in right triangles.*

5. *Demonstrate the use of trigonometric ratios (sine, cosine, and tangent) in solving right triangles.*

6. *Calculate an unknown side or an unknown angle in a right triangle, using appropriate technology.*

7. *Model and then solve given problem situations involving only one right triangle.*

Trigonometric ratios apply only to **right** triangles (triangles that have a 90° angle). Remember the longest side of a triangle is called the hypotenuse and the other two sides are called the legs.

The hypotenuse of a right triangle is always opposite the 90° angle. There are three trigonometric ratios we deal with in right triangles: *sine*, *cosine* and *tangent*. Each refers to the ratio of two sides in a right triangle relative to an angle(other than the right angle).

You can see from the triangle in the illustration below that the angle at *A* stays the same but the length of the sides may change based on the triangle chosen. However, the ratios of the lengths of the 3 sides will remain the same.

The ratios are:

$$\sin \theta = \frac{opposite}{hypotenuse}$$

$$\cos \theta = \frac{adjacent}{hypotenuse}$$

$$\tan \theta = \frac{opposite}{adjacent}$$

Sin is short for SINE, cos is short for COSINE and tan is short for TANGENT. θ is the symbol used to represent the angle of reference. We can remember these ratios as SOH CAH TOA.

The OPPOSITE is always the side across from the angle. Side BC is opposite angle A in $\triangle ABC$.

The ADJACENT is always the side right next to the angle (be careful not to accidentally identify the hypotenuse. Side AB is adjacent to angle A in $\triangle ABC$.

The HYPOTENUSE is the longest side and is always across from the 90° angle. Side AC is the hypotenuse in $\triangle ABC$.

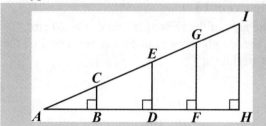

Example

If a ladder is resting against a tree and the base of the ladder forms a 68° angle with the ground 1.5 metres from the tree, how far up the tree does the ladder reach to the nearest tenth of a metre?

To solve this question, it is a good idea to first sketch a diagram of the information given. We are looking for the vertical distance between the ground and the top of the ladder. We are given angle A. The length

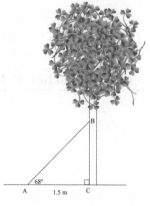

we're looking for, $\left(\overline{BC}\right)$ is opposite angle A.

We also know the length of the side adjacent to angle A, side $\left(\overline{AC}\right)$. $\left(\overline{AC}\right)$ 1.5 metres in length.

The 90° is where the tree meets the ground. It is important to acknowledge the presence of a right angle because without it, we could not use SOH CAH TOA.

$$\tan A = \frac{\overline{BC}}{\overline{AC}}$$

$$\tan 68° = \frac{\overline{BC}}{1.5 \text{ m}}$$

$$\left(\tan 68°\right)\left(1.5 \text{ m}\right) = \overline{BC}$$

$$3.7 \text{ m} \approx \overline{BC}$$

Related Questions: 1–11, NR3, 13, NR4, 14, NR7, NR9–11 36, 37,

8. *Relate expressions for volumes of pyramids to volumes of cones to volumes of cylinders.*

9. *Calculate and apply the rate of volume to surface area to solve design problems in three dimensions.*

A **prism** is a 3-D figure whose bases or ends have the same size and shape and are parallel to one another, and each of whose sides is a parallelogram. A cube is a prism.

The volume of any prism can be found using $V = Bh$ where V is the volume, B is the area of the base and h is the height.

The volume of a **pyramid** takes up $\frac{1}{3}$ the volume of a prism with the same base area. The formula for the volume of a pyramid is

$$V = \frac{1}{3}Bh$$

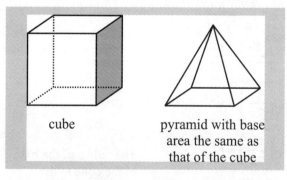

cube   pyramid with base area the same as that of the cube

The volume relationship is similar for cylinders and cones. A cylinder is a prism with a circle for a base. The area of a circle can be found using $V = \pi r^2$. If we use this as the base in the volume of the prism we find that the volume of a cylinder is $V = \pi r^2 h$.

The volume of a cone is $\dfrac{1}{3}$ the volume of a cylinder that has the same base. The volume of a cone is $V = \dfrac{1}{3}\pi r^2 h$.

Example

If a cone has a volume of 23 cm³ and is 7 cm high, what is the radius of the base of the cone, to the nearest tenth of a cm?

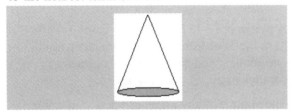

$$V = \frac{1}{3}\pi r^2 h$$

$$23 = \frac{1}{3}\pi r^2 7$$

$$(3)(23) = \left(\frac{1}{3}\pi r^2 7\right)(3)$$

$$\frac{69}{\pi} = \frac{\pi r^2 7}{\pi}$$

$$\left(\frac{69}{7\pi}\right) = \frac{r^2 7}{7}$$

$$\sqrt{\left(\frac{69}{7\pi}\right)} = \sqrt{r^2}$$

$$\sqrt{\left(\frac{69}{7\pi}\right)} = r$$

$$1.77 \approx r$$

$$1.8 \approx r$$

The radius of the base of the cone to the nearest tenth of a cm would be 1.8 cm.

Related Questions: 12, 18, 23, 25, 26, NR8

10. *Calculate and apply the rate of area to perimeter to solve design problems in two dimensions.*

Area and perimeter are directly related. An example is the area of a rectangle is length times width while the perimeter of the rectangle is two times the length plus two times the width. However, rectangles of different lengths of sides and widths can have the same area.

Example

A rectangle with an area of 20 cm² currently has a length of 5 cm and a width of 4 cm for a perimeter of 18 cm.

If the area of the rectangle remains at 20 cm², but the length changes to 10 cm, what will be the new perimeter?

$$A = lw$$

$$20 = 10w$$

$$\frac{20}{10} = \frac{10w}{10}$$

$$2 = w$$

$$P = 2l + 2w$$

$$P = 2(10) + 2(2)$$

$$P = 20 + 4$$

$$P = 24$$

The perimeter of the new rectangle will be 24 cm, but the area will remain fixed at 20 cm².

Related Questions: NR2, NR12

11. *Draw the plan and elevations of a 3-D object from sketches and models.*

12. *Sketch or build a 3-D object given the plan and elevation views.*

13. *Recognize and draw the locus of points in solving practical problems.*

There are no real hints for doing 3-D objects other than, if you can, use cube links to try and personally create 3-D objects. Cube links are sometimes called UNIFEX cubes and you can track them down easily by typing in "cube links math manipulatives" in a search engine like GOOGLE on the Internet. You can practice with them and also take them into the grade 9 provincial achievement test to use. For many students, visualizing in 3-dimensions is very challenging and requires a great deal of practice. If you can visualize 3-D plans without the cubes, you are well on your way.

A **locus of points** just means the set of all points or lines that satisfy or are determined by specific conditions.

For instance the locus of points that are all 3 cm from a given fixed point would be a circle.

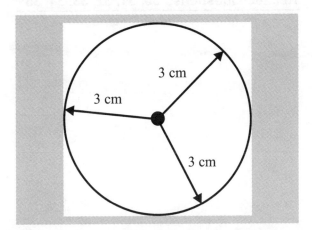

Related Questions: 16, 17, 19, 27–29, NR1, NR6

14. *Draw the image of a 2-D shape as a result of*
   - *a single transformation*
   - *a dilation*
   - *a combination of transformations and/or reflections*

15. *Identify the single transformation that connects a shape with its image.*

16. *Demonstrate that a triangle and its dilation image are similar.*

17. *Demonstrate the congruence of a triangle with its*
   - *translation image*
   - *rotation image*
   - *reflection image*

A **transformation** refers to a change in the x and/or y location of the points on a figure on the Cartesian plane.

A **translation** is a slide where a figure moves horizontally or vertically.

In the figure below, the moon figure at B is the translation image of the moon figure at A.
We can use mapping to describe the translation $(x, y) \rightarrow (x - 6, y - 5)$. This means that the figure has moved 6 units to the left and 5 units down A to B.

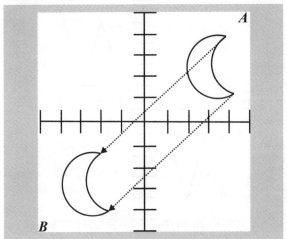

A **reflection** is when an object "flips" its orientation and produces an image that is a mirror to the original. The line of reflection (or mirror line) is the line about which the figure is reflected. Below we can see the reflection image and the line of reflection $\overline{AB}$

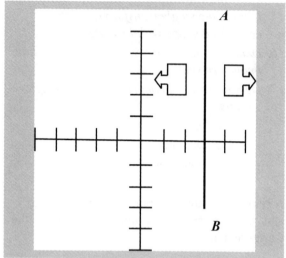

A **rotation** is a transformation in which a figure is turned or rotated about a point. In the figure below, the triangle has been rotated 180° about the origin of the Cartesian plane.

A 90° rotation is $\frac{1}{4}$ of a turn, a 180° rotation is $\frac{1}{2}$ of a turn, a 270° rotation is $\frac{3}{4}$ of a turn.

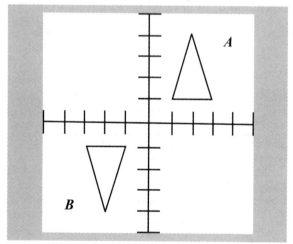

In the figure below, the triangle at A has been rotated 180° and also translated $(x, y) \longrightarrow (x + 4, y - 1)$.

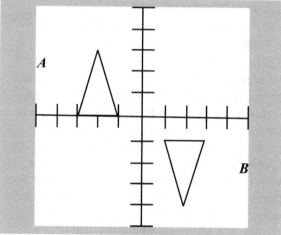

Notice that with these transformations, the images are only changing positions, not shape. Because the shape does not change at all, the resulting image of a triangle will have equal lengths of corresponding sides and equal measures of corresponding angles. This means that triangles that have a translation, rotation, reflection or any combination thereof, will be **congruent** with the resulting image.

Related Questions: 30, 31, 32, 33, 34, 35

1. A triangle has an angle A, where
    $\sin A = 0.496\ 5$. The measure of angle A, to
    the nearest degree, is

    A. $25°$

    B. $28°$

    C. $62°$

    D. $65°$

2. The **exact** value of $\sin A$ in the triangle
    shown below is

    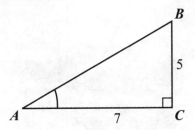

    A. $\sin A = \dfrac{5}{7}$ B. $\sin A = \dfrac{5}{\sqrt{74}}$

    C. $\sin A = \dfrac{7}{\sqrt{74}}$ D. $\sin A = 0.581\ 2$

3. In which of the following triangles does
    $\cos B = 0.8$?

    A. 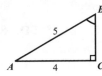   B.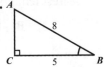

    C. 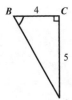   D.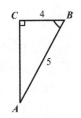

4. The measure of angle A in the following
    diagram is

    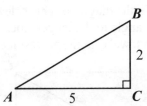

    A. $21.8°$ B. $23.6°$

    C. $66.4°$ D. $68.2°$

5. Given the diagram below of triangle ABC,
    which of the following equations is **not**
    correct?

    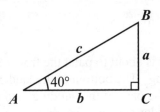

    A. $b = c \cos 40°$ B. $\sin 40° = \dfrac{b}{c}$

    C. $\tan 40° = \dfrac{a}{b}$ D. $b = c \sin 50°$

6. In the triangle below, $\sin B$ is equal to

    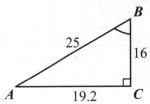

    A. $\dfrac{16}{25}$ B. $\dfrac{19.2}{25}$

    C. $\dfrac{16}{19.2}$ D. $\dfrac{19.2}{16}$

7. A rectangular garden 50 m in length will have a sidewalk built diagonally across it, as shown in the diagram. This sidewalk will be at a 32° angle to the longer side. The length of the sidewalk, to the nearest metre, will be

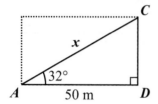

A. 42 m

B. 57 m

C. 59 m

D. 94 m

8. Kenda is about to paint the front of a building. The bottom of the ladder is 1.5 m from the base of the building, and the top of the ladder reaches a height of 5 m up the wall of the building. To the nearest tenth of a degree, what is the angle of the ladder to the ground?

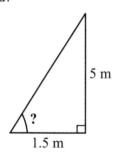

A. 16.7°

B. 17.5°

C. 72.5°

D. 73.3°

Use the following information to answer the next question.

There are hoodoos (tall rock formations) near Hoodoo Creek campground in Yoho National Park, British Columbia. From a viewpoint on one hoodoo, Mike estimates that he is 8 m away from the closest hoodoo, where his twin brother Spike stands.

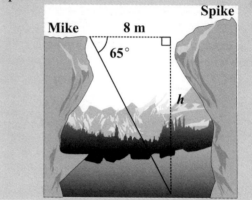

9. Given the information in the diagram, what is the approximate height of the hoodoo that Mike is standing on?

A. 7 m   B. 9 m   C. 17 m   D. 19 m

10. A certain hiking trail has a grade of about 15% (the trail climbs 15 m vertically for each 100 m of horizontal distance). What is the hiking trail's angle of elevation, to the nearest tenth of a degree?

A. 3.8°   B. 8.5°   C. 81.5°   D. 86.2°

Numerical Response

1. If a rotary sprinkler sprays water a distance of 5.5 m, what area of grass can it water?

_____
(In m², correct to one decimal place)

CHALLENGER QUESTION

Numerical Response

2. A circular table with a height of 1 m and a diameter of 2 m is covered with a square tablecloth. If the tablecloth drapes over the edge of the table so that the four corners just touch the floor, what is the total area of the tablecloth when laid flat?_____
(In m², correct to the nearest whole number)

Use the following information to answer the next two questions.

Mark stands at the top of a cliff. From the edge of the cliff, he can see his base camp in the valley below. Mark calculates that the distance from the edge of the cliff to his camp is 900 m. He also knows that he is standing 61 m higher than his camp.

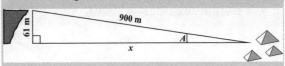

11. Mark climbs straight down from the cliff using a rope ladder. What is the distance, *x*, that he must now travel to get to the camp? (Assume the triangle formed is a right angle triangle, as shown in the diagram.)

A. 839.0 m

B. 897.9 m

C. 902.1 m

D. 961.0 m

Numerical Response

3. A person at the camp is looking at the top of the cliff and sees Mark. In the diagram, angle *A* is the angle of the person's line of sight above the horizontal. The measure of angle *A* is _____°.
(Round your answer to one decimal place.)

Use the following information to answer the next question.

When light is reflected off of a smooth surface, such as polished glass, the path it follows can easily be determined. Almost 2 000 years ago, Hero of Alexandria concluded that the angle at which light strikes a mirror (the angle of incidence) is exactly equal to the angle at which it reflects (the angle of reflection).

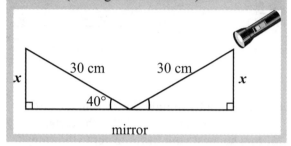

mirror

12. If the light from a flashlight reflects off of a mirror at a 40° angle and the distance the light travels to the mirror is 30 cm, then, rounded to the nearest tenth of a centimetre, how far is the flashlight from the mirror?

A. 19.3 cm

B. 23.0 cm

C. 25.2 cm

D. 46.7 cm

Use the following information to answer the next two questions.

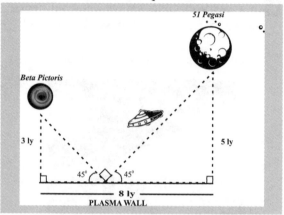

CHALLENGER QUESTION

13. An alien spaceship travelling from *Beta Pictoris* to *51 Pegasi* must first travel to a plasma wall for fuel as shown in the diagram below. What is the total distance the spaceship will travel, in light-years?

A. 9.43 light-years

B. 11.31 light-years

C. 11.66 light-years

D. 12.43 light-years

Numerical Response

4. Once the spaceship refuels, the captain receives a distress call from a spaceship stranded at the end of the plasma wall closest to *51 Pegasi*. If the captain travels to the stranded spaceship and then tows it back to *51 Pegasi*, how far will the spaceship have travelled from the time it got fuel until it reaches *51 Pegasi*? _____
(In light-years, correct to the nearest whole number)

Use the following information to answer the next question.

The Alaskan Pipeline extends 1 270 km and carries up to 2 million barrels of oil per day.

Numerical Response

5. If the diameter of the pipe is 1.5 m, what length of pipe will have a volume of 106 m^3? _____

(In metres, correct to one decimal place)

14. A glass has a diameter of 10 cm at the brim, and is 18 cm high. If the glass has the following shape, what is its volume?

A. 1 885 cm^3

B. 1 414 cm^3

C. 600 cm^3

D. 471 cm^3

15. Another 18 cm high glass with the same diameter has the following shape, where the cone and the stem are each half the height of the glass. How much liquid can this glass hold?

A. 942 cm^3

B. 707 cm^3

C. 236 cm^3

D. 150 cm^3

16. Which of the following diagrams represents the top, front, right, and left elevation of the object shown below?

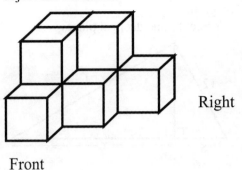

Right

Front

Top	Front	Right	Left

A.

B.

C.

D.

Numerical Response

6. An oscillating fan in the corner of a room is set to rotate through ninety degrees. If air can be felt up to 4.5 m from the fan, what area can be cooled by the fan?

_____

(In m^2, correct to one decimal place)

Numerical Response

7. What is the value of *x* in the following diagram? _____
(Correct to one decimal place)

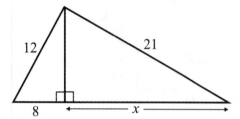

17. Which of the following diagrams represents the top, front, right, and left elevation of the object shown below?

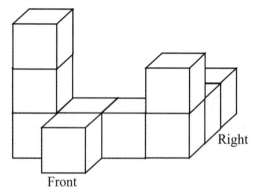

Top   Front   Right   Left

A.

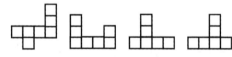

B.

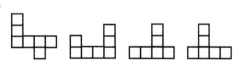

C.

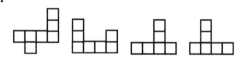

D.

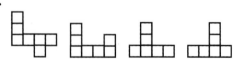

18. What are the similarity ratios of the triangles *ABC* and *ADF* shown in the diagram?

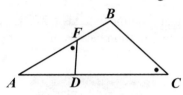

A. $\dfrac{AB}{AF} = \dfrac{AC}{AD} = \dfrac{BC}{FD}$

B. $\dfrac{AF}{AD} = \dfrac{AB}{AC} = \dfrac{FD}{CB}$

C. $\triangle ADF - \triangle ABC$

D. $\dfrac{AB}{AD} = \dfrac{AC}{AF} = \dfrac{BC}{DF}$

19. Which of the following sets of diagrams represents the Top, Right and Left, and Front elevations of Tom's new house?

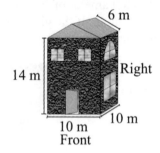

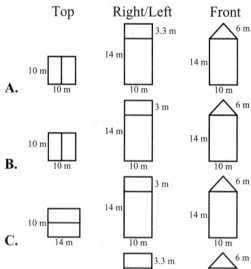

20. A military tent has a base of 4 m by 4 m, and the walls are 3 m high. The pyramid-shaped roof has a height of 3 m. What is the total volume of the tent?

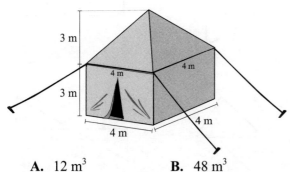

A. 12 m³

B. 48 m³

C. 60 m³

D. 64 m³

CHALLENGER QUESTION

21. How many rectangular **prisms** with different dimensions can be made using 20 sugar cubes?

A. 3   **B.** 4   **C.** 5   **D.** 6

Use the following information to answer the next question.

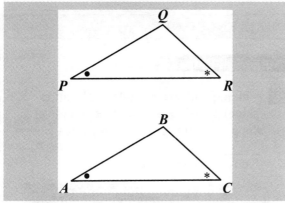

22. The two triangles shown above are

A. congruent triangles

B. similar triangles

C. right triangles

D. isosceles triangles

Use the following information to answer the next question.

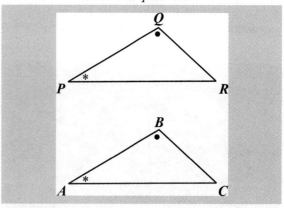

23. The similarity ratios of the triangles above are

A. $\dfrac{AB}{PR} = \dfrac{AC}{PQ} = \dfrac{BC}{QR}$

B. $\dfrac{AB}{PR} = \dfrac{PR}{AC} = \dfrac{BC}{QR}$

C. $\triangle ABC \sim \triangle PQR$

D. $\dfrac{PQ}{AB} = \dfrac{QR}{BC} = \dfrac{PR}{AC}$

24. Which of the following pairs of triangles are **not** congruent?

A.

B.

C.

D.

25. An engineering company must measure the width of a river before building a bridge. Given the information in the following diagram, what is the width of the river?

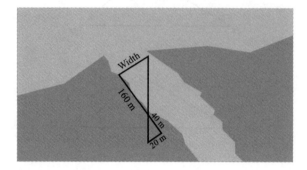

A. 40 m   **B.** 80 m

C. 160 m   **D.** 320 m

Numerical Response

8. In the following diagram, triangle *ADB* is similar to triangle *ABC*. If angle *A* is the same in both triangles, and angle *ADB* is equal to angle *ABC*, what is the value of *x*?

_____

(Correct to one decimal place)

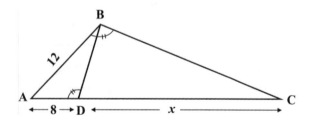

26. Which of the following pair of triangles is not certainly congruent?

A.   **B.**

C.   **D.**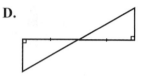

27. A security camera is mounted above an exhibit at a museum and can view everything within a circular region. The region scanned by the camera is a

A. pyramid

B. sphere

C. cone

D. prism

CHALLENGER QUESTION

Numerical Response

9. A hiking trail has an angle of elevation (slope) of 20°. How far must you travel along the trail to climb 30 m vertically?

_____

(Correct to one decimal place)

Use the following diagram to answer the next question

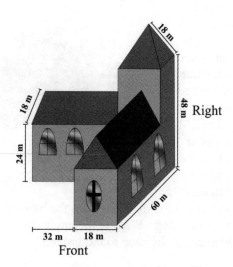

28. Given the diagram above, the correct views (front, top, right, and left elevations) of this 17th century European building are

A.

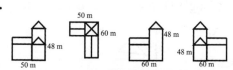

B.

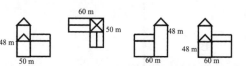

C.

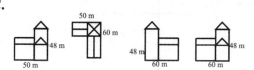

D.

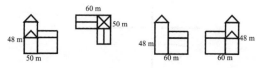

Use the following information to answer the next question.

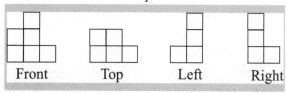

29. The front, top, left, and right views of an object are illustrated above. If the object is constructed from blocks that each have a volume of 10 cm^3, what is the total volume of the object?

A 50 cm^3 **B.** 60 cm^3

C. 70 cm^3 **D.** 80 cm^3

Use the following information to answer the next question.

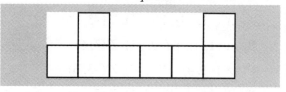

30. Which of the following figures is a reflection of the diagram above?

A. 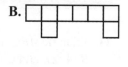   **B.**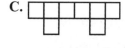

C.   **D.**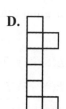

31. Triangle *PQR* is an image of triangle *LMN* obtained from the translation

$(x, y) \rightarrow (x + 1, y - 1)$ If triangle *LMN* has vertices at *L*(1, 1), *M*(1, –1), and *N*(–1, 1) then what are the coordinates of triangle *PQR*?

A. *P*(1, –1) *Q*(1, 1) *R*(–1, –1)

B. *P*(–1, 1) *Q*(–1, –1) *R*(1, 1)

C. *P*(0, 2) *Q*(0, 0) *R*(–2, 2)

D. *P*(2, 0) *Q*(2, –2) *R*(0, 0)

CHALLENGER QUESTION

32. Triangle *XYZ* has vertices at *X*(1, –4), *Y*(–2, 5), and *Z*(3, –6). If it is reflected in the line *x* = 0, what are the coordinates of the image *X′Y′Z′*?

A. *X′*(–1, –4), *Y′*(2, 5), *Z′*(–3, –6)

B. *X′*(1, 4), *Y′*(–2, –5), *Z′*(3, 6)

C. *X′*(–1, 4), *Y′*(2, –5), *Z′*(–3, 6)

D. *X′*(1, –4), *Y′*(–2, 5), *Z′*(3, –6)

CHALLENGER QUESTION

33. Triangle *ABC* has vertices at *A* (6, 8), *B* (4, 2), and C (2, 6). Triangle *ABC* is also an image obtained from the translation

$(x, y) \rightarrow (x + 2, y - 3)$ on triangle *EFG*, followed by a reflection in the *x*-axis. What are the coordinates of the vertices of the original triangle?

A. *E*(4, –11), *F*(2, –5), *G*(0, –9)

B. *E*(8, –5), *F*(6, 1), *G*(4, –3)

C. *E*(4, –5), *F*(2, 1), *G*(0, –3)

D. *E*(8, –11), *F*(6, –5), *G*(4, –9)

Numerical Response

10. A tree is supported by a rope that is tied to the tree and pegged to the ground. The height at which the rope is tied is three quarters of the distance from the base of the tree to the peg. What is the angle (in degrees) of the rope to the ground?

_____

(Correct to one decimal place)

34. Triangle *DEF* has vertices at *D*(2, 3), *E*(7, 4), and *F*(3, 6). Which of the following graphs shows the image of triangle *DEF* after a reflection in the *y*-axis?

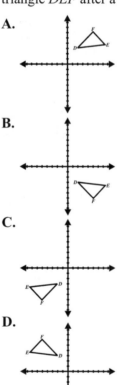

A.

B.

C.

D.

35. Quadrilateral *STUV* with vertices at
S(–3, 4), *T*(–4, –2), *U*(0, –4) and *V*(2, 3) is
rotated 180° about the origin to produce the
quadrilateral *ABCD*. What are the
coordinates of *ABCD*?

  A. *A*(1, –6), *B*(2, 0), *C*(–2, 2), *D*(–4, –5)

  B. *A*(–2, 5), *B*(–3, –1), *C*(1, –3), *D*(3, 4)

  C. *A*(3, –4), *B*(4, 2), *C*(0, 4), *D*(–2, –3)

  D. *A*(5, –2), *B*(6, 4), *C*(2, 6), *D*(0, –1)

*Use the following information to answer
the next question.*

A rescue helicopter is 80 m from a ship in
distress as shown in the diagram below.

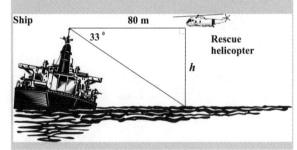

Numerical Response

11. How high above the water level is the
helicopter? _____
(Correct to the nearest metre)

*Use the following information to answer
the next question*

Recently, a team of four climbers from
Wyoming were the first to climb the northern
face of Trango Tower, one of the Himalayas'
most difficult ascents. Because of the height and
difficulty of the climb, it was accomplished in
stages. After a *base camp* was established at the
bottom, a second site was established higher up
the mountain. Since this site was perched on a
ledge, it was called a *hanging camp*.

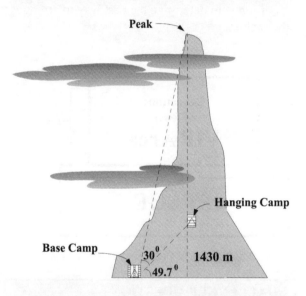

36. The line of sight of a person looking from
the *base camp* to the *hanging camp*, and
from the *base camp* to the peak, is shown in
the diagram above. The corresponding
angles of each view are also given. Given
that the *hanging camp* is 1 430 vertical
meters from the foot of the mountain, what
is the approximate height of Trango Tower
from the foot of the mountain to the peak?

  A. 2 290 m

  B. 5 290 m

  C. 5 370 m

  D. 6 675 m

Use the following information to answer the next question.

The promoters of a rock concert want to fence off a rectangular area directly in front of the stage for a VIP section. They will use 16 sections of fence. Each section is 1 m long. They plan to use the fence for 3 sides of the rectangular area. The front of the stage, or a part of it, will be used for the fourth side.

Note: the diagram below is just one way in which the fence sections could be arranged. Your job is to determine the best way to arrange the sections

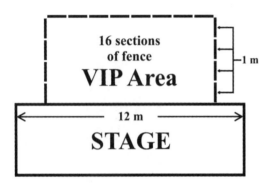

CHALLENGER QUESTION

Numerical Response

12. If the length of the stage is 12 m, what is the greatest area that can be fenced off using 16 m of fence? _____

Use the following information to answer the next question.

The "Drop of Doom" is an amusement park ride. Riders ride to the top of the 13-storey ride in a compartment. The compartment then releases and free-falls, taking the riders safely to the bottom. The drop takes about 4 seconds.

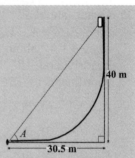

37. Sally stands at the end of the 30.5 m base of the Drop of Doom and looks up to see her friend Pat at the top of the ride 40 m above the ground. What is the angle of her line of sight above the horizontal (i.e., angle *A* in the diagram)?

A. 22.9°

B. 37.3°

C. 52.7°

D. 84.0°

Written Response

*Use the following information to answer
the next question.*

A commercially available motion detector has a
vertical range of 50°. Sasha wants to install a
detector at the end of a 2.3 m hallway.
However, it must be high enough that her 40 cm
tall dog, Fifi will not set off the alarm.

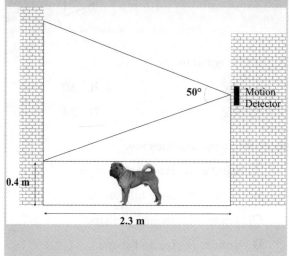

1. How high on the wall must the motion
detector be mounted?   **(3 marks)**

UNIT TEST 3 – SHAPE AND SPACE

Use the following diagram to answer the next question

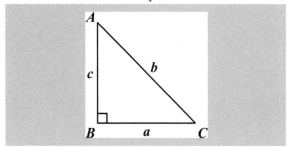

1. In the diagram, to solve for $\angle A$, you would use:

   A. $\sin A = \dfrac{c}{b}$

   B. $\tan A = \dfrac{b}{c}$

   C. $\tan A = \dfrac{a}{c}$

   D. $\cos A = \dfrac{a}{b}$

Use the following diagram to answer the next question

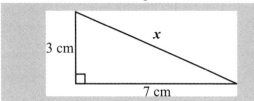

2. In the diagram, *x*, to the nearest hundredth, is equal to:

   A. 6.32 cm

   B. 7.62 cm

   C. 9.14 cm

   D. 10.00 cm

Use the following diagram to answer the next question

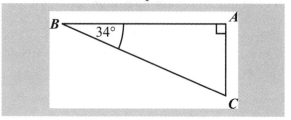

3. $\angle C$ is equal to

   A. 56°

   B. 50°

   C. 46°

   D. 34°

4. Congruent triangles are:

   A. similar in size but not shape

   B. similar in shape but not size

   C. not similar in size or shape

   D. similar in size and shape

Use the following diagrams to answer the next question

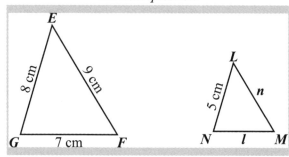

5. If $\angle E = \angle L$, $\angle F = \angle M$, and $\angle G = \angle N$, to the nearest hundredth, what are the lengths of *l* and *n*?

   A. $l = 5.63$ cm, $n = 4.38$ cm

   B. $l = 4.38$ cm, $n = 5.63$ cm

   C. $l = 6.38$ cm, $n = 4.63$ cm

   D. $l = 4.63$ cm, $n = 6.38$ cm

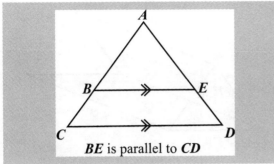

BE is parallel to **CD**

6. ∠*ABE* is equal to

    A. ∠*BAE*

    B. ∠*ACD*

    C. ∠*EDC*

    D. ∠*BEA*

7. The tangent ratio is

    A. $\dfrac{\text{opposite}}{\text{adjacent}}$

    B. $\dfrac{\text{adjacent}}{\text{opposite}}$

    C. $\dfrac{\text{opposite}}{\text{hypotenuse}}$

    D. $\dfrac{\text{adjacent}}{\text{hypotenuse}}$

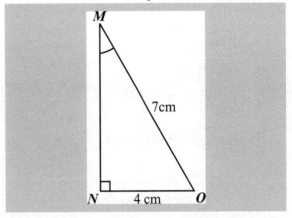

8. What is the measure of angle *M* to the nearest degree?

    A. 30°

    B. 35°

    C. 53°

    D. 55°

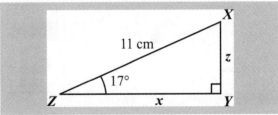

9. What is *x*, to the nearest tenth of a centimetre?

    A. 3.2 cm

    B. 10.5 cm

    C. 11.5 cm

    D. 25.6 cm

10. What keystrokes are used to find *M* in the equation $\tan M = \dfrac{4}{3}$?

    A. $\boxed{\tan}\ \boxed{4}\ \boxed{\div}\ \boxed{3}$

    B. $\boxed{\tan}\ \boxed{3}\ \boxed{\div}\ \boxed{4}$

    C. $\boxed{2nd}\ \boxed{\tan}\ \boxed{4}\ \boxed{\div}\ \boxed{3}$

    D. $\boxed{2nd}\ \boxed{\tan}\ \boxed{3}\ \boxed{\div}\ \boxed{4}$

*Use the following information to answer
the next question*

Anita is standing on the balcony of her
apartment, 12 m above the ground. Her friend,
Aly, is waiting for her on the ground at the
corner. The angle between the building and
Aly's line of sight is 84° as shown below.

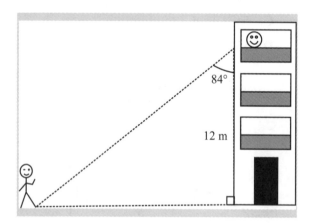

11. How far is Anita from Aly (to the nearest
tenth)?

    A. 114.8 m   **B.** 120.1 m

    C. 110.2 m   **D.** 96.4 m

*Use this diagram to answer
the next two questions.*

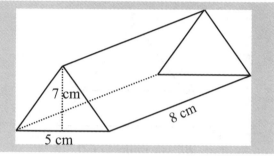

12. What is the surface area?

    A. 193.9 cm^2

    B. 228.9 cm^2

    C. 247.6 cm^2

    D. 212.6 cm^2

13. What is the volume?

    A. 280 cm^3

    B. 240 cm^3

    C. 200 cm^3

    D. 140 cm^3

*Use this diagram to answer
the next question.*

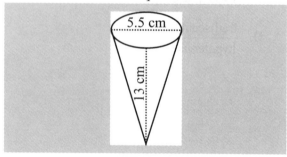

14. How much slushy will fill a snow cone if the
cone's diameter is 5.5 cm and height is
13 cm?

    A. 92 cm³

    B. 103 cm³

    C. 309 cm³

    D. 412 cm³

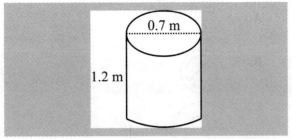

15. How much rain water (to the nearest hundredth) can be collected in this open-top barrel?

    A. 1.85 m^3

    B. 0.82 m^3

    C. 0.46 m^3

    D. 0.38 m^3

16. How much aluminum (to the nearest hundredth) is required to produce this barrel?

    A. 3.02 m^2 **B.** 1.71 m^2

    C. 5.24 m^2 **D.** 3.41 m^2

17. This cube has a surface area of 150 cm^2 What is the length of each side of the cube?

    A. 6 cm^3 **B.** 5 cm^2

    C. 5 cm   **D.** 6 cm

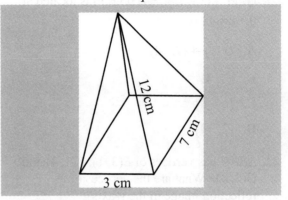

18. The area of the pyramid is

    A. 28 cm^3

    B. 64 cm^3

    C. 84 cm^3

    D. 126 cm^3

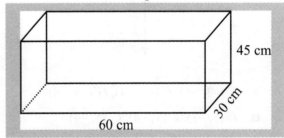

19. How much water does this tank hold?

    A. 81 cm^3

    B. 810 cm^3

    C. 8 100 cm^3

    D. 81 000 cm^3

20. In transformation, a translation image is a _____ from its original.

    A. slide

    B. rotation

    C. flip

    D. dilatation

21. Another way to write
$(x, y) \rightarrow (x - 7, y + 4)$ if (x, y) is located at the origin is

   A. $(x, y) \rightarrow (7, -4)$

   B. $\{7, 4\}$

   C. $[-7, 4]$

   D. $[7, -4]$

22. $\triangle EFG$ has vertices of $E(3, 1)$, $F(1, 4)$ and $G(5, 4)$. What are the vertices of its reflection image in the y-axis?

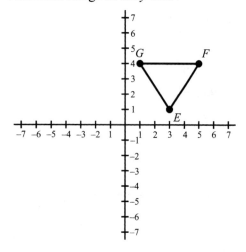

   A. $E'(-3, -1)$, $F'(-1, -4)$, $G'(-5, -4)$

   B. $E'(3, -1)$, $F'(1, -4)$, $G'(5, -4)$

   C. $E'(-3, 1)$, $F'(-1, 4)$, $G'(-5, 4)$

   D. none of the above

23. A $270°$ rotation is equal to

   A. $\dfrac{3}{4}$ turn clockwise

   B. $\dfrac{1}{2}$ turn clockwise

   C. $\dfrac{1}{2}$ turn counterclockwise

   D. $\dfrac{1}{4}$ turn clockwise

24. Which shape was produced with the help of a vertical reflection?

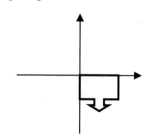

25. Using the following diagram, a $90°$ counter clockwise rotation from the origin of the following shape is

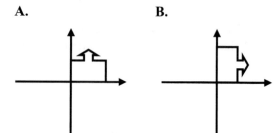

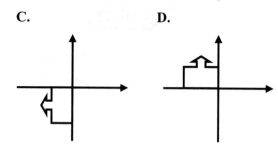

26. Which term is not related to dilatations?

   A. enlargements

   B. reductions

   C. flip

   D. scale factors

*Use this diagram to answer
the next question.*

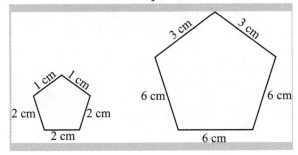

27. The scale factor from △*ABCDE* left to
△*A′B′C′D′E′* right is:

   A. 1

   B. 2

   C. 3

   D. 4

*Use the following information to answer
the next question.*

The vertices of ▱*ABCD* are
A(–3, –4), *B*(3, –3), *C*(1, 6) and *D*(–6, 3)

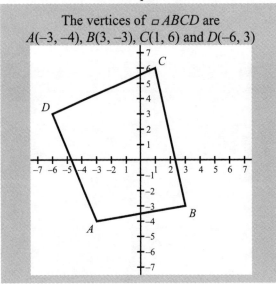

28. The only point inside the locus of the given
quadrilateral is:

   A. (–5, –4)   **B.** (3, 3)

   C. (0, –5)   **D.** (–3, 0)

*Use this diagram to answer
the next three questions.*

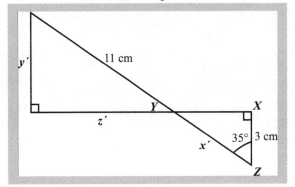

Numerical Response

1. To the nearest degree, what is ∠*Y* equal to?

2. What is the length of *y′* to the nearest tenth?

3. What is the scale factor between △*XYZ* and
△*X′Y′Z′* to the nearest whole number?

NOTES

Statistics and Probability

STATISTICS AND PROBABILITY

Table Of Correlations		
General Outcome	**Specific Outcome**	**Questions**
	Students are expected to:	
Collect and analyze experimental results expressed in two variables using technology as required.	1. Design, conduct, and report on an experiment to investigate a relationship between two variables.	1, 2, 3, 5
	2. Create scatter plots for discrete and continuous variables.	8, 23, 24
	3. Interpret a scatter plot to determine if there is an apparent relationship.	13
	4. Determine the lines of best fit from a scatter plot for an apparent linear relationship by: • inspection • using technology (equations are not expected)	4, 7
	5. Draw and justify conclusions from the line of best fit.	11, 12
	6. Assess the strengths, weaknesses, and biases of samples and data collection methods.	9, 10, 28, 30, 31
	7. Critique ways in which statistical information and conclusions are presented by the media and other sources.	6
Explain the use of probability and statistics in the solution of complex problems.	8. Recognize that decisions based on probability may be a combination of theoretical calculations, experimental results, and subjective judgements.	17, 25, 26, 29, NR6, NR7
	9. Demonstrate an understanding of the role of probability and statistics in society.	15, 27, NR2, NR4
	10. Solve problems involving the probability of independent events.	14, 16, 18, 19, 20, 21, 22, NR1, NR3, NR5

STATISTICS AND PROBABILITY

1. *Design, conduct and report on an experiment to investigate a relationship between two variables.*

Variables represent values that change, or vary. An example of completing this outcome would be to design an experiment about how high a ball bounces vs. the height you drop the ball from. You would need a ball and a metre stick. Hold the metre stick vertical and drop the ball from different heights and record how high the ball bounces each time. For instance, you could drop the ball 10 times starting at a height of 100 centimetres and increasing by 100 centimetres each time. Therefore, your second drop would be from 200 centimetres, your third from 300 centimetres and so on. Each time you would record how high the ball bounces back up the metre stick. You could then create a table that showed your information and use it in a report about your conclusion.
It may look like this:

Height Ball Dropped From (cm)	Height Ball Bounces (cm)
100	25
200	52
300	77
400	110
500	123
600	147
700	179
800	210
900	222
1000 (1 metre)	257

Your conclusion in your report could be that the higher the ball is when it is dropped, the higher the ball bounces.

Your report would include what you were trying to find out, the materials you used, how the experiment was conducted, your data (the values in the table) and your conclusion.

Related Questions: 1, 2, 3, 5

2. *Create scatter plots for discrete and continuous variables.*

A discrete variable is one that cannot take on all values within the limits of the variable. For example, responses to a five-point rating scale can only take on the values 1, 2, 3, 4, and 5. The variable cannot have the value 1.7. A variable such as a person's height can take on any value. Variables that can take on any value and therefore are not discrete are called continuous. For instance, the height the ball bounces to is a continuous variable; it could be any measurement on the metre stick. A scatter plot for the ball chart would look like this:

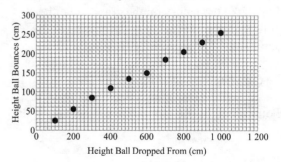

Height Ball Bounces

A scatter plot may or may not have a line connecting the plots. (The dots on the chart are the plots).

Related Questions: 8, 23, 24

3. *Interpret a scatter plot to determine if there is an apparent relationship.*

There would be a relationship for data if you see one set of data consistently increasing or decreasing when the other set of data increases or decreases. Looking at the scatter plot for the height of the bouncing ball, we can see that as the height the ball is dropped from increases, the height the ball bounces to increases, so there is an apparent relationship.

Related Questions: 13

4. *Determine the lines of best fit from a scatter plot for an apparent linear relationship by either inspection or using technology.*

5. *Draw and justify conclusions from the line of best fit.*

A line of best fit is a straight line that is as equidistant from the plots as possible. Ideally all plots would lie on the line, but since it is called the line of BEST fit, it is most likely that there will be some points that do not lie on the line. As such, the plots do not have to be **on** the best fit line. An apparent linear relationship means it looks like the values on the graph are either continuously increasing or decreasing at the same rate. Looking at the Height Ball Bounces scatter plot, we can see that a straight line could be drawn on the chart (and most plots would lie on that line). This means that an increase in bounce height corresponds to an increase in drop height.

Using Excel, you could use the line from the Drawing tool bar to create a line of best fit for this chart that would look like:

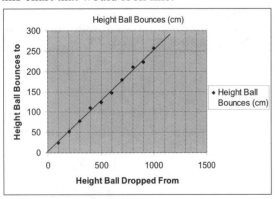

Notice that many of the plots are not on the best fit line. Using the line of best fit we can draw the conclusions that:

*   The height the ball bounces to is related to the height the ball bounces from.
*   The higher the ball is dropped from, the higher the height the ball will bounce to.

Related Questions: 4, 7, 11, 12

6. *Assess the strengths, weaknesses and biases of samples and data collection methods.*

7. *Critique ways in which statistical information and conclusions are presented by the media and other sources.*

8. *Recognize that decisions based on probability may be a combination of theoretical calculations, experimental results and subjective judgments.*

9. *Demonstrate an understanding of the role of probability and statistics in society.*

A bias is when information or data is presented in a manner that tries to sway the conclusions people will draw. For example, a headline could say that a cabinet minister has stepped down from his position, or the headline could say that a cabinet minister was fired. One headline makes a very different impression than the other.

A sample is small group, chosen from a larger group, which is examined in order to make estimates about the larger group. When you hear that Gallop did a poll about how Canadians will vote in the next election, and they asked 1000 people, those people are a sample. Their responses are used to represent how the population of Canadians of voting age will vote.

Data collection error can happen in several ways but usually is a result of a bias in the sample. For instance, if you do a survey and use a phone list provided by a church, you may get bias data on some issues. Or if a survey was done in a school that asked if the basketball team should have its way paid from student council funds for a basketball camp, but you only collect data by asking people in the school who play sports, you may get a different answer that if you pick a group of people at random.

If it is reported that a law was passed by a majority of 59% support an issue, would it be the same story if it was reported that a law passed despite 41% of people opposing it?

Many people use the probability and statistics they hear as one factor in making a decision. For instance, if the weather station says the forecast is for 30% chance of rain, but when you go outside it is humid and you see a solid dark sky, you may dress for rain or bring an umbrella. You are using your own judgment to conclude that there is a much higher probability of rain than 30%.

If you own a company that makes razors for men, would you direct your advertising towards events that have more men or women?
You would obviously direct your advertising dollars towards events that attract more men. You could find this out by looking at available statistics about the gender of the spectators at events.

For instance, which of the events in the table below would you send your advertising dollars towards if you own the razor company for men? (These statistics are not real).

Sport	% Men Spectators	% Female Spectators
Football	68	32
Boxing	82	18
Volleyball	35	65
Field Hockey	15	85

You would probably send your advertising dollars to the football and boxing sport based on these statistics.

Related Questions: 6, 9, 10, 15, 17, 28–31, NR2, NR4, NR5, NR6

10. *Solve problems involving the probability of independent events*

Probability is the total number of favorable outcomes divided by the total number of possible outcomes. For instance, if you have a single six–sided die and you want to know the probability of rolling a four, four would be the favorable outcome and there is only one side of a die that has a four, so the number of favorable outcomes would be one. The total number of possible outcomes for a six-sided die is six.
$\frac{1}{6} = 0.1666...$ to change this to a percent we multiply by 100. $0.1666... \times 100 = 16.666...\%$ rounded to one decimal place would be 16.7% Independent events are events whose outcomes are not affected by each other. For instance, what is the probability of rolling a 4 on a six-sided die and drawing a two from a deck of cards?

First we find the probability of rolling a 4 which we know is $\frac{1}{6}$. The probability of drawing a two is $\frac{4}{52}$ (remember that there are 4 different twos in a deck of cards). To find the probability of both of these independent events occurring, we would multiply them together. $\frac{1}{6} \times \frac{4}{52} = \frac{4}{312}$ and reduce the answer $\frac{4}{312} \div \frac{4}{4} = \frac{1}{78}$. If we wanted to change $\frac{1}{78}$ to a percent, we would divide 1 by 78 $\left(\frac{1}{78} = 0.128 \right)$. Then multiply by one hundred ($0.0128 \times 100 = 1.28\%$) which rounded to the nearest tenth would be 1.3%. So we can say that there is a 1.28% chance of rolling a four on a die and drawing a two from a deck of cards simultaneously.

Related Questions: 14, 16, 18–22, NR1, NR2, NR3

Some of the questions in this unit will require the student to graph the data provided. If you have a graphing calculator or computer, enter the data into the appropriate graphing spreadsheet program. Otherwise, plot any graphs you may require on graph paper.

Use the following information to answer the next three questions.

Immigrants to Canada by Birthplace and Years of Residence, 1994-95

1. Prior to 1985, the largest number of immigrants to Canada originated from

   A. Latin America

   B. Europe

   C. Asia

   D. Australia and New Zealand

2. Prior to 1985, approximately what percentage of immigrants came from Asia ?

   A. 17%   B. 25%

   C. 55%   D. 65%

3. The percentage of Canada's immigrants from one region has decreased dramatically in recent years. From which world region is this?

   A. Europe

   B. Latin America

   C. Asia

   D. Africa

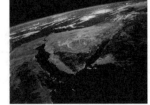

Use the following table to answer the next question.

Year	Number of Dentists in Canada
1980	10 325
1985	12 075
1990	13 025

4. Assuming the trend continued, approximately how many dentists were there in 1995?

   A. 12 800   B. 13 550

   C. 13 975   D. 14 975

Use the following data table to answer the next two questions.

Name	Resting Rate	Recovery Time
Renu	78	15
Vic	54	7
Reg	72	15
Gary	60	9
Liz	66	12

5. According to research, the resting heart rate of a fit individual tends to be lower than that of an unfit person, because the heart becomes more efficient with regular exercise. Given this fact, the people above, ordered from most fit to least fit, are

   A. Reg, Liz, Renu, Gary, and Vic

   B. Renu, Reg, Liz, Gary, and Vic

   C. Vic, Gary, Renu, Liz, and Reg

   D. Vic, Gary, Liz, Reg, and Renu

6. The data collected on these five people do not necessarily provide strong evidence of the correlation between better fitness and lower resting heart rates. What is the most serious limitation of the data?

A. The difference in recovery rates between men and women is not taken into account in the data.

B. There is not enough variety in the fitness levels of the individuals being tested.

C. The sample size is not large enough to generalize across a population.

D. There is no attempt to account for differences in the height and weight of these individuals.

Use the following information to answer the next question.

Year	All fatal and injury collisions in which the driver had consumed alcohol before the accident (%)
1991	38.5
1992	37.1
1993	30.3
1994	25.7
1995	26.6

7. Which of the following statements is **not** supported by the information in the chart?

A. The percentage of alcohol-related injury collisions is lower in 1995 than in most previous years.

B. The largest one-year decline in alcohol-related injury collisions was between 1992 and 1993.

C. Alcohol will probably be involved in less than 10% of all injury collisions by the year 2000.

D. The decrease in alcohol-related injury collisions is not steady and may be levelling off.

8. Shirley is doing some research on the weekly income of high school students. Which of the following scatter plots is the **most likely** plot of her results?

A.

B.

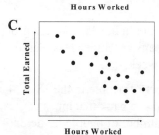

C.

D.

Hours Worked

Use the following information to answer the next two questions.

Frequency of Bank Machine Use (%)			
Age (years)	Never	1 – 2 times per week	3 or more times per week
18 – 24	18	40	42
25 – 34	20	45	35
35 – 44	29	43	28
45 – 54	42	40	18
55 – 64	53	38	9
65+	75	21	4

9. The age group that tends to use the machines most often is

   A. 18 – 24   B. 25 – 34

   C. 45 – 54   D. 65+

10. Which of the following statements **cannot** be inferred from the table?

    A. Of the people in the 45 – 54 age group, 40% use bank machines once or twice per week.

    B. Of the people in the 25 – 34 age group, 80% use bank machines at least once a week.

    C. Of the people in the 35 – 44 age group, 72% use bank machines less than three times per week.

    D. The number of people in the 18 – 24 age group who use bank machines is greater than the number of people in the 25 – 34 age group who use bank machines.

Use the following graph to answer the next two questions.

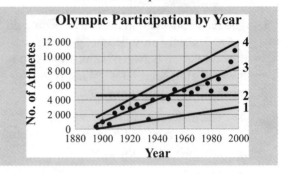

11. The trend indicated by the scatter plot above can be reasonably attributed to each of the following factors **except** for an increase in the

    A. number of athletes for each event

    B. number of participating nations

    C. number of events

    D. frequency of the Olympic Games

12. Of the four labelled lines on the graph above, which line best represents the data?

    A. 1   B. 2

    C. 3   D. 4

Use the following scatterplot to answer the next question.

Final Marks vs. Attendance

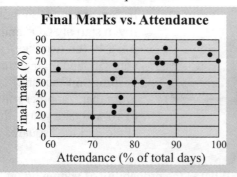

CHALLENGER QUESTION

13. Which of the following statements best describes the correlation between attendance and a student's final marks?

A. Some students attain better grades because they have better attendance.

B. Some students have better attendance because they attain good grades.

C. There is no correlation between attendance and grades.

D. There is a correlation between attendance and grades, but one does not necessarily imply the other.

Use the following information to answer the next question.

A carnival game advertises that everyone who plays can win a prize. To play the game, contestants pull any one of 50 strings from a barrel. The other end of each string is attached to a button that determines whether the player wins a "small," "medium," or "large" prize. Suppose that only two strings are connected to "large" buttons, eight to "medium" buttons, and the rest to "Small."

14. The probability of winning either a large or medium prize is

A. $\dfrac{1}{5}$ **B.** $\dfrac{1}{25}$ **C.** $\dfrac{4}{25}$ **D.** $\dfrac{8}{25}$

Use the following information to answer the next question.

The following information was gathered by Statistics Canada in a survey of Canadian men and women under 45 years of age.

Percentage of Total Income Spent on Living Sporting Events

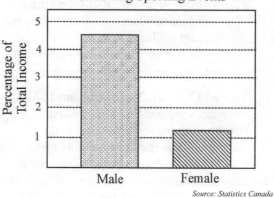

Source: Statistics Canada

15. A conclusion that can be drawn from this survey is that

A. males generally spend more money than females

B. single females spend about 25% less money than single males

C. males under 45 years of age spend about 25% more money on sporting events than females

D. females under the age of 45 spend a smaller percentage of their income on live sporting events than do males.

CHALLENGER QUESTION

Numerical Response

1. Alesha has a 52-card deck, a dime, and a 6-sided die. She draws one card from the deck, flips the coin, and rolls the die. The combined probability of drawing a face card (Jack, Queen, or King), flipping heads, **and** rolling a 3 or higher is 1 out of _____. (Correct to one decimal place)

16. Tom and Joni are 2 of 20 students in Mrs. Feldman's math class. She needs a volunteer to deliver a message to the custodian. She thinks of a number from 1 to 40 and asks each of her students to write their guess on a piece of paper. What is the likelihood of Tom and Joni guessing the same number?

A. $\dfrac{1}{40}$ B. $\dfrac{1}{20}$

C. $\dfrac{1}{18}$ D. $\dfrac{1}{2}$

Use the following information to answer the next question.

A Las Vegas roulette wheel has 38 numbers (1–36, 0, and 00). The 0 and 00 are green in colour and of the other 36 numbers, 18 are red and 18 are black.

17. What is the probability of getting a green number on one spin of the roulette wheel?

A. $\dfrac{1}{38}$ B. $\dfrac{1}{36}$

C. $\dfrac{1}{19}$ D. $\dfrac{1}{2}$

CHALLENGER QUESTION

In the game of Monopoly, if you start at "GO" and roll a 10 (on two dice) you will land on the "Just Visiting/Jail" square. From there, another roll of 10 will take you to the "Free Parking" square.

18. What is the probability of ending up on "Free Parking" by rolling a 10 followed by another 10?

A. $\dfrac{1}{36}$

B. $\dfrac{1}{100}$

C. $\dfrac{1}{144}$

D. $\dfrac{1}{324}$

CHALLENGER QUESTION

19. The probability of two particular independent events occurring is $\dfrac{1}{12}$. If the first event is rolling a 5 on a die, then the second event could be

A. randomly selecting the ace of hearts out of a deck of 52 cards

B. randomly selecting a red ace out of a deck of 52 cards

C. randomly selecting a heart out of a deck of 52 cards

D. randomly selecting a red card out of a deck of 52 cards

20. A 6-sided die is rolled 3 times and the results are tallied. Which of the following results is most likely?

    A. All 3 rolls are the same number.

    B. All 3 numbers are different.

    C. All 3 numbers are odd.

    D. The numbers 1, 2, and 3 are each rolled once.

Numerical Response

2. In the 2002 World Cup of soccer held in Korea and Japan, 32 teams competed. During World Cup play, teams were divided into 8 groups of 4, with each group having 1 top seed. If all of the teams were equally rated, then what was the probability of a top seed winning the World Cup?_____
(Correct to two decimal places)

21. Sasha flips 3 nickels while Arun flips 2 quarters. Which of the following outcomes has the **lowest** probability of occurring?

    A. Sasha flips heads on all three nickels

    B. Arun flips tails on both quarters

    C. Sasha gets two heads and one tail

    D. Arun gets one head and one tail

22. Jake is playing a game that requires him to roll a fair eight-sided die. Each side of the die bears a different number from 1 to 8. If he rolls a 1 or an 8, he loses his turn. He continues to play if he rolls 2, 3, 4, 5, 6, or 7. The probability that Jake **does not** roll 1 or 8 in his first 30 rolls is

    A. 8.7×10^{-19}

    B. 0.000 18

    C. 0.000 24

    D. 0.75

Use the following information to answer the next question.

Karl Malone of the Los Angeles Lakers led his team to the 2004 NBA final, which they lost to the Detroit Pistons in six games. Malone's free throw percentage for the season was 75%.

Numerical Response

3. If Malone is awarded two free throws, what is the probability that he makes both attempts?_____
(Correct to two decimal places) (Assume each attempt is an independent event, that is, what happens on the first attempt does not influence his second attempt.)

Use the following information for the next two questions.

The following table of information compares certain physical properties of the 9 planets in our solar system. The values have been given in terms of Earth units to make the comparisons easier to interpret. For example, the distance from the sun to Earth is one astronomical unit, so the table shows that Mars is about one and a half (1.52) times farther from the sun than is Earth.

Planet	Distance from Sun	Radius	Surface Gravity
Mercury	0.39	0.38	0.38
Venus	0.72	0.95	0.91
Earth	1.00	1.00	1.00
Mars	1.52	0.53	0.39
Jupiter	5.20	11.2	2.74
Saturn	9.54	9.42	1.17
Uranus	19.18	4.10	0.94
Neptune	30.06	3.88	1.15
Pluto	39.44	0.18	0.03

23. Students in a grade 9 math class are asked to describe the correlation between the radii of the planets and their distances from the sun. The students were told that they could use a calculator, computer, or graph paper to plot the data sets. Which of the following statements best describes the correlation between the two data sets ?

   A. There is no correlation between these two measures.

   B. There is a strong linear correlation between these two measures.

   C. There is a partial correlation (a best-fit line applies to some points on the graph).

   D. There is a non-linear correlation (i.e., there is a best-fit curve but no best-fit line).

24. The students were also asked to plot the radius versus surface gravity of the planets. What conclusion could the students draw from the graph?

   A. The surface gravity depends directly on the radius of the planet.

   B. The surface gravity depends somewhat on the radius, but there appear to be other factors involved as well.

   C. The surface gravity does not depend on the radius of the planet.

   D. The surface gravity depends inversely on the radius (the larger the radius, the lower the gravity).

Numerical Response

4. If two coins are flipped at the same time, what is the probability that they land the same way (either both heads or both tails)?

_____

(Correct to two decimal places)

Numerical Response

5. Sandy has been studying for her math exam all week because she wants to go to the beach on the weekend. On Friday morning, she hears on the radio that there is a 35% chance of rain for Saturday and that it is twice as likely to rain on Sunday. Given this forecast, what is the probability, expressed as a whole number/percent, that it will **not** rain on Sunday?

_____

Numerical Response

6. A red, a blue, a purple, and a green 6-sided die are rolled, and the number and colour of each die is recorded.
How many different outcomes are possible?

_____

25. A newspaper asks readers to call a special pay telephone line to express their views on a controversial issue. The results of this poll could be misleading because

A. the sample space could be too large.

B. anybody who wanted to, could call in.

C. people who did not subscribe to the newspaper might still respond to the poll.

D. the price of the telephone call could deter some people from calling in.

Use the following information to answer the next question.

Mario Lemieux's hockey statistics for the 2000–01 hockey season are shown on the table below.

Games Played	43
Goals	35
Assists	41
Points	76
Game-Winning Goals	5
Shots on Goal	171
Shooting Percentage	20.5

26. The ratio of the number of times that Lemieux scored a goal to the number of times he did not score is

A. 1:5 **B.** 1:4

C. 35:171 **D.** 35:136

27. A company is doing a survey to determine which type of drink adults like better: soft drinks, fruit juices, or water. A representative sample could be obtained by

A. polling the spectators at a basketball game.

B. doing a random telephone survey.

C. surveying all the employees in an office building.

D. polling the students and teachers at a local high school.

28. A sports magazine placed a questionnaire on the back page to find out what people thought of a proposal for taxpayers to pay for a new sports facility. Which of the following statements describes a potential source of bias in this type of survey?

A. Since all of the readers are males, they would all say they are in favour of building the facility.

B. Since all the readers would complete the questionnaire, the results would be hard to tabulate.

C. Since there are different opinions on the issue, it would be difficult to tell exactly what the readers thought of the proposal.

D. Since many of the readers who would look at the magazine are sports fans, they would probably only provide favourable opinions.

Written Response

1. The following line graph compares the average household taxable income for all of Canada against the average taxable income for households in a small Saskatchewan town. The solid black line shows the data collected from 5 300 surveys conducted by Statistics Canada. The dashed line represents the results of a civic poll of 187 residents in the small town.

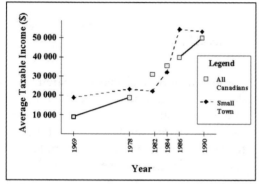

Source: Statistics Canada

a) State two possible explanations for the differences in the graphs.

(2 marks)

b) Explain how the weather might affect the average taxable income in the town in Saskatchewan more than the national average.

(1 mark)

2. At the end of the 2002 – 2003 National Hockey League season, a total of 104 players had achieved 800 or more career points, and Wayne Gretzky, with 2 857 career points, led all NHL players in points by a large margin (Source: National Hockey League Official Guide and Record Book). The following table summarizes the list of players, indicating the number of players in each 100-point range. The histogram further illustrates the distribution of players achieving each of these milestones.

All-Time Points (regular season)

Point Range	Number of Players	Histogram
800–899	24	************************
900–999	14	**************
1 000–1 099	20	********************
1 100–1 199	8	********
1 200–1 299	14	**************
1 300–1 399	9	*********
1 400–1 499	5	*****
1 500–1 599	3	***
1 600–1 699	2	**
1 700–1 799	2	**
1 800–1 899	2	**
1 900–1 999	–	
2 000–2 099	–	
2 100–2 199	–	
2 200–2 299	–	
2 300–2 399	–	
2 400–2 499	–	
2 500–2 599	–	
2 600–2 699	–	
2 700–2 799	–	
2 800–2 899	1	*
2 900+	–	

a) How might this information be used to compare Gretzky's achievements in hockey with the best players in other sports, such as football, baseball, and basketball?

(1 mark)

b) Complete the following line graph by plotting and connecting points for each **200**-point interval, with each point representing the **total** number of players to have achieved that plateau.

(3 marks)

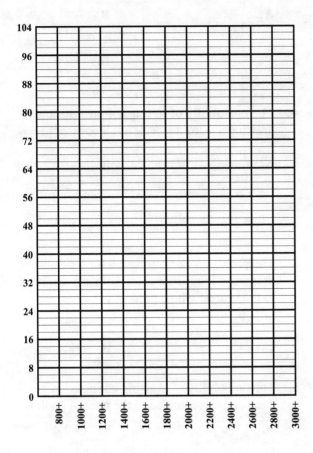

UNIT TEST 4 – STATISTICS AND PROBABILITY

Use the following information to answer the next question.

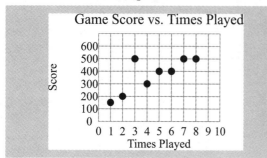

1. The scatter plot shows a boy's score while playing a computer game for the first ten times. The score that is farthest from the line of best fit is

   A. (2, 200)   B. (3, 500)

   C. (6, 400)   D. (7, 500)

2. In her purse, Mengya has 3 red, 6 yellow, 4 multi-coloured and 2 blue hair clips. If Mengya randomly pulls one hair clip out of her purse without looking, the odds of the hair clip being red are

   A. $\dfrac{1}{3}$ B. $\dfrac{1}{6}$

   C. $\dfrac{3}{8}$ D. $\dfrac{1}{5}$

3. If we roll one die, what is the probability of a four coming up?

   A. $\dfrac{1}{4}$ B. $\dfrac{1}{6}$

   C. $\dfrac{4}{6}$ D. $\dfrac{4}{1}$

4. The probability of rolling a 4 on a die and drawing a 4 from a deck of cards is

   A. $\dfrac{1}{6}$ B. $\dfrac{1}{52}$

   C. $\dfrac{5}{52}$ D. $\dfrac{1}{78}$

5. The probability of rolling a 6 on a die and drawing a king from a deck of cards rounded to the nearest whole percent is

   A. 8%   B. 10%

   C. 21%   D. 1%

6. The probability of drawing a king from a deck of cards rounded to the nearest tenth is

   A. 7.7%   B. 19.2%

   C. 3.8%   D. 25.9%

7. As the price of oil steadily increases, the Alberta government steadily gets more money in royalties. Which graph shows the relationship between the steadily rising oil prices and the steadily increasing royalties?

A.

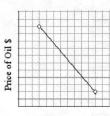

B.

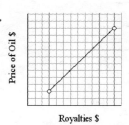

C.

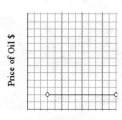

D.

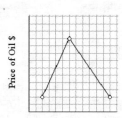

8. Royinder has a bag of bubblegum balls. There are 4 blue, 8 red, 6 white, and 2 black. If Royinder reaches in the bag without looking and picks one out, what is the probability that the bubblegum ball is white to the nearest percent?

A. 10%   **B.** 20%

C. 30%   **D.** 40%

9. If you did an experiment where you dropped a ball from different heights and recorded the data above. Which scatter plot would be the correct one to show the data?

Height Ball Dropped From (cm)	Height Ball Bounces (cm)
100	25
200	55
300	80
400	110
500	125
600	150
700	180
800	210
900	220
1 000 (1 metre)	255

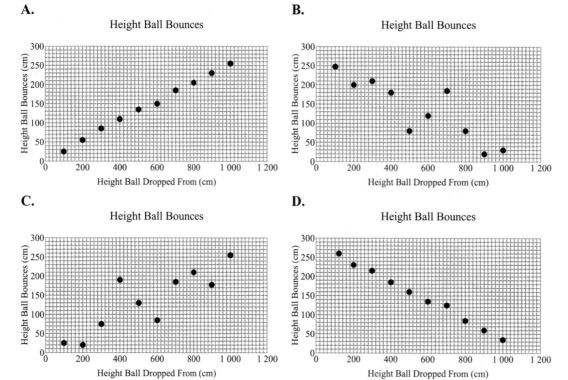

A.

B.

C.

D.

Use the following information to answer the next two questions.

Household Internet use at home by Internet activity
(All households)

	1999	2000	2001	2002	2003
	% of all households				
E-mail	26.3	37.4	46.1	48.9	52.1
Electronic banking	8.0	14.7	21.6	26.2	30.8
Purchasing goods and services	5.5	9.6	12.7	15.7	18.6
Medical or health information	15.6	22.9	30.1	32.8	35.6
Formal education/training	9.2	19.0	22.9	24.3	24.9
Government information	12.7	18.9	25.6	29.2	32.2
General browsing	24.3	36.2	44.3	46.1	48.5
Playing games	12.3	18.2	24.4	25.7	27.9
Chat groups	7.5	11.0	13.7	14.0	14.4
Other Internet services	10.0	17.7	21.1	24.8	23.5
Obtain and save music	7.8	17.8	23.3	24.3	20.6
Listen to the radio	5.0	9.3	12.3	12.3	13.1
Find sports related information	..	17.3	22.1	23.8	24.6
Financial information	..	18.5	22.8	23.5	25.0
View the news	..	20.4	26.2	27.2	30.2
Travel information/arrangements	..	21.9	27.4	30.4	33.6
Search for a job	..	12.2	16.2	18.0	19.6

.. : not available for a specific period of time.
Source: Statistics Canada, CANSIM, table (for fee) 358-0006 and Catalogue no. 56F0003X (free).
Last modified: 2005-02-18.

10. Which of the following conclusions **cannot** be made based on the data in the table?

  A. From 1999 to 2003 the number of households using e-mail roughly doubled.

  B. The use of the Internet for formal education/training is decreasing over time.

  C. The use of the Internet for financial information is increasing over time.

  D. From 1999 to 2003 the number of households using chat groups roughly doubled.

11. Which of the following conclusions **can** be made based on the data in the table?

  A. Overall, household use of the Internet is decreasing.

  B. The amount of use of the Internet depends on the time of day.

  C. Overall, household use of the Internet is increasing.

  D. Overall, household use of the Internet depends on the type of computer in the house.

Use the following information to answer the next question.

Jo-Anne, a grade 9 student in Somewhere Junior High, is trying to show the student council that there is more support for spending money on sports than there is for buying new microwaves for the lunch program. Jo-Anne does a survey after school during her girls volleyball practice of all the junior high students around her. She tallies up the responses to her question: "Should the student council buy yet more microwaves for the lunch program or buy much needed equipment so that our teams can compete better with other schools?", and then graphs the answer with result below.

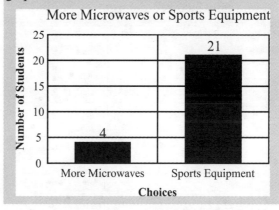

12. Which of the following is not an example of bias in Jo-Anne's survey?

 A. The majority of students in the survey have something to do with volleyball.

 B. A bar graph was used to show the results.

 C. Microwaves are referred to as "yet more" while sports equipment is referred to as "much needed".

 D. Boys will probably be underrepresented in the survey.

13. If you were going to do research on the best car to buy, which of the following sources would be your best choice to find unbiased comparative information?

 A. Ford Motor Company.com

 B. Toyota.com

 C. Car and Driver.com

 D. Nissan.com

14. Generally, the more years of education, the greater the average yearly income.
Which of the following scatter plots is most likely to represent the amount of education vs. yearly income?

A.
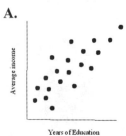

B.
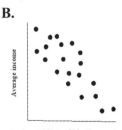

C.
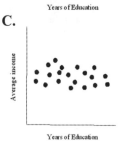

D.

15. What is the probability of spinning each spinner once and ending up with blue on each spinner?

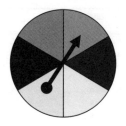 

 A. $\frac{1}{6}$

 B. $\frac{1}{36}$

 C. $\frac{1}{12}$

 D. $\frac{2}{6}$

16. All samples should be

 A. Random and unbiased

 B. Concise and to the point

 C. Honest and web-based

 D. Primary and secondary

Numerical Response

1. To the nearest tenth, what is the percent probability of rolling a 3 on a die?

_____

2. In reduced fraction form, what is the probability of rolling a 2 on a die and drawing a red ace from a deck of cards?

_____

3. To the nearest tenth, what is the percent probability of rolling a 5 on a die and drawing a black ace from a deck of cards?

_____

SOLUTIONS – NUMBER CONCEPTS

1. C	14. D	25. D	35. D	NR9. 2.5
2. B	15. D	26. C	36. A	45. A
3. D	NR1. 8	27. B	37. B	46. C
4. B	16. D	28. D	38. D	NR10. 2.4
5. C	17. C	29. A	39. B	NR11. 3
6. D	18. C	NR3. 27.0	40. C	47. A
7. A	19. D	30. C	41. D	48. C
8. B	20. B	31. B	42. D	49. D
9. C	21. B	NR4. 15.3	NR6. 11	50. B
10. D	NR2. 0.2	32. D	43. C	51. C
11. C	22. B	33. C	44. B	52. C
12. C	23. C	NR5. 4.8	NR7. 9	WR1. See Solution
13. C	24. A	34. A	NR8. 225	WR2. See Solution

1. C

When $\frac{3}{7}$ is converted to a decimal, it can
be represented as 0.428 571 428 571... or
$0.\overline{428\ 571}$, which is a repeating decimal.
A is incorrect because irrational numbers
can **only** be expressed as non-repeating,
non-terminating decimals.

B is incorrect since $\frac{3}{7}$ is a repeating

decimal.
D is incorrect since integers include **only**
the natural numbers, their negatives and 0.

2. B

Statement **i** is false because the set of whole
numbers contains the number 0 and the set
of natural numbers do not.
Therefore, natural numbers are a subset of
whole numbers and not the reverse.
Statement **ii** is correct since any integer a
can be expressed as the ratio of two

integers, i.e., $\frac{a}{b}$, where a is the given

integer and $b = 1$.

Statement **iii** is false, since rational
numbers and irrational numbers are sets
that are independent of one another.
A number **cannot** belong to both sets.

3. D

You are told that the area for the bottom of
a pyramid is $A = 10\ 000\ \text{m}^2$

The formula for the area (A) of a square is
$A = s^2$, where s is the length of one of the
sides.

Therefore, $s^2 = 10\ 000\ \text{m}^2$
To find the number that multiplied by itself
to give 10 000, take the square root of both
sides.

$$\sqrt{s^2} = \sqrt{10\ 000\ \text{m}^2}$$
$$s = 100\ \text{m}$$

Therefore, the length of one side of the
pyramid is 100 m.

4. B

A rational number can be represented as $\frac{a}{b}$, where a and b are integers and $b \neq 0$.

In **A**, $\sqrt{15-6}$ equals $\sqrt{9}=3$, which is rational.

In **B**, $\sqrt{3.9}$ equals 1.974 841 76....

This is a non-repeating, non-terminating decimal, so it cannot be represented as a rational number.

In **C**, $\frac{5}{11}$ is rational by definition.

It is already in the form of a fraction.

In **D**, $-\sqrt{25}$ equals $-(5) = -5$ which is rational.

5. C

In **A**, the number $\frac{1}{2}$ is a rational number.

(in the form $\frac{a}{b}$, where a and b are integers).

However, the number $\frac{1}{2}$ is NOT an integer.

In **B**, the number $\frac{1}{2}$ is a rational number,

(in the form $\frac{a}{b}$, where a and b are integers).

However, the number $\frac{1}{2}$ is NOT a natural number.

In **D**, the number $\frac{1}{2}$ is equal to 0.5, which is a terminating decimal, so it is not an irrational number.

6. D

$\pi = 3.141\ 592\ 6...$is non-terminating, non-repeating. Therefore, π is **always** irrational, it is **never** rational. Even though $\pi = \frac{c}{d}$,

either c or d must be irrational.

7. A

An irrational number can only be expressed as a non-terminating, non-repeating decimal.

In **A**, $-\sqrt{80} = -(8.944\ 27\ldots) = -8.944\ 27\ldots,$

As this decimal does not repeat or terminate, it is an example of an irrational number. (Students should note that the square root of **any** number that is not a perfect square will always be irrational)

In **B**, $\sqrt{25}$ equals $+5$ or -5, both of which are integers.

In **C**, $\sqrt{\frac{16}{4}} = \sqrt{4} = +2$ or -2, both of which are integers.

In **D**, $-\sqrt{81} = -9$, which is an integer.

8. B

The set of rational and the set of irrational numbers are distinct, i.e., they do not contain any common values. Therefore, **C** and **D** are not correct representations of the real number system. The set of **rational** numbers includes the set of integers, whole numbers, and natural numbers.

9. C

By definition, a **rational number** can be expressed as $\frac{a}{b}$, where a and b are integers and $b \neq 0$

10. D

Recall that the correct order of operations is as follows:

B – Brackets or   P – Parentheses
E – Exponent
D – Division, or
M – Multiplication
A – Addition, or
S – Subtraction

From the calculator keystroke sequence given in the question, 36 and 76 are in brackets so they must be added before the sum is multiplied by 99. This is not the case in sequence **A** and **C** where 99 and 36 are multiplied first. According to the order of operations, 75 is subtracted from 150 before this difference is divided by 32. **B** is wrong since 75 is first divided by 32.

11. C

The square root of any natural number will have exactly one positive and one negative solution. Therefore, **C** is correct.

12. C

The coefficient is the number that multiplies the variable. In this case, x^5 is the variable and $-\dfrac{3}{8}$ is the coefficient.

13. C

We are asked to combine the different working rates of Renu, Jason, and Michelle to find how long it will take them to finish the assignment. We are given the rates of each student.

Renu: 1 assignment in 9 h or $\dfrac{1}{9}$ of the assignment in 1 h.

Jason: 1 assignment in 12 h or $\dfrac{1}{12}$ of the assignment in 1 h.

Michelle: 1 assignment in 18 h or $\dfrac{1}{18}$ of the assignment in 1 h. Therefore, if all 3 people work on the same assignment at their individual rates they can complete:

$\left(\dfrac{1}{9}+\dfrac{1}{12}+\dfrac{1}{18}\right)$ of the assignment in 1 h.

$\dfrac{1}{9}+\dfrac{1}{12}+\dfrac{1}{18}=\dfrac{4}{36}+\dfrac{3}{36}+\dfrac{2}{36}=\dfrac{9}{36}=\dfrac{1}{4}$

That is, they can complete $\dfrac{1}{4}$ of the assignment in 1 h. Therefore, to complete the assignment, it will take them 4 h.

14. D

In the expression $-\dfrac{3}{5}x^2$, the base is x, the coefficient is $-\dfrac{3}{5}$, and the exponent is 2.

A, **B**, and **C** are all correct. x^2 will always be positive regardless of the value of x. However, multiplying a positive value by the coefficient $-\left(\dfrac{3}{5}\right)$ will always result in a negative number. Hence, **D** is not correct.

15. D

The number 2 is the coefficient of the term $\left(\dfrac{x}{y}\right)^m$ and m is the exponent with a base of $\left(\dfrac{x}{y}\right)$.

NR1. 8

From the exponent rules, everything within the brackets is raised to a power of 3, including the coefficient. Therefore, $(2x)^3 = 2^3 x^3$ Since $2^3 = 2 \times 2 \times 2 = 8$ the coefficient is 8.

16. D

To add these numbers, they must have like bases that are raised to the same exponent. Since this is not the case, we must express them in another form. Since 2.3×10^{12} is equal to 23×10^{11} we can rewrite the equation as

$(6 \times 10^{11}) + (23 \times 10^{11}) = (6 + 23) \times 10^{11}$
$= 29 \times 10^{11}$

However, using scientific notation, it would be incorrect to leave an answer as 29×10^{11}. Therefore, it must be expressed in the form 2.9×10^{12}.

17. C

Applying the exponent rules, we must raise both the coefficient and the variable to the exponent outside the brackets. We can use one of two methods to then find the answer.

Method 1

$$(-a^2)^{-3}$$
$$=(-1a^2)^{-3}$$
$$=(-1)^{-3} \times (a^2)^{-3}$$
$$=-1 \times a^{-6}$$
$$=-a^{-6}$$

Method 2

Since we have a negative exponent, we can express $(-a^2)^{-3}$ as $\dfrac{1}{(-a^2)^3} = \dfrac{1}{-a^6} = -a^{-6}$.

18. C

You can expand each of the powers to see which choice simplifies to $-\dfrac{1}{16}$.

A. $\left(\dfrac{1}{2}\right)^{-4} = \dfrac{1}{\left(\dfrac{1}{2}\right)^4} = \dfrac{1}{\dfrac{1}{16}} = 16$

(Simplify $\dfrac{1}{\dfrac{1}{16}}$ by multiplying the numerator and the denominator by 16).

B. $(-2)^{-4} = \dfrac{1}{(-2)^4} = \dfrac{1}{16}$

C. $-(2)^{-4} = -\dfrac{1}{(2)^4} = -\dfrac{1}{16}$

D. $2^{-4} = \dfrac{1}{(2)^4} = \dfrac{1}{16}$

19. D

Although this expression looks complex, there are some steps we can take to quickly simplify it.
Simplify the numerator

$$2x^2y^3 \times \dfrac{1}{2x^2y^3} = 1$$

Simplify the denominator: we can see that the terms $((3xy^6) (4x^4y^{-1}))$ and (xy) both have an exponent of 0. Using exponent rules, we know that any number raised to an exponent of 0 equals 1.

Therefore, the expression reduces to $\dfrac{1}{1} = 1$

20. B

Since we are multiplying and dividing terms, we can use exponent rules to add and subtract the exponents of terms with like bases. By simplifying the numerator, we get

$$(4x^3y^2)(4x^5y^6)$$
$$=(4 \times 4)(x^{3+5})(y^{2+6})$$
$$=16x^8y^8$$

The expression then becomes

$$\dfrac{16x^8y^8}{2x^3y^4} = \left(\dfrac{16}{2}\right)(x^{8-3}y^{8-4}) = 8x^5y^4$$

21. B

We can first simplify the expression using exponent laws.

$$\frac{(2b^3)}{2^{-3}(b^2)}=80$$

(Simplify the left side by dividing the numerator and denominator by b^2.)

$$\frac{2b}{2^{-3}}=80$$

$$2b=(80)2^{-3}$$

(Multiply both sides by 2^{-3} to remove the denominator.)

$$2b=(80)\left(\frac{1}{80}\right)$$

$$2b=10$$

$$b=5$$

NR2. 0.2

By using exponent laws, we find

$$n^2n^{-3}=5$$

$$n^{2+(-3)}=5$$

$$n^{-1}=5$$

$$n^{-1}=5$$

$$\frac{1}{n}=5$$

(Multiply both sides by n.)

$1=5n$ and $n=\frac{1}{5}$

Correct to the nearest tenth, $n=0.2$

22. B

We can use exponent laws to reduce the given expression.

$$\frac{4x^3y^2}{3xy^4}=\frac{4}{3}x^{3-1}y^{2-4}=\frac{4}{3}x^2y^{-2}$$

23. C

This question requires the application of the Exponent Laws to determine which statement is incorrect.
A. $15^{11}\times15^{21}=15^{11+21}=15^{32}$
This is a true statement.

B. $202^{18}\times202^{-70}=202^{18+(-70)}=202^{-52}$
This is a true statement.

C. $1\,500^3\times1\,500^0=0$ is **not** a true statement because
$1\,500^3\times1\,500^0=1\,500^3$
and **not** equal to 0.

D. $142^0\times142^0=142^{0+0}=142^0=1$
This is a true statement as any base raised to the exponent 0 is 1.

24. A

We are told that the total amount collected from the sales of 3 different sizes of chocolate bars equals $1\,037.50. Although we know the price and the quantities sold of two of the bars, we only know the price of the third. If we denote the number of 200 g bars sold as x, we have the following relationship:
 (Number of 500 g bars sold
   × price of 500 g bars)
+ (Number of 300 g bars sold
   × price of 300 g bars)
+ (Number of 200 g bars sold
   × price of 200 g bars)
= 1 037.50.
By substituting the given values into this equation, we get
$(140\times2.50)+(190\times1.75)+(x\times1.25)$
 $=1\,037.50$
$350+332.50+1.25x=1\,037.50$
Subtract 682.50 from both sides
$682.50+1.25x=1\,037.50$
$1.25x=355$
(Divide both sides by 1.25.)
$x=284$

25. D

We are told that the total number of hours completed by the graduating class of 3 different diplomas offered at a college equals 164 800. We are given the number of hours required as well as the number of students graduating for two of the three programs. For the third program, we only know the number of hours required. If we denote the number of students in the third program as n, we have the following relationship.

(Total number of students in the programming or networking diplomas × number of hours required to complete the courses)
+ (Total number of students in the business diploma × number of hours required to complete the course)
= 164 800

By substituting the given values into this equation, we get
$(120 \times 1\,160) + (n \times 640) = 164\,800$
$139\,200 + 640n$　　　(Subtract 139 200
$= 164\,800$　　　　　　from both sides)
$640n = 25\,600$　　　(Divide both sides
$n = 40$　　　　　　　by 640)

There are 40 students taking the business course.

26. C

From the information in the question, we know that the charge for power usage is $8.30 plus $0.07 for each kWh used, or $0.07 \times$ kWh This can be expressed as $[\$8.30 + (0.07 \times kWh)]$

However, a tax of 7% is applied to the entire bill. This means the bill is multiplied by 1.07 to take into account the tax levied on the original amount. Therefore, the monthly power bill can be calculated using the equation

$T = (8.30 + 0.07 \times kWh) \times 1.07$

27. B

To find the number of kilowatt hours (kWh) used during the month, substitute $t = \$40.34$ into the previously derived equation.
$(8.30 + 0.07 \times kWh) \times 1.07 = 40.34$
　　　　　　(Divide both sides by 1.07)
$8.30 + 0.07\ kWh = 37.7$
　　　　　　(Subtract 8.30 from both sides)
$0.07\ kWh = 29.4$
　　　　　　(Divide both sides by 0.07)
number of $kWh = \dfrac{29.4}{0.07} = 420$

28. D

From the information in the question, we know that Mia will earn $5.50 per hour for 7 hours per day over 10 days.
Her earnings during this period are
$5.5 \times 7 \times 10$
She is also paid a daily commission of 5% on the total amount of merchandise she sells ($350.00 \times 0.05 \times 10$) Therefore, Mia's total earnings (x) will be

$x = (5.50 \times 7 \times 10) + (350 \times 0.05 \times 10)$
$x = 385 + 175$
$x = \$560$

Mia will earn $560.00.

29. A

According to the exponent laws, when dividing powers with the same base, SUBTRACT the exponents,
$a^b \div a^c = a^{b-c}$

NR3. 27

We are told that the formula for the volume

of a cylinder is $V = \frac{4}{3}\pi r^3$

To find the radius of the ball, substitute $V = 36\pi$ into the formula.

$36\pi = \frac{4}{3}\pi r^3$	(Divide both sides by π)
$36 = \frac{4}{3}r^3$	(Multiply both sides by 3)
$108 = 4r^3$	(Divide both sides by 4)
$r^3 = 27.0$	
$r = 3$	$(3 \times 3 \times 3 = 37)$

30. C

We are told that the tuxedo costs $1 500 and that Jean paid for it by making a down payment of $700 and financing the remainder for one year at an interest rate of $\frac{1}{2}$ of 1 percent per month. Therefore, the interest rate for one year is $\frac{1}{2} \times 12 = 6\%$.

To calculate the total amount paid for the tuxedo, first find the outstanding balance.
$1 500 – $700 = $800
Now, calculate the interest on the outstanding balance after one year.
Let x be the interest.

$$\frac{x}{800} = \frac{6}{100}$$
$$x = 800 \times 0.06$$
$$x = \$48$$

Now, add the interest to the cost of the tuxedo.

$48 + $1 500 = $1 548

31. B

We are given that the tuxedo costs $1 500 and that Jean paid for it by making a down payment of $700 and financing the remainder for one year. We are also given that he owes $844 after one year.
To calculate the interest rate he was charged on the outstanding balance, first calculate the outstanding balance.
$1 500 – $700 = $800
Subtract this amount from the total amount he owed after one year to find the amount of interest he paid.
$844 – $800 = $44.
We can then calculate the interest rate he was charged on the outstanding balance of $800. Let x be the interest rate.

$$\frac{x}{100} = \frac{44}{800} \quad x \times 800 = 44 \times 100$$
$$x = \frac{4\,400}{800} \quad x = 5.5\%$$

NR4. 15.3

The volume of paper (V_p) on the roll can be found by subtracting the volume of the cardboard tube (V_c) from the total volume of the roll (V_t) Drawing a diagram will help to visualize this relationship.

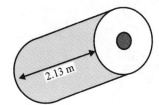
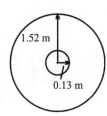

Given that the formula for a cylinder is $V = \pi r^2 h$ where h is the height of the cylinder and r is the radius of the base, we have

$$(V_p) = (V_t) - (V_c)$$

$$(V_p) = \left((\pi(1.52)^2(2.13)) - (\pi(0.13)^2(2.13))\right)$$

$$= 4.921152\pi - 0.035997\pi$$

$$= 4.885155\pi$$

$$\approx 15.339187 \text{ m}^3$$

$$\approx 15.3 \text{ m}^3$$

The volume of the paper on the roll is 15.3 m^3 (rounded to the nearest tenth).

32. D

Using exponent laws, we can evaluate the two terms in this expression separately. Evaluate the first term by converting the terms to the same base of 2.

$$\frac{4^4}{2^6} = \frac{(2^2)^4}{2^6} = \frac{2^8}{2^6} = 2^{8-6} = 2^2 = 4$$

Evaluate the second term by converting the terms to the base of 3.

$$\frac{(3^4)(27^2)}{(9^2)^2} = \frac{(3^4)(3^3)^2}{((3^2)^2)^2}$$

$$= \frac{3^4 \times 3^{3\times2}}{3^{2\times2\times2}} = \frac{3^4 \times 3^6}{3^8}$$

$$3^{4+6-8} = 3^2 = 9$$

By substituting these values for the first and second terms, we get $4 \div 9 = \dfrac{4}{9}$.

33. C

To simplify $\sqrt{c^4 \div c^2}$, we can use exponent laws to reduce the expression within the radical.

$$c^4 \div c^2 = c^{4-2} c^2$$

Therefore, $\sqrt{c^2} = c$.

NR5. 4.8

Given that the formula for the rate of acceleration is

$$a = \frac{V_f - V_i}{t}\text{, we are asked to find out how}$$

many seconds it will take to reach a final velocity of 26.7 m/s when the uniform acceleration is 5.56 m/s^2.

Substituting $a = 5.56$, $V_i = 0$ and $V_f = 26.7$ into the formula, we get

$$5.56 = \frac{26.7 - 0}{t}$$

(Multiply both sides by t.)

$$5.33t = 26.7$$

(Divide both sides by 5.56.)

$$t = \frac{26.7}{5.56} = 4.8$$

Therefore, it will take 4.8 seconds to reach a final velocity of 26.7 m/s.

34. A

Using exponent laws,

$$\frac{(3x^3t^5)(4x^2t^7)^2}{(8x^2t^7)(x^3t^{-8})}$$

$$= \frac{3x^3t^5(4)^2(x^2)^2(t^7)^2}{8x^2t^7x^3t^{-8}} \qquad \text{(Simplify)}$$

$$\frac{(3\times16)x^{3+4}t^{5+14}}{8x^5t^{-1}} \qquad \text{(Collect like terms)}$$

$$= \frac{48x^7t^{19}}{8x^5t^{-1}} \qquad \text{(Simplify)}$$

$$= \frac{48}{8}x^{7-5}t^{19-(-1)}$$

$$= 6x^2t^{20}$$

35. D

Using exponent laws,

$$\frac{(x^{-8}) \div x^5}{(x^2)^3(x^0)} = \frac{x^{-8-5}}{x^{2\times3}(1)}$$

$$\frac{x^{-13}}{x^6} = x^{-13-6}$$

$$x^{-19} = \frac{1}{x^{19}}$$

36. A

Using exponent laws, $\dfrac{(6^2)^2 \times 3^{-3}}{10^4 \div 5^4}$ can be written as

$$\dfrac{(3^2 \times 2^2)^2 \times 3^{-3}}{5^4 \times 2^4 \div 5^4} \qquad \text{(Simplify)}$$

$$= \dfrac{3^4 \times 2^4 \times 3^{-3}}{5^4 \times 2^4 \div 5^4} \qquad \text{(Collect like terms)}$$

$$= \dfrac{3^1 \times 2^4}{2^4}$$

$$= 3^1 = 3$$

37. B

Using exponent laws,

$$\dfrac{\left(\dfrac{1}{2}\right)^3 \left(\dfrac{1}{2}\right)^{-2}}{\left(\dfrac{1}{3}\right)^2 \left(\dfrac{1}{4}\right)^2} = \dfrac{\left(\dfrac{1}{2}\right)^{3+(-2)}}{\left(\dfrac{1}{3}\right)^{-2} \left(\left(\dfrac{1}{2}\right)^2\right)}$$

Rewriting $\left(\dfrac{1}{3}\right)^{-2}$ with positive exponents, we get

$$\dfrac{\left(\dfrac{1}{2}\right)\left(\dfrac{1}{2}\right)^2}{\left(\dfrac{1}{2}\right)^4} = \left(\dfrac{1}{2}\right)^{1-4}\left(\dfrac{1}{3}\right)^2 = \left(\dfrac{1}{2}\right)^{-3}\left(\dfrac{1}{3}\right)^2$$

$$= \dfrac{\left(\dfrac{1}{3}\right)^2}{\left(\dfrac{1}{2}\right)^3} = \dfrac{\dfrac{1}{3^2}}{\dfrac{1}{2^3}} = \dfrac{\dfrac{1}{9}}{\dfrac{1}{8}} = \dfrac{8}{9}$$

38. D

Before substituting $x = -3$ and $y = -2$ into this equation, we can simplify the expression using exponent rules,

$$\dfrac{(x^3)^2 (y^{-2})^3}{y^{-7}} = \dfrac{x^6 y^{-6}}{y^{-7}} = x^6 y^{-6-(-7)} = x^6 y.$$

By substituting $x = -3$ and $y = -2$, we get $(-3)^6(-2) = -1\,458$.

39. B

Recall from the laws of exponents that

$$\left(\dfrac{x}{y}\right)^n = \dfrac{x^n}{y^n}.$$

Since both 7^2 and 3^2 are powers that have a common exponent, $\dfrac{7^2}{3^2}$ can be rewritten as

$$\left(\dfrac{7}{3}\right)^2.$$

40. C

From the information given in the question, we are asked to combine the different painting rates of Jake, Susan, and Ted to find how long it will take them to paint a house. We are given the rates of each painter:

Jake: 1 house every 4 hours or $\dfrac{1}{4}$ of a house in 1 hour.

Susan: 1 house every 5 hours or $\dfrac{1}{5}$ of a house in 1 hour.

Ted: 1 house every 20 hours or $\dfrac{1}{20}$ of a house in 1 hour.

Therefore, if all 3 people work on the same house at their individual rates they can paint:

$$\left(\dfrac{1}{4} + \dfrac{1}{5} + \dfrac{1}{20}\right) \text{ of a house in 1 hour.}$$

That is, $\dfrac{10}{20} = \dfrac{1}{2}$ house in 1 hour.

Therefore, to paint a complete house it will take them 2 hours

41. D

Given that the average number of points per game is 2.25, the total points scored by both players in 68 games is

$68 \times 2.25 = 153$

By subtracting the points contributed by player A we get,

$153 - 85 = 68$

Hence, 68 is the number of points scored by player B.

42. D

From the information given in the question, to calculate c, substitute $n = 6$ into the equation $c = 2^n - 1$

$c = 2^6 - 1$

$c = 64 - 1$

$c = 63$

The total number of cards purchased after 6 shows is 63.

NR6. 11

We must first use the information given in the question to determine how many cards Miro would have after 9 shows.

By substituting $n = 9$ into the equation, we get

$c = 2^9 - 1 = 512 - 1 = 511$

Since each case can hold up to 50 cards, divide the number of cards by 50 to find the number of cases.

$\dfrac{511}{50} = 10.22$

Note: We need to find the minimum number of cases needed to store **all** the cards. Therefore, the total number of cases needed to hold all of the cards is 11 (even though the 11th case would not be completely full).

43. C

Since these powers are too large to calculate on a calculator, we must find an alternate strategy for solving this question. We can look for some initial patterns in the choices that we are given and quickly eliminate those that cannot possibly have 43 as the last two digits.

For example, 5 to any power will always result in a 5 as the last digit. As well any power of 6 ends with a 6 as the last digit. Therefore, both **A** and **B** are not correct.

Raising 8 to any power means multiplying two or more even numbers. This will always result in an even number.

Since 43 is an odd number **D** cannot be correct.

Therefore, **C** must be right.

44. B

From the information in the question, we are told that x which is equal to 6.3×10^9 is divided by $10y$, where $y = 9.0 \times 10^{-3}$

By rewriting this, we get

$$\frac{x}{10y} = \frac{6.3 \times 10^9}{10(9.0 \times 10^{-3})} = \frac{6.3 \times 10^9}{9.0 \times 10^{-2}}$$

By using exponent laws, we get

$$\frac{6.3}{9.0} \times 10^{9-(-2)} = 0.7 \times 10^{11} = 7.0 \times 10^{10}$$

NR7. 9

Before substituting for x and y, we can use exponent laws to simplify the given expression.

$$\frac{(x^{-2})^4 \div y^{14}}{3x} \times \frac{(x^2)^6(y^2)^8}{5y}$$

$$\frac{x^{(-8+12)}y^{(-14+16)}}{(3x)(5y)} = \frac{x^4 y^2}{15xy} = \frac{x^3 y}{15}$$

By substituting $x = 3$ and $y = 5$, we get

$$\frac{27(5)}{15} = 9$$

NR8. 225

By using exponent laws, we can simplify the given expression.

$$\frac{(4^{-2})^2(5^3)}{5(6^{-4} \div 6^{-2} \times 4^{-3})} = \frac{(4^{-4})(5^3)}{5^1(6^{-4-(-2)})(4^{-3})}$$

$$\frac{4^{-4(-3)} \times 5^{3-1}}{6^{-2}} = \frac{(4^{-4})(5)^2}{6^{-2}}$$

Rewrite with positive exponents.

$$\frac{(5^2)(6^2)}{4^1} = \frac{25 \times 36}{4} = 225$$

NR9. 2.5

Using exponent laws:

$$\frac{n}{m} = \frac{4.0 \times 10^{-206}}{1.6 \times 10^{-206}} = \frac{40}{1.6} \times 10^{-206-(-206)}$$

$$= 2.5 \times 10^0 = 2.5$$

Therefore, n is 2.5 times larger than m.

45. A

Although this is a simple division problem, we must be careful when converting the total mass (50 kg) and the mass of a single bacterium (1×10^{-5} g) to like units.
If we choose to use grams as the standard unit to work with, then 50 kg = 50 000 g or 5×10^4 g. Therefore, using exponent laws,

$$\frac{5 \times 10^4}{1 \times 10^{-5}} = \left(\frac{5}{1}\right) \times 10^{4-(-5)} = 5 \times 10^9$$

46. C

From the information given, the volume of the asteroid is $\frac{1}{9}$ the volume of Earth, that is,

$$(1.08 \times 10^{12}) \times \frac{1}{9} = \frac{1.08}{9} \times 10^{12}$$

$$= 0.12 \times 10^{12} = 1.2 \times 10^{11} \text{km}^3.$$

NR10. 2.4

Substituting $x = 9.84 \times 10^{-23}$ and

$y = 4.10 \times 10^{-28}$ into the expression $\frac{x}{y}$,

we get:

$$\frac{x}{y} = \frac{9.84 \times 10^{-23}}{4.10 \times 10^{-28}}$$

$$= \frac{9.84}{4.10} \times 10^{-23-(-28)} = 2.4 \times 10^5$$

Therefore, in the form $Q = 10^w$, $w = 5$ and $Q = 2.4$

NR11. 3

If we examine the given expression, we can quickly reduce $(b^0)(c)^{-1}$ to c^{-1} since any value of b raised to an exponent of 0 will equal 1.

Substituting $c = \frac{1}{3}$, we get $\left(\frac{1}{3}\right)^{-1} = 3$

Alternatively, we could solve the problem by substituting the values for b and c into the expression and simplifying.

$$(b^0)(c)^{-1} = (-2)^0 \left(\frac{1}{3}\right)^{-1} = (1)\left(\frac{1}{3}\right)^{-1} = \frac{1}{\frac{1}{3}} = 3$$

47. A

We can solve this problem by inspection. By examining sequence B, we can see that according to the order of operations, instead of 6.6 being first subtracted from 12.2, as it is in the original equation, it is divided by 2. Sequence A, on the other hand, does allow 6.6 to be first subtracted from 12.2 before being divided by 2. It does this by incorporating an "equal sign" into the sequence immediately after 6.6 is entered.

48. C

To find the number of stars in the universe, multiply the number of stars in a typical galaxy (10^{11}) by the number of galaxies (10^{11}).
$$10^{11} \times 10^{11} = 10^{11+11} = 10^{22}$$

49. D

Applying exponent laws, we must divide the mass of Earth by that of the sun.

Therefore, $\dfrac{6 \times 10^{24}}{2 \times 10^{30}} = \left(\dfrac{6}{2}\right) \times 10^{24-30}$

$= 3 \times 10^{-6}$

50. B

From the information provided, we can set up the following relationship to find the distance to the farthest visible galaxy.

$\dfrac{10^5}{1} = \dfrac{10^{25}}{x}$, where x is the number of hours it takes to travel to the farthest visible galaxy.

Therefore, cross-multiplying, we get $(10^5)x = 10^{25}$

$x = \dfrac{10^{25}}{10^5} = 10^{25-5}$ $x = 10^{20}$ hours.

51. C

In this question, we are looking for the difference in time between (2.5×10^8) years ago and (7.5×10^7) years ago. Therefore, we need to find $(2.5 \times 10^8) - (7.5 \times 10^7)$ Rewriting (7.5×10^7) as (0.75×10^8) so that the exponents on base are the same, we get $(2.5 \times 10^8) - (0.75 \times 10^8) = 1.75 \times 10^8$ years.

52. C

We are given that 1 150 000 L of water are filtered through the Dolphin Lagoon every 3 h. To find out how much water flows through the lagoon in 24 h, multiply the amount that is filtered in 3 h by $8(24 \div 3 = 8)$. 1 150 000 × 8 = 9 200 000 L Rewriting this amount in scientific notation 9 200 000 = 9.2×10^6 L

Written Response

1. a) Reading from the mass column of the table, the planet with the largest mass is Jupiter, at 317.8 Earth masses. The smallest planet is Pluto, at 0.004 Earth masses.

The ratio is $\dfrac{317.8}{0.004} = 79\ 450$

(1 point)

The nearest power of ten is 100 000 (since 79 450 is closer to 100 000 than it is to 1 000), for a ratio of **10^5**.

(1 point)

b) Reading from the revolution period column of the table, we find that Pluto requires 247.7 years to revolve around the sun, while Mercury takes only 0.24 years. The ratio is $\dfrac{247.7}{0.24}$

$= 1\ 032.08$ **(1 point)**

So, Mercury will make about **1 032** revolutions in the time it takes Pluto to make one. **(1 point)**

Reading from the radius column of the table (which is directly proportional to diameter), the smaller planets are those with a radius of less than 1.00 Earth radius. There are **four** such planets; namely, Mercury, Venus, Mars, and Pluto. **(1 point)**

d) Since one particle requires one millisecond of computer time,
$$\frac{1}{10^{-3}} = 10^3 = 1\,000$$ particles can be handled during each second of the simulation. Since there are $60 \times 60 \times 25 = 90\,000$ seconds in 25 hours, the total size of the model can be $(10^3) \times (9 \times 10^4) = 9 \times 10^7$ particles.

2. Since the larger loader can fill the entire silo in 60 minutes, it fills $\dfrac{1}{60}$ of the silo in one minute. Similarly, the smaller loader fills $\dfrac{1}{90}$ of the silo in one minute.

(1 point)

Working together, they can fill $\dfrac{1}{60} + \dfrac{1}{90}$ of the silo in one minute. Using a common denominator, we find that $\dfrac{2}{180} + \dfrac{3}{180} = \dfrac{5}{180}$ of the silo is filled each minute.

(1 point)

Since $\dfrac{5}{180}$ of the silo is filled in one minute, the total number of minutes to fill the silo is the reciprocal. The reciprocal is the number that is multiplied to an original number to yield a product of 1. The reciprocal of $\dfrac{5}{180}$ is $\dfrac{180}{5}$. Taking the reciprocal tells us that the entire silo will be filled in $\dfrac{180}{5} = 36$ minutes.

(1 point)

A general formula for solving problems that combine different rates is $\dfrac{1}{R} = \dfrac{1}{R_1} + \dfrac{1}{R_2} + \dots$ where R_1 is the first rate, R_2 is the second rate, and R is the total of all rates. $\dfrac{1}{R}$ is the reciprocal of R. Applying the formula to this question, we get $\dfrac{1}{T} = \dfrac{1}{L} + \dfrac{1}{S}$ where L is the time it takes for the larger loader, S is the time it takes for the smaller loader, and T is the total time needed using both loaders.

ANSWERS AND SOLUTIONS
NUMBER CONCEPTS – UNIT TEST 1

1. A	7. A	13. D	19. C	25. D
2. D	8. B	14. A	20. D	26. A
3. D	9. D	15. D	21. C	WR1. See Solution
4. C	10. D	16. B	22. B	WR2. See Solution
5. B	11. A	17. C	23. B	WR3. See Solution
6. B	12. A	18. A	24. D	

1. A

Remember the natural numbers are all the numbers in the sequence 1, 2, 3, …
and that whole numbers, integers and rational numbers all include the natural numbers.

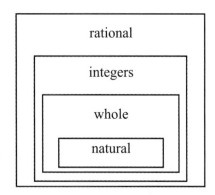

2. D

Numbers with terminating decimal belong to the rational number system only which is represented with the letter Q

3. D

Integers include all numbers in the sequence …, –3, –2, –1, 0, 1, 2, 3,…

4. C

Any number divided by 0 is undefined and therefore not in the rational number system.

5. B

All radicals have two square roots, a positive and a negative. The positive square root is called the principal square root.

6. B

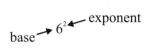

7. A

Expanded form in this case means expanding the power using multiplication. Everything in the brackets is multiplied against itself 4 times. **B**, **C**, and **D** are all in simplified form.

8. B

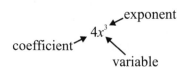

9. D

Remember that exponents are a short cut for showing multiplication of the same terms. Since the expanded form shows the same term multiplied by itself three times, the expression can be simplified by taking one of the terms and raising it to an exponent of 3.

10. D

$$\text{Area} = s^2; \ s = 2x^2y^3$$
$$\text{Area} = (2x^2y^3)^2$$
$$\text{Area} = 4x^4y^6$$

11. A

Anything raised to the exponent of 0 is equal to 1. (Note that in the second set of brackets, the number 3 does not have an exponent of 0, only the x does)

$$4(x^0) \ (3x^0)$$
$$= 4(1) \ (3 \times 1)$$
$$= 12$$

12. A

Divide the two coefficients by the Greatest Common Factor (5) and remember to subtract exponents when dividing.

13. D

A cube has all sides equal.
Volume = length × width × height
Remember to add the exponents when you multiply them.

$$(3x^3y^4) \ (3x^3y^4) \ (3x^3y^4)$$
$$= 27x^9y^{12}$$

or

$$(3x^3y^4)^3 = 27x^9y^{12}$$ by applying the exponent of 3 to everything inside the brackets.

14. A

Any number raised to an exponent of 0 is 1 and a negative exponent means the power belongs in the denominator of the fraction.

$$3^0 - 2^{-3}$$
$$3^0 - \frac{1}{2^3}$$
$$1 - \frac{1}{8}$$
$$\frac{7}{8}$$

15. D

The first number in scientific notation must have only a **single digit** before the decimal place. The digit before the decimal place must be greater than or equal to 1 and less than 10. The base of power must always be 10 when using scientific notation.
Moving the decimal place to the right results in a negative exponent.

16. B

Dividing by 0 makes an expression undefined, so $y \neq 0$.

17. C

The expression first can be written as $\frac{1}{2^4}$.

However, by using a negative exponent, we can move the power up and write it as 2^{-4}

18. A

Positive exponents move the decimal place to the right. In this case the decimal place moves to the right 8 times and 0's are filled in each time. 2 followed by 8 zeros is 200 000 000.

19. C

The whole numbers (3 and 3) multiply together and the exponents are added because the bases are both 10.

$$(3 \times 10^{15}) \times (3 \times 10^9)$$
$$(3)(3) \times 10^{15+9}$$
$$9 \times 10^{24}$$

20. D

Remember that standard form is the form you usually see numbers in.

$$(4 \times 10^{-19}) \times (2 \times 10^{22})$$
$$(4)(2) \times 10^{-19+22}$$
$$8 \times 10^3$$
$$8 \times 1 \ 000$$
$$8 \ 000$$

21. C

The –2 is multiplied by itself 5 times, so that means it can be written as $(-2)^5$. Remember that everything in the brackets is raised to the exponent.

22. B

Remember that when you get 0.012 as an answer you need to convert it to scientific notation, and that when you move the decimal place to the right, it results in a negative exponent.

23. B

Division of powers results in subtraction of exponents. Simplify first and then substitute the numbers

$$\frac{x^5 y^6}{x^3 y^3}$$

$$\left(x^{5-3}\right)\left(y^{6-3}\right)$$

$$x^2 y^3; x = 3, y = -2$$

$$\left(3^2\right)\left(-2^3\right)$$

$$(9)(-8)$$

$$-72$$

24. D

The exponent affects everything in the brackets.

$$\left(\frac{2x^2}{3y^3}\right)^3$$

$$\left(\frac{2x^2}{3y^3}\right)\left(\frac{2x^2}{3y^3}\right)\left(\frac{2x^2}{3y^3}\right)$$

$$\frac{(2 \times 2 \times 2)\left(x^{2 \times 3}\right)}{(3 \times 3 \times 3)\left(y^{3 \times 3}\right)}$$

$$\frac{8x^6}{27y^9}$$

25. D

The negative sign outside the brackets means that the entire expression is made negative after the exponent is applied to the term inside the brackets.

$$-\left(-2x^3\right)\left(-2x^3\right)\left(-2x^3\right)\left(-2x^3\right)$$

Consider that there are five negative signs being multiplied together. An odd number of negative signs being multiplied together results in a negative answer

$$-\left(-2x^3\right)\left(-2x^3\right)\left(-2x^3\right)\left(-2x^3\right)$$

$$-(-2)(-2)(-2)(-2)\left(x^{3+3+3+3}\right)$$

$$-16x^{12}$$

26. A

Simplify in the brackets first and then remember that the exponent outside the bracket affects both the numerator and the denominator.

$$\left(\frac{4x^3 y^8}{2x^5 y^6}\right)^3$$

$$\left(\frac{2y^2}{x^2}\right)^3$$

$$\frac{(2)(2)(2)\left(y^{2 \times 3}\right)}{x^{2 \times 3}}$$

$$\frac{8y^6}{x^6}$$

Written Response

1. There are 12 months in the year. Harold makes $275.23 for each month. This means Harold would make $3 302.76 in a year.

12 × $275.23
$3 302.76

2. We substitute in the values in the equation and solve for the answer.

$$\text{Speed} = \frac{\text{Distance}}{\text{Time}}$$

Distance = 198 000 000 000 km,

Time = 8 000 hr

$$\text{Speed} = \frac{198\,000\,000\,000 \text{ km}}{8\,000 \text{ hr}}$$

$$\text{Speed} = \frac{1.98 \times 10^{11} \text{ km}}{8 \times 10^{3} \text{ hr}}$$

$$\text{Speed} = 0.2475 \times 10^{8} \text{ km/hr}$$

$$\text{Speed} = 2.475 \times 10^{7} \text{ km/hr}$$

3. Looking at a chart we see that the number of pennies is increasing exponentially **using** a base of 2.

Number of pennies	days	Exponential Form
1	1	2^{0}
2	2	2^{1}
4	3	2^{2}
8	4	2^{3}

At the end of a month with 31 days there will be 2^{30} pennies which is $10\,737\,418\,24$ pennies in total. This is equivalent to \$10 737 418.24! Because these are pennies, it takes 100 of them to make \$1.00, so you need to divide the number of pennies by 100 to get the value in dollars.

SOLUTIONS – PATTERNS AND RELATIONS

1. D	10. C	20. A	29. B	39. C
NR1. 2	NR4. 75	21. C	30. C	40. B
NR2. 2.0	11. B	22. A	31. C	41. A
2. D	12. B	23. B	32. D	NR9. 3
3. A	13. D	24. A	33. C	NR10. 35
4. D	14. A	25. D	34. A	42. A
NR3. 60	NR5. 792	NR6. 0.45	NR8. 12	43. B
5. C	15. B	26. C	35. C	44. D
6. D	16. A	NR7. 1.25	36. D	45. B
7. A	17. C	27. B	37. C	NR11. 10
8. A	18. D	28. A	38. C	WR1. See Solution
9. D	19. A			

1. D

We are given the equation
$-4x + 6 = 2x - 12$
which when simplified, is
$-6x = -18$, or $x = 3$.
To determine which arrangement of tiles is not a valid representation of the original equation, translate each into its equivalent algebraic form. We can then compare the algebraic expressions.
Recall that

$$\boxed{} = x \qquad \blacksquare = +1$$
$$\boxed{} = -x \qquad \square = -1$$

In **A**, the algebra tiles represent the equation $-6x = -18$. When solved, $x = 3$
In **B**, the algebra tiles represent the equation $x = 3$.

In **C**, the algebra tiles represent the equation $3x = 9$, which can be simplified to $x = 3$.

In **D**, the algebra tiles represent the equation $-2x + x + 3 = -6$, which can be simplified to $x = 9$.

Therefore, **A**, **B**, and **C** are all equivalent forms of the equation $-4x + 6 = 2x - 12$.

NR1. 2

Remember that
$$\boxed{} = x \qquad \blacksquare = +1$$
$$\boxed{} = -x \qquad \square = -1$$

Therefore, the algebra tile arrangement is equivalent to the algebraic expression,
$4x + 3 = 11$

Simplifying, we get $4x = 8 \Rightarrow x = 2$
Therefore, the value of x is 2.

NR2. 2.0

We are given that $\boxed{}$ equals $\frac{1}{3}x$.

Therefore, $\boxed{}$ equals $\frac{1}{2}x$.

The arrangement of algebra tiles in this question is equivalent to the algebraic equation

$\frac{1}{2}x = 3x - 5$ (Multiply both sides by 2)
$x = 6x - 10$ (Subtract 6x from both sides)
$-5x = -10$ (Divide both sides by –5)
$x = 2$

Therefore, correct to one decimal place,
$x = 2.0$

2. D

To solve for x, use the distributive property to multiply each term inside the brackets by the term outside the brackets.
Therefore,

$2(3x + 5) = 5(x - 7)$
$6x + = 5x - 35$

(Subtract $5x$ from both sides).

$x + 10 = -35$

(Subtract 10 from both sides).

$x = -45$

3. A

From the information given in the question, one CD costs x dollars and a CD is $7.00 more than a tape. If the cost of one CD is x, then
$x - 7$ is the cost of one tape.
Since Maggie wants to buy 3 CDs, the cost is $3(x)$. Similarly, 6 tapes cost $6(x - 7)$.
The total purchase price (P):

$P = 3x + 6(x - 7)$
$P = 3x + 6x - 42$
$P = 9x - 42$

4. D

We are told that after an initial payment of 20%, the balance of the purchase price will be payable in 3 equal payments.
If $x =$ one payment, then

$$x = \frac{300 - (300)(0.20)}{3}$$

(Multiply both sides by 3 to eliminate the fraction)

$3x = 300 - (300)(0.20)$

At this point, it is important to compare this answer with the 4 choices given. It would appear that by adding (300) (0.20) to both sides the result is

$0.2(300) + 3x = 300$(This is option **D**)
While the previous method yields the correct answer, it is still recommended that students solve for x and substitute its value back into the 4 choices to verify.

$3x = 300 - 60 \qquad 3x = 240 \qquad x = 80$

We know that the correct solution is $x = 80$.

To determine which equation correctly represents the solution to the question, substitute $x = 80$ into each equation to see which equation is correct (in other words to see which equation has its left side equal to its right side).

NR3. 60

To correctly determine the value of each of the remaining 3 payments, subtract the down payment from the total purchase price and divide the remaining amount into 3 equal payments.

Purchase price = $300
Initial Down Payment
= 40% of $300 = $120

Balance Outstanding
= $300 – $120 = $180.

This balance must be divided into 3 equal parts.

$$\frac{\$180}{3} = \$60$$

Therefore, each remaining payment is $60.

5. C

Given that $3x = 4 - 2x$, by adding $2x$ to both sides, we get $5x = 4$

6. **D**

To solve for x in the expression:
$0.25x - 15.3 = 0.75x + 12.5$
　　　　　　　　(Collect like terms)

$(0.25x - 0.75x) = (12.5 + 15.3)$
$-0.5x = 27.8$

　　　　　　　　(Divide both sides by -0.5)
$x = -55.6$

Note: The collection of like terms could happen on opposite sides of the equal side as follows:

$0.25x - 15.3 = 0.75x + 12.5$

　　　　　　　　(Collect like terms and then divide both sides by 0.5)

7. **A**

Using the distributive property, the factor outside the bracket must be multiplied by every term inside the bracket.

$7(3x - 2) = -4(6 - 5x)$
$21x - 14 = -24 + 20x$

　　　　　　　　(Subtract $20x$ from both sides).
$x - 14 = -24$

　　　　　　　　(Add 14 to both sides).
$x = -10$

In **A**, $x - 10 = 0$ simplifies to $x = 10$. Therefore, **A** is not equivalent to the original expression.
B, **C**, and **D** are equivalent forms of $x = -10$.

8. **A**

Solve for x.
$238 + 3.70x \geq 460$
　　　　　　　　(Subtract 238 from both sides.)

$3.70x \geq 222$
　　　　　　　　(Divide both sides by 3.70.)
$x \geq 60$
After at least 60 hours of work, Molly will have enough money to purchase the bike.

9. **D**

The basic cost of the car rental is $195.00. To this we must add the charge for exceeding 100 km. Since x is defined as the number of kilometres over 100, the $0.25 charge applies to x and may be expressed as $0.25x$. Therefore, the total cost (c) of renting the car is
$c = 195 + 0.25x$.

10. **C**

We are told that the clothing company paid $569 for the tuxedo. We are also told that the garment is rented for $109 but that Derks must pay $10 for cleaning each time the tuxedo is rented.

Let x be the number of times that the tuxedo must be rented to earn $569.

To solve for x, we can use the following equation:

$(109 - 10)\, x = 569$

(The $(109 - 10)$ represents the actual amount of money the company earns on each rental due to the fee they must pay to have it dry cleaned)

$99x = 569$ 　　　 $x = \dfrac{569}{99}$ 　　　 $x = 5.75$

The number of times that the tuxedo is rented must be a whole number. Since the tuxedo must earn at least $569 to pay for itself, round the answer up to the next integer, which is 6.

NR4. 75

From the information provided in the question, we need to find what mark Enrico needs in his fifth course to qualify for a scholarship. To get a scholarship, the sum of Enrico's marks in 5 subjects, divided by 5, should be at least 80.

Method 1

If we let x = his mark for the fifth subject, then we have the following expression.

$$\frac{79 + 86 + 83 + 77 + x}{5} \geq 80.$$

(Multiplying both sides by 5).

$79 + 86 + 83 + 77 + x \geq 400$
$325 + x \geq 400$

(Subtract 325 from both sides).

$x \geq 75$

Method 2

To average 80% over 5 subjects, he would need a total of 400 marks ($80 \times 5 = 400$). If we subtract the marks he already has from 400, we will find what mark he needs on his fifth subject
$400 - 79 - 86 - 83 - 77 = 75$
Therefore, Enrico needs at least 75% on his last subject to achieve a final average of 80% over five subjects.

11. B

We are told that twice as much was spent on refurbishing a specialty suite as was on each regular suite. Let x be the cost of refurbishing a specialty suite. So, $\frac{1}{2}x$ is the cost of refurbishing a regular room.

$189\left(\frac{x}{2}\right) + 9(x) = 7\,000\,000$

$94.5x + 9x = 7\,000\,000$
$103.5x = 7\,000\,000$
$x = \dfrac{7\,000\,000}{103.5}$
$x = 67\,632.85$

12. B

From the information in the question, we are told that the cost of the Internet service is $30.00 per month, plus $0.75 for each additional hour after the first 20 hours. The total Internet bill (t) equals $30 + 0.75x$ where x is the number of hours online after 20 hours.
Note: Questions like this require students to be able to take statements and correctly translate them into mathematical equations. It is important for students to **read** the information carefully and determine exactly what is needed to solve the problem.

13. D

From the information in the question, each girl sells 5 boxes to their own families, so together, they immediately collect a total of $20.00.
$5 \times 2.00 \times 2 = 20.00$
They then collect $2.00 for every box sold after that. If they sell x boxes, they will collect $2.00x$. By combining these, we get
$t = 2.00x + 20.00$.

14. A

Given the information in the question, we know that it will cost $0.50 to play the arcade game, plus $0.25 each time the player chooses to continue the same game. The total cost (t) is $t = 0.50 + 0.25c$, where c is the number of times that a player continues the same game.

NR5. 792

By substituting the values of $x = 2$, and $y = 3$ into the expression $2x^4y^3 - 9x^3y^0$ we get

$$\left(2(2)^4(3)^3\right) - \left(9(2)^3(3)^0\right)$$
$= (2)\,(16)\,(27) - (9)\,(8)\,(1)$
$= 864 - 72$
$= 792$

15. B

We are told that from a perfect score of 10, a final score (s) is arrived at by subtracting 0.1 for every mistake. Since a deduction is made for each mistake, if m mistakes are made, the total of all deductions is $0.1m$. Therefore, the equation that can be used to calculate a gymnast's final score (s) is $s = 10 - 0.1m$.

16. A

Creating a chart of the given information may be helpful in solving this question.

Clock Number	Time	Difference	Factor Multiplied By
1	12:10		
		10 min	
2	12:20		2
		20 min	
3	12:40		2
		40 min	
4	1:20		

We can see that the time difference between successive clocks has been multiplied by a factor of 2 to arrive at the time difference for the next two successive clocks in the sequence.

17. C

Since the time intervals between the clocks increase by a factor of 2, the next clock will be 80 minutes ahead. (40×2)

Adding 80 minutes to the time on the fourth clock will give us the time of the next clock in the sequence.

1:20 + 80 min = 2:40.

18. D

Given that $A = \dfrac{1}{2}bh$, we can rearrange this formula by multiplying both sides by 2. $2A = bh$, therefore **A** is true.

Since $2A = bh$, dividing both sides by b we get $\dfrac{2A}{b} = h$, therefore **B** is true.

Using the original formula $A = \dfrac{1}{2}bh$, if we divide both sides by h, we get $\dfrac{A}{h} = \dfrac{1}{2}b$, therefore **C** is true.

D, which states $\dfrac{1}{2}A = bh$, is incorrect.

19. A

To find the equation that is equivalent to $\dfrac{9x+15}{3} = 18$, we can rewrite it as

$\dfrac{9x}{3} + \dfrac{15}{3} = 18$, which simplifies to

$3x + 5 = 18 \Rightarrow 3x = 13$

Another way to look at this equation is as follows:
$\dfrac{9x+15}{3} = 18$
$9x + 15 = 54$ (Multiply both sides by 3)
$9x = 39$ (Even though 39 can NOT be divided by 9, it can be divided by 3)

$3x = 13$

20. A

To find which equation is equivalent to $\dfrac{9x}{2} + \dfrac{3}{5} = \dfrac{1}{5}$, simplify by subtracting $\dfrac{3}{5}$ from both sides.
$\dfrac{9x}{2} = \dfrac{-2}{5}$
Cross multiply leaving
$45x = -4$ (Add 4 to both sides).
$45x + 4 = 0$

21. C

You are told that at sea level, the temperature is 32°C and the temperature will drop C for every 1 000 m increase in altitude. Since each 1 000 m increase in altitude results in a 1°C decrease in temperature, you must divide the altitude (*a*) by 1 000 to determine how many degrees the temperature changes.

The temperature (*t*) can be determined by subtracting the temperature change from the original temperature.

$$t = 32 - \left(\frac{a}{1\,000}\right) \times 1$$

However, since multiplying by 1 does not change the value of and expression, the 1 is left out of the final equation:

$$t = 32 - \left(\frac{a}{1\,000}\right) \text{ or } t = 32 - \frac{a}{1\,000}$$

22. A

Since you are trying to find the temperature at an altitude of 50 000 m, substitute *a* = 50 000 into the equation derived in the previous solution.

$$t = 32°C - \frac{50\,000}{1\,000}$$
$$t = 32 - 50$$
$$t = -18°C$$

23. B

From the information given in the question, we must divide the tensile strength of graphite by that of steel to find out by what factor they differ. Applying the exponent laws for powers,

$$\frac{770 \times 10^6}{500 \times 10^6} = \left(\frac{700}{500}\right) \times 10^{6-6}$$
$$= \frac{700}{500} \times 1 = 1.54$$

Therefore, graphite is 1.54 times stronger than steel.

24. A

To find out how much denser steel is compared to graphite, we must divide the density of steel by the density of graphite. This question is similar to the previous one, however, we must be careful when dividing powers with rational bases, especially when the bases are DIFFERENT.

Method I

Using Exponent Rules

$$\frac{20 \times \left(\frac{3}{4}\right)^4}{20 \times \left(\frac{1}{2}\right)^4} = \left(\frac{20}{20}\right) \times \frac{\left(\frac{3}{4}\right)^4}{\left(\frac{1}{2}\right)^4}$$

$$= 1 \times \frac{\frac{81}{256}}{\frac{1}{16}} = \frac{81}{256} \times \frac{16}{1} = \frac{1\,296}{256} = \frac{81}{16}$$

$$= \frac{3 \times 3 \times 3 \times 3}{2 \times 2 \times 2 \times 2} = \left(\frac{3}{2}\right)^4$$

Method II

The number $\left(\frac{3}{4}\right)^4$ can be rewritten as

$\left[\left(\frac{3}{2}\right)\left(\frac{1}{2}\right)\right]^4$ so the question can be simplified to

$$\frac{20 \times \left[\left(\frac{3}{2}\right)\left(\frac{1}{2}\right)\right]^4}{20 \times \left(\frac{1}{2}\right)^4} = \frac{20}{20} \times \frac{1 \times \left(\frac{3}{2}\right)^4 \left(\frac{1}{2}\right)^4}{\left(\frac{1}{2}\right)^4}$$

$$= 1 \times \left(\frac{3}{2}\right)^4 = \left(\frac{3}{2}\right)^4$$

(since $\left(\frac{1}{2}\right)^4$ in both the numerator and denominator reduce to 1)

25. D

To translate the arrangement of algebra tiles into its algebraic form, we must remember that

$$\blacksquare = x^2 \quad \boxed{} = x \quad \square = +1$$
$$\square = -x^2 \quad \boxed{} = -x \quad \square = -1$$

Therefore, the arrangement of algebra tiles, written algebraically, is

$$(4x^2 - 6x + 2) + (3x^2 - 2x - 4)$$

By collecting like terms, we get
$(4x^2 + 3x^2 - 6x - 2x + 2 - 4)$
$= 7x^2 - 8x - 2$

NR6. **0.45**

The average number of home runs per game is found by dividing the number of home runs earned by the number of games played.

$$\frac{70}{155} = 0.4516$$

Rounded to two decimal places, the correct answer is 0.45.

26. C

From the information given in the question, we know that Sosa hit 66 home runs and he needed to surpass 70 home runs to exceed McGwire's total. Assuming that he maintained the same home run pace $\left(\frac{66}{159}\right)$, the equation that can be used to project the number of **additional games** needed to exceed McGwire's home run total is

$$66 + x\left(\frac{66}{159}\right) > 70, \text{ where } x \text{ is the number}$$

of additional games needed to exceed McGwire's home run total.

NR7. **1.25**

To solve this inequality for y, first, collect like terms.

$$\frac{2y}{3} + 2y > 5 - \frac{4y}{3}$$

$$\frac{4y}{3} \qquad \text{(Add to both sides)}.$$

$$\left(\frac{2y}{3} + \frac{4y}{3}\right) + 2y > 5 \quad \text{(Collect like terms)}.$$

$$\frac{6}{3}y + 2y > 5$$

(Note: $\frac{6}{3}y = 2y$, therefore $2y + 2y = 4y$)

$$4y > 5$$

Correct to two decimal places, $y > 1.25$.

27. B

To find the correct number line display, we must first solve for m.

$3m - 1 > -4$ \qquad (Add 1 to both sides)
$3m > -3$ \qquad (Divide both sides by 3)
$m > -1$

B is correct since (**B**) indicates greater than, (but not equal to – open hole) whereas in **A**, the closed hole indicates greater than or equal to.

28. A

To find out how many times faster the race car is then the sprinter, divide the speed of the race car by the speed of the sprinter. Using exponent laws,

$$\frac{(2.1)^8}{(2.1)^5} = (2.1)^{8-5} = (2.1)^3 = 9.3.$$

Therefore, the race car is 9.3 times faster than the sprinter.

29. B

We can draw a diagram of the series of events to help us solve this problem. We must recognize that after the first student has been told the news, every 10 seconds there after, twice as many more people know the news compared with the number of new people at the previous level. This is shown below.

Total number of new students who hear the news		Time (in sec)

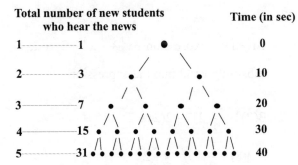

1	1	0
2	3	10
3	7	20
4	15	30
5	31	40

The total number of people who know the news is determined by adding all previous levels. To reach 31 people, it will require five rounds of "telling." If it takes 10 s between each round, it will take 40 s for all 31 students to know that a substitute teacher is coming.

30. C

From the information in the question, we know that Jill is paid $6.25/h for an 8 hour day.

(8×6.25)

Added to this is her commission of $3.00 for every pair of shoes sold $(n) \Rightarrow 3n$
Combining these two expressions, we get
$a = 8(6.25) + 3n$

31. C

Rewrite $\frac{4}{x} + \frac{3}{5} = \frac{1}{5}$, using the lowest common denominator $5x$.

$$\frac{20}{5x} + \frac{3x}{5x} = \frac{1x}{5x} \qquad \text{The } \frac{1x}{5x} \text{ reduces to } \frac{1}{5}.$$

$$\frac{20 + 3x}{5x} = \frac{1}{5}$$

32. D

To determine which factor is common to both $20x^2 - 125$ and we must factor each expression completely and then determine which factor is common to both.
Factor $20x^2 - 125$
(take out common factor of 5)
$5(4x^2 - 25)$

Using difference of squares, factor $(4x^2 - 25)$ into its two factors.

$5(2x - 5)(2x + 5)$

Factor $15x^2 + 5x - 70$
(take out common factor of 5)
$5(3x^2 + x - 14)$
(factor the trinomial into its two factors)
$5(3x + 7)(x - 2)$

Therefore, we can see that the only factor that is common to both expressions is 5.

33. C

Given the information in the equation, after 5 730 years only $\frac{1}{2}$ of a given sample of carbon-14 will remain. After another 5 730 years, or 11 460 total years, only $\frac{1}{4}$ (one half of a half or $\frac{1}{2}$ of $\frac{1}{2}$) will remain. After another 5 730 years, or about 17 000 total years, only $\frac{1}{2}$ of $\frac{1}{2}$ of $\frac{1}{2}$ (or $\frac{1}{8}$) of the original amount will remain.

Recall: We are told that the wood is 3 half-lives old.

$$\left(\frac{1}{2}\right)^3 = \frac{1}{8}$$

34. A

To completely factor the expression, we must first collect like terms.

$4x^2 + 4x - 10 + 4x - 2x^2$
$= (4x^2 - 2x^2) + (4x + 4x) - 10$
$= 2x^2 + 8x - 10$

(Take out a common factor of 2)

$= 2(x^2 + 4x - 5)$

Within the brackets, we have a trinomial that can be further factored to
$(x - 1)(x + 5)$

Therefore, the fully factored form is
$2(x - 1)(x + 5)$.

NR8. 12

When dividing $9n^4 + 36n^3 + 15n^2 + 21n$ by $3n$, we must remove a factor of $3n$ from each term in the expression

$$\frac{9n^4 + 36n^3 + 15n^2 + 21n}{3n}$$
$$= \frac{9n^4}{3n} + \frac{36n^3}{3n} + \frac{15n^2}{3n} + \frac{21n}{3n}$$
$$= 3n^3 + 12n^2 + 5n + 7$$

Therefore, 12 is the coefficient of the n^2 term in the **quotient**.

35. C

Solve for x.
$5x + 5 < 3(2x + 2)$
$5x + 5 < 6x + 6$
$5x - 6x < 6 - 5$

(Simplify and collect like terms.)
$-x < 1$ (Multiply both sides by –1.)
$x < -1$

Note: You should remember that when an inequality is multiplied or divided by a negative number, the sign **must** be reversed.

The number line that corresponds to a solution of $x > -1$ is one that includes all numbers to the LEFT of –1 and has an OPEN hole at the –1.

36. D

The numerical coefficient multiplies the variables.

$\dfrac{3x^4 y^5}{4}$ is equal to $\dfrac{3}{4} \times x^4 y^5$

The coefficient is $\dfrac{3}{4}$ and the variables are $x^4 y^5$

37. C

Given the expression $3x^3 + \dfrac{1}{2}x^4 - 2x + 2$, substitute $x = 2$ into the expression

$3(2)^3 + \dfrac{1}{2}(2)^4 - 2(2) + 2$

$= 3(8) + \dfrac{1}{2}(16) - 4 + 2$

$= 24 + 8 - 4 + 2 = 30$

38. C

Before evaluating the expression for the given values, we can simplify by collecting like terms.

$3p^3 + 14q^2 + y^3 - 2p^3$
$= (3p^3 - 2p^3) + 14q^2 + y^3$

(combine like terms)
$= p^3 + 14q^2 + y^3$

(Substitute $p = 1$, $q = -2$, and $y = -3$)

$= (1)^3 + 14(-2)^2 + (-3)^3$
$= 1 + 56 + (-27) = 30$

39. C

Simplify by collecting like terms.

$(6x^2 + 4x - 7) + (2x^2 - 4x - 3)$
$= (6x^2 + 2x^2 + 4x - 4x - 7 - 3)$
$= 8x^2 + 0x - 10 = -10$

40. B

To calculate Earth's mass, we must rearrange the expression to solve for m_1

$$F = G\frac{m_1 m_2}{d^2}$$

(Multiply both sides by d^2)

$$Fd^2 = Gm_1 m_2$$

(Divide both sides by (Gm_2))

$$\frac{Fd^2}{Gm_2} = m_1$$

41. A

To add the trinomials, collect like terms.

$4x^2 + 3x - 9 + (6x^2 + 2x + 2)$
$= 6x^2 + 4x^2 + 3x + 2x - 9 + 2$
$= 10x^2 + 5x - 7$

NR9. 3

Before we collect like terms, we must multiply the terms in the second set of brackets by the negative sign out in front.

$5x^3 - 2x^2 + 8x - 1$
$- (-2x^2 + 5x^3 - 4 + 8x)$ can be rewritten as
$5x^3 - 2x^2 + 8x - 1 + 2x^2 - 5x^3 + 4 - 8x$
$(5x^3 - 5x^3) + (-2x^2 + 2x^2)$
$+ (8x - 8x) - 1 + 4$

Simplify by collecting like terms.
$= 3$
It is not necessary to substitute for x to solve this problem since the expression reduces to 3.

NR10. 35

When these two binomials are multiplied, we get

$(2x + 3)(3x + 4)$
$= 6x^2 + 17x + 12$.
Therefore, we need
6 "x^2" tiles + 17 "x" tiles + 12 unit tiles
= 35 tiles

42. A

Multiply the expressions using the distributive property.

$7x(5x^2 + 3x + 14) = 35x^3 + 21x^2 + 98x$

43. B

Use the distributive property.

$(8g^2 + 11g - 3)(6h^3 t^5)$
$48g^2 h^3 t^5 + 66ght^5 - 18h^3 t^5$

44. D

We need to find which of the expressions is not a factor of the given trinomial.
First, we can take out a common factor of 3.

$3n^2 + 9n - 84 = 3(n^2 + 3n - 28)$

The factors of the trinomial inside the brackets are $(n + 7)(n - 4)$
The 3 factors are 3, $n + 7$, and $n - 4$.
Therefore $(n + 4)$, choice **D** is not a factor.

45. B

We can factor each expression separately and find what factor is common to both.
The factors of $x^2 + 2x - 15$ are

$(x - 3)(x + 5)$

The factors of $x^2 + x - 20$ are $(x - 4)(x + 5)$
Therefore, $(x + 5)$ is the common factor.

NR11. 10

The degree of a polynomial is the highest sum of the exponents in any one term of the polynomial. The degree of the original expression is 5 (in the term $11p^5$).
When $7q^2 r^3$ is multiplied by this term, the resulting term, $77p^5 q^2 r^3$ will have a degree of 10 (5 + 2 + 3).

Written Response

1. For two binomials of the form $(a + b)(c + d)$, the FOIL method of multiplication combines four pairs of variables to produce $ac + ad + bc + bd$. A negative (or subtraction) sign is carried through all combinations.

a) $(7x^3y^2 - 4z)(x^2 - 5z^3)$
$7x^3y^2x^2 - 35x^3y^2z - 4x^2z + 20z\,z^3$
$7x^5y^2 - 35x^3y^2z^3 - 4x^2z + 20z^4$

(2 marks)

b) $(2x + 3y)(3x - 4y)$
$6x^2 - 8xy + 9xy - 12y^2$
$3x^2 + xy - 12y^2$

(2 marks)

c) Multiply the last two binomials first:

$x(x + 1)(x - 1)$
$= x(x^2 - x + x - 1)$
$= x(x^2 - 1)$
$= x^3 - x$

OR

Multiplying the first binomial by x:
$x(x + 1)(x - 1)$
$= (x^2 + x)(x - 1)$
$= x^3 - x^2 + x^2 - x$
$= x^3 - x$

(3 marks)

ANSWERS AND SOLUTIONS – UNIT TEST 2
PATTERNS AND RELATIONS

1. A	8. B	15. D	22. D	28. D
2. C	9. D	16. D	23. C	29. B
3. B	10. A	17. C	24. A	30. C
4. D	11. D	18. A	25. C	NR1. 112
5. A	12. B	19. B	26. B	NR2. 5
6. B	13. C	20. A	27. B	NR3. 117
7. D	14. C	21. C		

1.   A

$3(2)^2 + 2(-5) + 4$
$= 3(4) + (-10) + 4$
$= 12 - 10 + 4 = 6$

2.   C

$(5x^2)(3y)(2xy)$
$= (5)(3)(2)(x^2)(y)(x)(y)$
$= 30x^3y^2$

3.   B

$$\frac{-7a^2bc^3}{21a^3b^2c}$$

$$= \left(\frac{-7}{21}\right)\left(\frac{a^2}{a^3}\right)\left(\frac{b}{b^2}\right)\left(\frac{c^3}{c}\right)$$

$$= \left(\frac{-1}{3}\right)\left(\frac{1}{a}\right)\left(\frac{1}{b}\right)\left(\frac{c^2}{1}\right) = -\frac{c^2}{3ab}$$

4.   D.

$$-3e^2 + 4ef - 6f^3$$
$$\underline{+e^2 - 2ef + 2f^3}$$
$$-2e^2 + 2ef - 4f^3$$

5.   A

$P = 2l + 2w$
$P = 16r^2 + 2r - 2$
$l = 7r^2 + 3r - 4$

$16r^2 + 2r - 2 = 2(7r2 + 3r - 4) + 2w$
$16r^2 + 2r - 2 = (14r^2 + 6r - 8) + 2w$
$\left(16r^2 + 2r - 2\right) - \left(14r^2 + 6r - 8\right) = 2w$
$16r^2 + 2r - 2 - 14r^2 - 6r + 8 = 2w$
$2r^2 - 4r + 6 = 2w$
$$\frac{2r^2 - 4r + 6}{2} = w$$
$r^2 - 2r + 3 = w$

6.   B

The pattern is dividing each number by 3.

7.   D

A quarter is worth $0.25 so take the value of the quarter and multiply it by the number of quarters needed to make up $10.00.
$$\frac{\$10.00}{0.25} = 40 \text{ quarters per roll.}$$

8.   B

$7m - 10 + 3m = 60$
$10m - 10 = 60$
$10m - 10 + 10 = 60 + 10$
$10m = 70$
$m = 7$

9. **D**

    $3x^2 + 2x - 4$

10. **A**

    $$\frac{x}{7} + 5 = 3$$

    $$\frac{x}{7} + 5 - 5 = 3 - 5$$

    $$(7)\frac{x}{7} = -2(7)$$

    $$x = -14$$

11. **D**

    $3x + 9 = 7x - 19$
    $3x - 3x + 9 + 19 = 7x - 3x - 19 + 19$
    $28 = 4x$
    $x = 7$

12. **B**

    $$\frac{y+1}{7} = \frac{12}{21}$$

    By cross multiplying, we get
    $(21)\,(y + 1) = (12)\,(7)$
    $21y + 21 = 84$
    $21y + 21 - 21 = 84 - 21$
    $21y = 63$
    $y = 3$

13. **C**

    $Ef - fg + g$ if $e = 7, f = 3$, and $g = -5$
    $= (7)\,(3) - (3)(-5) + (-5)$
    $= 21 - (-15) + (-5)$
    $= 21 + 15 - 5$
    $= 31$

14. **C**

    $4xy^3z = 5^{\text{th}}$ degree
    $7x^3yz = 5^{\text{th}}$ degree
    $3x^3y^2z = 6^{\text{th}}$ degree
    Add each term's exponents; the term with
    the highest degree determines the degree of
    the polynomial. In this case, the degree is
    six.

15. **D**

    $3m^2np^3, 15m^3n^3p^4, 36m^2n^2p^3$
    3 is a common factor to all three terms.
    m^2, n, p^3 are all common to the three terms,
    thus the GCF for these three expressions is
    $3m^2np^3$.
    To verify, divide each term by $3m^2np^3$.
    This will show that there are not any further
    common factors.

16. **D**

    $4a(2a + 3) - 2a(a + 2)$
    $= 8a^2 + 12a - 2a^2 - 4a$
    $= 6a^2 + 8a$

17. **C**

    $$\frac{12a^2b + 15ab^2 - 18a^2b^2}{-3ab}$$

    $$= \left(\frac{12a^2b}{-3ab}\right) + \left(\frac{15ab^2}{-3ab}\right) - \left(\frac{18a^2b^2}{-3ab}\right)$$

    $$= -4a - 5b + 6ab$$

18. **A**

    $$(4ef)(ef + 4e - 7g) = 4e^2f^2 + 16e^2f - 28efg$$

19. **B**

    $(-y + 2)\,(-5)$
    $= -2y^2 + 5y + 4y - 10$
    $= -2y^2 + 9y - 10$

20. A

$m^2 - 2m - 15$ – find two numbers that give
a sum of -2 and a product of -15
$\rightarrow +3$ and -5
So the factors for the trinomial are
$(m + 3)(m - 5)$

21. C

Using the method of difference of squares,
$(x + 9)(x - 9)$
$= x^2 - 9x + 9x - 81$ (verify)
$= x^2 - 81$

22. D

$(3e - 5f)2 = (3e - 5f)(3e - 5f)$
$= 9e^2 - 15ef - 15ef + 25f^2$
$= 9e^2 - 30ef + 25f^2$

23. C

$$\frac{15m^2n^2}{2mn^2} \times \frac{2m^3n}{3m^2n^2}$$
$$= \left(\frac{15}{2}\right)\left(\frac{m^2}{m}\right)\left(\frac{n^2}{n^2}\right) \times \left(\frac{2}{3}\right)\left(\frac{m^3}{m^2}\right)\left(\frac{n}{n^2}\right)$$
$$= \left(\frac{30}{6}\right)\left(\frac{m^5}{m^3}\right)\left(\frac{n^3}{n^4}\right)$$
$$= \frac{5m^2}{n}, n \neq 0$$

24. A

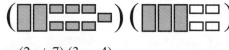

$= (2x + 7)(3x - 4)$
$= 6x^2 - 8x + 21x - 28$
$= 6x^2 + 13x - 28$

25. C

$(3x - 2)(x + 5)$
$= 3x^2 + 15x - 2x - 10$
$= 3x^2 + 13x - 10$

26. B

$(x - 3)(x^2 + 2x - 4)$
$= x^3 + 2x^2 - 4x - 3x^2 - 6x + 12$
$= x^3 - x^2 - 10x + 12$

27. B

$$\frac{x+3}{4} + \frac{x-2}{2}$$
$$= \frac{x+3}{4} + \frac{2x-4}{4}$$
$$= \frac{x + 2x + 3 - 4}{4}$$
$$= \frac{3x - 1}{4}$$

28. D

$4(x + 2) - 3(2x + 5)$
$= 4x + 8 - 6x - 15$
$= -2x - 7$

29. B

$4x^2 - 16x - 48$
$= (x^2 - 4x - 12)$
$= 4(x - 6)(x + 2)$

$x^2 - 4x - 12$--find two numbers that give a
sum of -4 and a product of -12
$\rightarrow$The two numbers are $+2$ and -6.
So the factors for the trinomial are
$(x - 6)(x + 2)$

30. C

A coefficient is a number that is multiplied
by a variable.

NR1. 112

Area of shaded and white rectangles together (large shape):
$$A = (6a^3b^2)(3a^2b)$$
$$= 18a^5b^3$$
$$= 18(1^5)(2^3)$$
$$= 18(8)$$
$$= 144 \text{ cm}^2$$

Area of white rectangle alone (inside of large shape):
$$A = (2ab^3)(ab)$$
$$= 2a^2b^4$$
$$= 2(1^2)(2^4)$$
$$= 2(16)$$
$$= 32 \text{ cm}^2$$

Area of shaded area
= Area of large shape – Area inside shape:
$$A = 144 - 32$$
$$= 112 \text{ cm}^2$$

NR2. 5

After adding like terms
$$\rightarrow 3e^2 + 2ef^3 - 2e^4g + 6fg$$
Add the exponents from each term:
$3e^2 \rightarrow$ degree 2
$2ef^3 \rightarrow$ degree 4
$-2e^4g \rightarrow$ degree 5
$6fg \rightarrow$ degree 2
5 degrees is the highest $\therefore$ the resulting polynomial is of degree 5.

NR3. 117

Row 1 numbers increase by 2. Row 2 is 3 greater than the number in row 1. Row 3 is the product of row 1 and 2. Row 4 is the difference between row 3 and row 2.

2	4	6	8	10
5	7	9	11	13
10	28	54	88	130
5	21	45	77	**117**

ANSWERS AND SOLUTIONS – SHAPE AND SPACE

1. B	NR1. 95.0	16. B	24. D	32. A
2. B	NR2. 8	NR6. 15.9	25. B	33. C
3. D	11. B	NR7. 19.0	NR8. 10.0	NR10. 36.9
4. A	NR3. 3.87	17. A	26. C	34. D
5. B	12. A	18. D	27. C	35. C
6. B	13. B	19. A	NR9. 87.7	NR11. 52
7. C	NR4. 10	20. D	28. A	36. D
8. D	NR5. 60.0	21. B	29. D	NR12. 32
9. C	14. D	22. B	30. B	37. C
10. B	15. C	23. D	31. D	WR1. See Solution

1. B

From the information in the question, we are told that
Sin $A = 0.469\,5$
Using the $[\sin^{-1}]$ or [inv] key on our calculator, we find that
$A = 28°$

2. B

Recall that $\sin A = \dfrac{\text{opposite}}{\text{hypotenuse}}$

Therefore, $\sin A = \dfrac{5}{\text{hypotenuse}}$

To calculate the length of the hypotenuse (c), use the Pythagorean Theorem.
$c^2 = a^2 + b^2 \qquad \Rightarrow \qquad c^2 = 5^2 + 7^2$
$c^2 = 25 + 49 \qquad \Rightarrow \qquad c^2 = 74$
　(Take the square root of both
　sides of the equation)
$c = \sqrt{74}$　　(Since we are finding length, use only the positive root)

Therefore, $\sin A = \dfrac{5}{\sqrt{74}}$

Note: Answer **D** is incorrect because the question asks for the **exact** value of sin A. The exact answer is an irrational number, i.e., a non-repeating, non-terminating decimal. Answer **D** is an approximation of sin A, but is not the exact value.

3. D

We are told that cos $B = 0.8$. Since the cosine ratio is the ratio of the side adjacent over the hypotenuse, we must find the triangle where this ratio is equal to 0.8.

In **A**, we must first determine the length of the side adjacent using the Pythagorean theorem.

$(BC)^2 = (AB)^2 - (AC)^2 = 5^2 - 4^2$
$= 25 - 16 = 9$

Therefore, $BC = \sqrt{9} = 3$ and
$\cos B = \dfrac{BC}{AB} = \dfrac{3}{5} = 0.6$

In **B**, $\cos B = \dfrac{BC}{AB} = \dfrac{5}{8} = 0.625$

In **C**, we need to find the length of the hypotenuse AB
$AB^2 = BC^2 + AC^2 = 4^2 + 5^2$
$= 16 + 25 = 41$

Therefore, $AB = \sqrt{41}$, and
$\cos B = \dfrac{BC}{AB} = \dfrac{4}{\sqrt{41}} \approx 0.62$

In **D**, $\cos B = \dfrac{BC}{AB} = \dfrac{4}{5} = 0.8$

4. **A**

    Using the information in the diagram, we can use the tangent ratio to find the measure of angle A.

    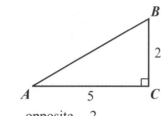

    $$\tan A = \frac{\text{opposite}}{\text{adjacent}} = \frac{2}{5}$$

    $\tan A = 0.4$

    Using the [tan^{-1}] or [inv] [tan] key, we find $A = 21.8°$

5. **B**

    In **A**, the cosine ratio is used to solve for b.

    $$\cos A = \frac{\text{adjacent}}{\text{hypotenuse}} = \frac{b}{c} \quad \cos 40° = \frac{b}{c}$$

    Multiplying both sides of the equation by c, we get $b = c \times \cos 40°$

    Hence, the equation in **A** can be used to solve for b.

    In **B**, $\sin 40°$ is given as $\frac{b}{c}$.

    However, if we look at the diagram, we can see that $\sin 40° = \frac{a}{c}$ (recall that $\sin = \frac{\text{opp}}{\text{hyp}}$).

    Therefore, the equation in **B** is wrong and cannot be used to derive a value for side b.
    In **C**, the tangent ratio is used to solve for b.

    $$\tan A = \frac{\text{opposite}}{\text{adjacent}}, \quad \tan 40° = \frac{a}{b}$$

    Therefore, **C** can be used to solve for side b.
    In **D**, the sine ratio is used to solve for b. Given that we have a right angle triangle and that the sum of all angles within a triangle equals 180°, angle B must equal 50° (180° − 90° − 40°).

    Therefore,

    $$\sin B = \frac{\text{opposite}}{\text{hypotenuse}}, \quad \sin 50° = \frac{b}{c}$$

    Multiplying both sides by c, we get
    $b = c \times \sin 50°$
    Therefore, **D** can be used to solve for b.
    The only equation that cannot be used is **B**.

6. **B**

    Recall that the sine ratio is the ratio of the length of the side opposite over the length of the hypotenuse. Using the information from the diagram, the length of the side opposite to B is 19.2 and the length of the hypotenuse is 25.

    $$\sin B = \frac{\text{opp}}{\text{hyp}} = \frac{19.2}{25}$$

7. **C**

    From the diagram, we can see that triangle ACD is a right triangle, where $\overline{AC}$ (the sidewalk) is the hypotenuse, $\overline{AD}$ is the length of the garden (50 m), $\overline{CD}$ is the width, and angle A is 32°. Given this information, we can use the cosine ratio to determine the length of the sidewalk (hypotenuse).

    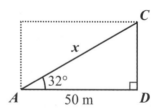

    $$\cos A = \frac{\text{adjacent}}{\text{hypotenuse}}$$

    (Let x = the length of the sidewalk)

    $$\cos 32° = \frac{50}{x}$$

    (Multiply both sides of the equation by x)
    $x(\cos 32°) = 50$
    (Using cosine, we find that $\cos 32° \approx 0.848…$
    So, $x \times 0.848 \approx 50$)
    (Divide both sides of the equation by 0.848)
    $x \approx 59$ m

8. D

Given the information in the diagram, we can use the tangent ratio to calculate the measure of the unknown angle.

If we let A be the measure of the unknown angle then,

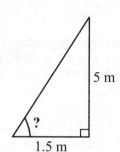

5 m

?

1.5 m

$$\tan A = \frac{\text{opposite}}{\text{adjacent}}$$

$$= \frac{5}{1.5} = 3.3\overline{3}.$$

Taking the inverse tan (or $\tan^{-1}$) of $3.3\overline{3}$, we find that
$A \approx 73.300\ 7...°$

Therefore, the angle that the ladder makes with the ground is $73.3°$.

9. C

From the diagram, we have a right triangle with one angle equal to $65°$. The side adjacent to that angle is 8 m and the side opposite to that angle is the height of Mike's hoodoo, which we will call x.

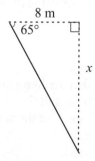

8 m

$65°$

x

$$\tan\theta = \frac{\text{opposite}}{\text{adjacent}}$$

$$\tan 65° = \frac{x}{8}$$

Multiply both sides of the equation by 8.
$$\tan 65° = 2.144\ 5...$$
$$8\tan 65° = x$$
$$8(2.144\ 5...) = x$$
$$17 \approx x$$

10. B

It may be helpful to sketch a diagram of the information in the question.

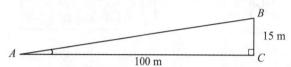

B

15 m

A

100 m

C

Since the angle of elevation is the angle formed by the horizontal and $\overline{AB}$, the angle of elevation is angle A.

To find the measure of angle A, we can use the tan ratio since we are told that the ratio of the side opposite to the side adjacent equals 0.15.

$$\tan A = \frac{\text{opposite}}{\text{adjacent}} = \frac{15}{100} = 0.15$$

Using the [inv] [tan] or [$\tan^{-1}$] key on our calculator, we find that
$A = 8.530\ 7...° \approx 8.5°$

NR1. 95.0

From the diagram, we can see that we are looking for the area of a circle with radius of 5.5 m. Recall that the formula for the area of a circle is $A = \pi r^2$
(Use the approximation 3.14 for π)

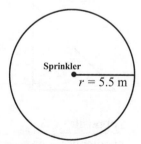

Sprinkler

$r = 5.5$ m

$A \approx 3.14(5.5)^2$
$A \approx 3.14\ (30.25) \approx 94.985$
Correct to one decimal place, $A = 95.0$ m^2

NR2. 8

Side View of Table

Modified Top View
of Tablecloth

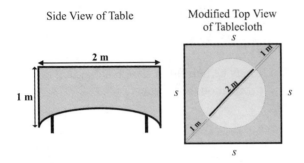

Method I

Recall that the formula for area of a square is $A = s^2$, where s is the length of one side of the square.

We can see from the diagram that we can determine the length of the diagonal of the square tablecloth. Starting at a corner of the tablecloth, the distance from the corner (touching the floor) to the edge of the table is 1 m; the distance across the table is 2 m and the distance from the edge of the table to the opposite corner of the tablecloth is 1m. The length of the diagonal is

$1\text{ m} + 2\text{ m} + 1\text{ m} = 4\text{ m}.$

We also know that the diagonal of a square forms a 45° angle with each side.

Therefore, knowing the length of a diagonal (hypotenuse), we can use either sine or cosine ratio to determine the length of a side.

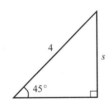

$$\sin 45° = \frac{\text{opposite}}{\text{hypotenuse}} = \frac{s}{4}$$

$(\sin 45° \approx 0.707\ 10... \approx 0.71)$

Therefore, $0.71 = \dfrac{s}{4}$

(Multiply both sides by 4)

$S \approx 2.84\text{ m}$

Now, we can solve for the area of the tablecloth

$A = s^2$

$A = (2.84\text{ m})^2$

$A = 8.065\ 6\text{ m}^2$

$A = 8\text{ m}^2$ (to the nearest whole number)

Method II

The length of the diagonal is
$1\text{ m} + 2\text{ m} + 1\text{ m} = 4\text{ m}$. We can use either the Pythagorean Theorem or trigonometry to find the length of a side.

$A^2 + b^2 = c^2$

Since a and b are both sides of the square, (and are therefore equal in length), we can substitute s for each, and c is the length of the hypotenuse, which is 4.

$s^2 + s^2 = (4)^2$

$2s^2 = 16$ (Gather like terms.)

$s^2 = 8$ (Divide both sides by 2.)

Now, we can solve for the area of the tablecloth.

$A = s^2$ $s^2 = 8$, so $A = 8$

Correct to the nearest whole number, the area is 8 m^2

11. B

We are told that the hypotenuse, z, is 900 m and that the height, y, is 61 m. We can use Pythagorean theorem to determine the length of the base, x.

$z^2 = x^2 + y^2,$ (Solving for x)

$x = \sqrt{z^2 - y^2}$ $\Rightarrow$ $x = \sqrt{900^2 - 61^2}$

$x = \sqrt{810\ 000 - 3\ 721} = \sqrt{806\ 279}$

$x \approx 897.9\text{ m}$

NR3. 3.9

We are told that the hypotenuse of the triangle is 900 m and that the side opposite angle A is 61 m. Use the sine ratio to find angle A.

$$\sin A = \frac{\text{opposite}}{\text{hypotenuse}}$$

$$\sin A = \frac{61}{900} = 0.06\overline{7}$$

$A \approx 3.87°$

12. A

The diagram gives us the angle of incidence equals the angle of reflection to be 40°. Since the angle of incidence equals the angle of the reflection, the angle of incidence is also 40°. In the diagram, the distance between the flashlight and the mirror is the side of the right triangle opposite the 40° angle.

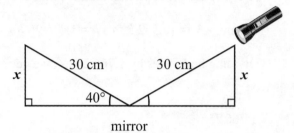

mirror

We know that the hypotenuse of the triangle is 30 cm, so we can use the sine ratio to determine the distance between the flashlight and the mirror. Let x equal the distance between the flashlight and the mirror.

$$\frac{x}{30} = \sin 40°$$

(sin 40 ≈ 0.642 78... ≈ 0.643)

Therefore, $\frac{x}{30} \approx 0.643$

(Multiply both sides of the equation by 30 cm)

$x \approx 30 \times 0.643$
$x \approx 19.3$

13. B

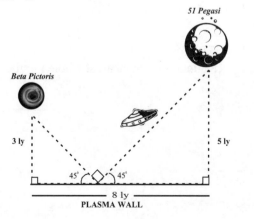

Method I

From the diagram, we can see that as the spaceship travels from *Beta Pictoris* to the plasma wall, the distance it travels is equal to the length of the hypotenuse of the first (left) right triangle. As it continues its journey, the second leg of the trip is the hypotenuse of the second right triangle.

In the first triangle, we are given the length of one side as 3 ly and the angle opposite as 45°. We can use the sine ratio to find the length of the hypotenuse.

If we call this distance x, then

$\sin 45° = \frac{3}{x}$ (Multiply both sides by x)

$x \sin 45° = 3$ (Divide both sides by sin 45°)

$x = \frac{3}{\sin 45°}$

As sin 45° = 0.707 10... ≈ 0.707

$x \approx \frac{3}{0.707} \approx 4.24$ light-years

In the second triangle, we are given the length of one side as 5 ly and the angle opposite as 45°. If we call the length of the hypotenuse y, then we can use the sine ratio to calculate this distance.

$\sin 45° = \frac{5}{y}$ (Multiply both sides by y.)

$y \sin 45° = 5$

(Divide both sides by sin 45°)

$y = \frac{5}{\sin 45°}$

As 45° = 0.707 10... ≈ 0.707

$y = \frac{5}{0.707} = 7.07$ light-years

Adding the two distances gives us the total length of the trip.

4.24 light-years + 7.07 light-years
= 11.31 light-years

Method II

Because the two angles the spaceship makes with the plasma wall are both 45° the legs of each right triangle are equal. Thus, we can use Pythagorean theorem to calculate the hypotenuse of each triangle to be $\sqrt{3^3 + 3^2} = \sqrt{18}$ and $\sqrt{52 + 52} = \sqrt{50}$

Add the two together to calculate the distance travelled.

Distance
$= \sqrt{18} + \sqrt{50}$
≈ 11.31 light-years

NR4. **10**

We are asked to determine the total distance travelled from the fuel station to *51 Pegasi* if an additional stop is made at the right end of the plasma wall.

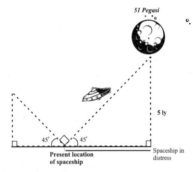

We need to determine the distance between the rescue spaceship and the spaceship in distress (*x*). Using the tan ratio, we have

$\tan\theta = \dfrac{\text{opp}}{\text{adj}}$ $\tan 45° = \dfrac{5}{x}$

$(x)(\tan 45°) = 5$

$x = \dfrac{5}{\tan 45°} = \dfrac{5}{1} = 5$ ly

Since we already know that the distance from the right side of the plasma wall to *51 Pegasi* is 5 light-years, then the total distance travelled is
5 light-years + 5 light-years
= 10 light-years

NR5. **60.0**

Recall that the formula for volume of a cylinder is $V = \pi r^2 h$, where r is the radius of the base and h is the height of the cylinder.

Therefore, $106 \text{ m}^3 = \pi \left(\dfrac{1.5 \text{ m}}{2}\right)^2 h$

$\left(\text{Remember that } r = \dfrac{d}{2}\right)$

(we will use the approximation 3.14 for π)

$106 \text{ m}^3 = 3.14\ (0.562\ 5 \text{ m}^2)\ h \approx 1.776\ 25\ h$

Dividing both sides by 1.766 25 m², we get

$\dfrac{106}{1.766\ 25} = h$

$60 \approx h$

Rounded to one decimal place, $h = 60.0$ m

14. D

From the information given, the glass forms a cone with a **radius** of 5 cm and a height of 18 cm.

The formula for volume of a cone is

$V = \dfrac{1}{3}\pi r^2 h$

$V = \dfrac{1}{3}\pi \left(\dfrac{10 \text{ cm}}{2}\right)^2 \times 18 \text{ cm}$

$V \approx \dfrac{1}{3}\times 3.14 \times 25 \text{ cm}^2 \times 18 \text{ cm}$

$V = 471 \text{ cm}^3$
(Rounded to the nearest whole number)

15. C

The glass in this question is still a cone, with a radius of 5 cm, but the height has now been reduced to 9 cm (half the height of the entire glass). We can still use the formula for the volume of a cone to determine how much liquid the glass holds.

$$V = \frac{1}{3}\pi r^2 h$$

$$V = \frac{1}{3}\pi \left(\frac{10 \text{ cm}}{2}\right)^2 (9) \text{ cm}$$

(remember that the height of the cone is $\frac{1}{2}$ the height of the cone in the previous question.)

$$V \approx \frac{1}{3} \times 3.14 \times 25 \text{ cm}^2 \times 9 \text{ cm}$$

$$V = 236 \text{ cm}^3$$

(Rounded to the nearest whole number)

16. B

When the object in the diagram is viewed from the top, a total of 6 blocks should be visible. **C** and **D** can be eliminated since only 5 blocks are shown in the top views. When the object is viewed from the front, a base of 3 blocks should be visible, with 2 blocks stacked on the second level, 1 over the middle block of the base, and the other over the left-most block. Only the Front elevation illustrated in **B** shows this arrangement.

NR6. **15.9**

The area cooled by the fan can be described as a $\frac{1}{4}$ circle with radius equal to 4.5 m.

Recall that the formula for the area of a circle is $A = \pi r^2$

Therefore, the area covered by $\frac{1}{4}$ of a circle is

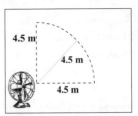

$$A = \frac{1}{4}\pi r^2$$

$$A = \frac{1}{4}\pi (4.5 \text{ m})^2$$

$$= \frac{1}{4}\pi (20.25 \text{ m}^2)$$

$$= 15.9 \text{ m}^2$$

(rounded to one decimal place)

NR7. **19.0**

This question can be solved using two steps.

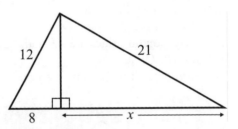

Step 1.
Determine the height in the diagram.
Using the Pythagorean Theorem, we know that
$$c^2 = a^2 + b^2 \qquad \text{(for a right triangle)}$$
From the triangle on the left,
$$12^2 = 8^2 + y^2$$
$$144 = 64 + y^2$$
$80 = y^2$, therefore, $y = \sqrt{80}$ represents the height of the triangle. We can now solve for x.

Step 2
Using the Pythagorean theorem again,
$$c^2 = a^2 + b^2$$
$$(21)^2 = (\sqrt{80})^2 + x^2$$
$$441 = 80 + x^2$$
$$361 = x^2$$
$$x = \sqrt{361} \approx 19$$
Therefore, the value of x correct to one decimal place is 19.0.

17. A

Any front profile of this object must have 3 blocks stacked on the left and 2 blocks stacked on the right with only a single level of blocks in the middle two positions. Only **A** and **C** have this arrangement. **A** and **C** differ only in their right and left profiles. The right profile of the object should show 3 stacked blocks sitting with 1 block to the left and 2 blocks to the right. Therefore, only the view in **A** can be correct.

18. D

To determine if the triangles are similar, we need to see if corresponding angles are equal. In this case, triangles ADF, and ABC share angle A. We are also given that angle F and angle C are equal. Therefore, having two matching angles means that the third angles must also the same.
Therefore, angle B = angle D.
The corresponding sides are AF and AC; AD and AB; DF and BC.
Therefore, the similarity ratios are:

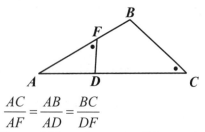

$$\frac{AC}{AF} = \frac{AB}{AD} = \frac{BC}{DF}$$

Note: Although answer **C** is true, it does not display similarity **ratios** (which is what the question asked for), so it is not the correct answer.

19. A

Since the base of the house is 10 m × 10 m, only **A** and **B** have the correct top view. **A** and **B** only different in the height of the roof in the right and left profile. Draw the profile of the roof:

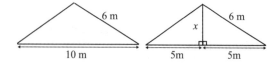

Let x be the height of the roof. Solve for x using the Pythagorean theorem.

$$6^2 = 5^2 + x^2$$
$$36 = 25 + x^2$$
$$x^2 = 36 - 25$$
$$x^2 = 11$$
$$x = \sqrt{11}$$
$$x \approx 3.3$$

The height of the roof is 3.3 m, therefore **A** is correct.

20. D

The roof of the tent forms a pyramid with a square base. The walls form a rectangular prism. We can determine the volume of the prism and the volume of the pyramid separately and then add the two volumes.
Volume of base = length × width × height

$$V_{base} = 4 \times 4 \times 3 = 48 \text{ m}^3$$

The formula for the volume of a pyramid is $V = \frac{1}{3}lwh$, where l is the length, w is the width, and h is the height.
We have also seen the volume of a pyramid to be $V = \frac{1}{3}lwh$, where B is the area of the base. However, the area of the base is the same as $l \times w$, so both formulas are actually the same.

$$V_{top} = \frac{4 \times 4 \times 3}{3} = 16 \text{m}^3$$

Volume of tent = Volume of base
                        + Volume of top
$$V = 48 \text{ m}^3 + 16 \text{ m}^3$$
$$V = 64 \text{ m}^3$$

21. B

A rectangular prism has 3 dimensions (length, width, and height). If the volume of the rectangle is always 20 cubes, how many ways can we change the number of cubes in each dimension and still maintain the overall shape as a rectangular prism? One method of finding the answer is simply by finding how many different ways we can factor the number 20 into exactly 3 factors (dimensions). We can factor 20 as follows

$1 \times 1 \times 20 = 20$
$1 \times 2 \times 10 = 20$
$1 \times 4 \times 5 = 20$
$2 \times 2 \times 5 = 20$

Note: All other boxes are obtained by turning or rotating one of the 4 boxes above and so do not count as a separate solution(boxes turned on their sides still have the same overall dimensions).

22. B

Since two of the corresponding angles in each triangle are the same, the third angle in each triangle must also be equal. Therefore, the triangles must be similar. Information regarding the other aspects of the triangle are not provided. Therefore, we are unable to conclude whether **A**, **C**, or **D** are correct. We can only be certain that the triangles are similar, so **B** is correct.

23. D

From the diagram, side AB corresponds to side PQ. Also, side BC corresponds to side QR Therefore, side AC must correspond to side PR.

Therefore, the ratios are $\dfrac{AB}{PQ} = \dfrac{BC}{QR} = \dfrac{AC}{PR}$.

This can be rewritten as $\dfrac{PQ}{AB} = \dfrac{QR}{BC} = \dfrac{PR}{AC}$.

24. D

Congruent triangles are the same size and shape. Examining the diagrams, we can see that triangles AFD and ABC in **D** are definitely not the same size (though they are similar).

A.

B.

C.

D.

25. B

If we can show that the 2 triangles are similar, we can use the ratios of corresponding sides to determine the width of the river.

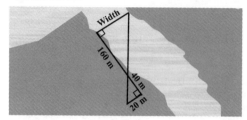

Recall from the opposite angle theorem that opposite angles are equal, so we have two triangles where two corresponding angles are equal. Therefore, the third angle in each triangle is equal meaning that the two triangles are similar.

The side of the triangle that is the width (w) of the river, corresponds to the 20 m side of the smaller triangle. The 160 m side of the larger triangle corresponds to the 40 m side of the smaller triangle. The ratios then are

$\dfrac{w}{20} = \dfrac{160}{40}$ Cross-multiplying, we get

$40\,w = 3\,200$ $\Rightarrow$ $w = 80$

NR8. 10.0

Sketch a diagram to separate the triangles and identify the corresponding sides and angles.

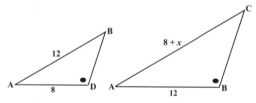

Using similarity ratios,

$$\dfrac{AC}{AB(\text{left triangle})} = \dfrac{AB(\text{right triangle})}{AD}$$

$\dfrac{8+x}{12} = \dfrac{12}{8}$ $\left(\dfrac{12}{8} \text{ can be reduced to } \dfrac{3}{2}\right)$

$\dfrac{8+x}{12} = \dfrac{3}{2}$ (Cross-multiply)

$16 + 2x = 36$ (Subtract 16 from both sides)
$2x = 20$ $x = 10.0$
$x = 10.0$ (Remember to record your answer to one decimal place.)

26.

Two triangles are congruent when the corresponding sides and angles are equal. If no information is provided about the sides of the triangles, then a conclusion about congruency is not possible. In **A**, **B**, and **D** some information is provided about the sides, which allows us to prove that the triangles are congruent. In **C**, no information regarding the sides is provided that will help us to establish congruency.

27. C

Sketch a diagram. In profile, we see that the area from ceiling to floor must be triangular. Since we are told that the base of this shape is circular, the volume scanned by the camera can be described as a cone.

NR9. 87.7

Draw a diagram.
Let x be the distance you must travel along the trail to climb 30 m.

Using the sine ratio,

$\sin\theta = \dfrac{\text{opposite}}{\text{hypotenuse}}$

$\sin 20° = \dfrac{30 \text{ m}}{x}$ (multiply both sides by x)

$x\sin 20° = 30 \text{ m},$ that is,

$x = \dfrac{30 \text{ m}}{\sin 20°} = \dfrac{30}{0.342\ldots}$

$x = 87.7 \text{ m}$

28. A

Start by comparing the front views. When the original is viewed from the front, the steeple is on the right. We can therefore eliminate **B** and **D** (which have the steeple on the left). Comparing **A** and **C**, the top view is the same but the side views differ. When the original is viewed from the right, the steeple is on the right and from the left the steeple is on the left. This corresponds to the views in answer **A**.

29. D

To find the volume of the object, we must first determine the number of blocks that were used. From the top view, we can see that the base has 5 blocks. The left and right views show that the object has a height of 3 blocks, and no blocks are stacked on the back row of blocks. The front view confirms that the middle block is stacked 3 high has a stack of 3 blocks and the left side is stacked 2 high. Using this information, we can draw a diagram of the object.
We can see from the diagram that a total of 8 blocks were used to construct this object. As each block has a volume of 10 cm, the volume of the object is 80 cm.

30. B

In a reflection, the shape of an object does not change. Since **C** does not have the same shape as the original, it can beimmeditly eliminated. A reflection requires an axis of symmetry across which the reflection occurs. Answer **B** is a reflection; the axis of symmetry being a horizontal line. Choices **A** and **D** are both rotations of the original but are not reflections.

31. D

For any point on LMN with coordinate (x, y), the corresponding point on PQR is $(x + 1, y - 1)$. So,
$L(1, 1)$ corresponds to
$$P(1 + 1, 1 - 1) \rightarrow P(2, 0);$$
$M(1, -1)$ corresponds to
$$Q(1 + 1, -1 - 1) \rightarrow Q(2, -2);$$
$N(-1, 1)$ corresponds to
$$R(-1 + 1, 1 - 1) \rightarrow R(0, 0).$$

32. A

As a point, $A(x, y)$ is reflected in the line $x = 0$. The point and its image $A(x, y)$ will be the same distance from the reflection line. Since $x = 0$ is the y-axis, the distance of a point from the y-axis is determined by its x-coordinate.

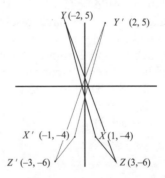

The reflection of point $A(x, y)$ in the line $x = 0$ is $A'(-x, y)$
Therefore, the y-coordinate does not change and the x-coordinate is multiplied by -1
From the information in the diagram, if triangle XYZ is reflected in the line $x = 0$, then the coordinates of the reflected image are

$X(1, -4)$	$\rightarrow$	$X'(-1, -4)$
$Y(-2, 5)$	$\rightarrow$	$Y'(2, 5)$
$Z(3, -6)$	$\rightarrow$	$Z'(-3, -6)$

33. C

From the information in the question, we are told that *EFG* was translated; $(x, y) \rightarrow (x + 2, y - 3)$, and then reflected in the *x*-axis to obtain *ABC*. To find the coordinates of *EFG*, we must reverse the steps of the reflection and then the translation. Since *EFG* was reflected in the *x*-axis, the *x*-coordinates have remained the same but the *y*-coordinates have been multiplied by –1. Therefore, the reflection in the *x*-axis is $(x, -y)$. Given that the vertices of *ABC* are *A*(6, 8), *B*(4, 2), and *C*(2, 6) The coordinates prior to the reflection would have been $A'(6, -8)$, $B'(4, -2)$, and $C'(2, -6)$.
To reverse the effect of the translation, we must get the original *x*-coordinates and *y*-coordinates. Therefore, the nature of the translation would be $(x + 2, y - 3) \rightarrow (z, y)$. To make $x + 2 = x$ we have to subtract 2, and to make $y - 3 = y$ we have to add 3. So, by subtracting 2 from each *x*-coordinate and adding 3 to each *y*-coordinate, we get
$A'(6 - 2, -8 + 3) \rightarrow E(4, -5)$
$B'(4 - 2, -2 + 3) \rightarrow F(2, 1)$
$C'(2 - 2, -6 + 3) \rightarrow G'(0, -3)$

NR10. 36.9

Sketch a diagram of the information. Let *x* equal the distance from the base of the tree to the peg. Then 75*x* equals the distance from the base of the tree to the point at which the rope is tied to the tree. Using the tangent ratio:

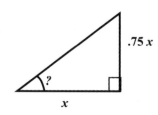

$$\tan\theta = \frac{\text{opposite}}{\text{adjacent}} = \frac{0.75x}{x} = 0.75$$

(The *x*'s are eliminated)
As $\tan\theta = 0.75, \theta = 36.9°$

34. D

(See question 32 for an explanation of a reflection in the *y*-axis.)

Since this reflection has the effect of multiplying the *x*-coordinates by –1, *DEF* reflected in the *y*-axis is
$D(2, 3) \rightarrow D'(-2\ 3)$
$E(7, 4) \rightarrow E'(-7, 4)$
$F(3, 6) \rightarrow F'(-3, 6)$
If we plot the reflected points on a coordinate plane, the graph would be identical to **D**.

35. C

Quadrilateral *STUV* with vertices at $S(-3, 4)$, $T(-4, -2)$, $U(0, -4)$, and $V(2, 3)$ is shown in the following diagram.

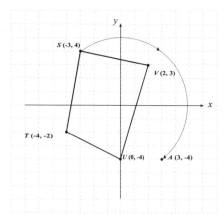

If *STUV* is rotated clockwise 180° about the origin, then each vertex of the quadrilateral is rotated 180°. That is, each vertex rotates into the opposite quadrant. For example, $S(-3, 4)$ moves from the second quadrant to the fourth quadrant to point $A(3, -4)$. The signs of both the *x* and the *y* coordinates change. The coordinates of the transformed figure are:
$S(-3, 4) \rightarrow A(3, -4)$
$T(-4, -2) \rightarrow B(4, 2)$
$U(0, -4) \rightarrow C(0, 4)$
$V(2, 3) \rightarrow D(-2, -3)$

NR11.52

To find the height, h, we must set up a trigonometric ratio using the given information.

$$\tan = \frac{\text{opp}}{\text{adj}}$$

$$\tan 33° = \frac{h}{80} \qquad \text{(Multiply both sides by 80.)}$$

$80 \tan 33° = h$

$80(0.649\,4) \approx h$

$h = 52 \text{ m} \qquad \text{(correct to the nearest metre)}$

36. D

Let x = the height of Trango Tower.
Let y = the base of the triangles, that is, a horizontal line segment from the base camp to the base of the mountain directly below the hanging camp.
First, solve for y.

$$\tan 49.7 = \frac{1\,430}{y}$$

$y \times \tan 49.7° = 1\,430$

$$y = \frac{1\,430}{\tan 49.7°}$$

$y \approx 1\,213 \text{ m}$

Use this value for y to solve for x.

$$\tan(30 + 49.7)° = \frac{x}{1\,213}$$

$1\,213\,(\tan 79.7°) = x$

$= 6\,675 \text{ m}$

NR12.32

To determine the largest area that we can fence off with the stage and 16 m of fence, let L equal the length of the fenced area and W the width. We know that the area of a rectangle can be calculated by multiplying its length by its width. We also know that the length of 3 sides of this rectangle (not including the side next to the stage) will be 16 m long (the length of the available fencing). Set up a table of values.

Width (m)	Length (m)	$2W + L = $ 16?	Area $(L \times W)$
1	14	16	14
2	12	16	24
3	10	16	30
4	8	16	32
5	6	16	30
6	4	16	24

You may continue with the table to calculate all possible values for the length and width and you will determine that the maximum area is 32 m^2

37. C

Using the information in the diagram, we can use the tangent ratio to calculate the measure of the unknown angle. Since A is the unknown angle, then

$$\tan A = \frac{\text{opposite}}{\text{adjacent}} = \frac{40}{30.5} = 1.31\ldots$$

Taking the inverse tan (or $\tan^{-1}$) of 1.31..., we find that

$A = 52.67\ldots° \approx 52.7°$

Therefore, the angle of Sally's line of sight to the ground is approximately 52.7°.

Written Response

1. Since the motion detector has a range of 50°, it spans 25° above and 25° below the horizontal, as shown in the diagram.

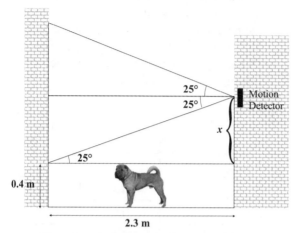

The triangle below the horizontal is congruent to the triangle above the level of Fifi's head, so the angle to the opposite wall is also 25° from the horizontal. The height of this triangle, shown as x on the diagram, can be computed with a trigonometric ratio:

$$\tan 25° = \frac{x}{2.3} \quad \Rightarrow \quad x = 1.07 \text{ m} \quad \textbf{(2 marks)}$$

So, the detector must be mounted at a height of $x + 0.4 = 1.07 + 0.4 = \textbf{1.47}$ m above the ground. **(1 mark)**

ANSWERS AND SOLUTIONS
SHAPE AND SPACE — UNIT TEST 3

1. C	8. B	15. C	22. C	NR1. 55
2. B	9. B	16. A	23. A	NR2. 9.0
3. A	10. C	17. C	24. D	NR3. 3
4. D	11. A	18. C	25. B	
5. B	12. A	19. D	26. C	
6. B	13. D	20. A	27. C	
7. A	14. B	21. C	28. D	

1. C

SOH CAH TOA $\rightarrow \tan = \dfrac{\text{opposite}}{\text{adjacent}}$

2. B

$a^2 + b^2 = c^2$

$3^2 + 7^2 = c^2$

$c^2 = 9 + 49$

$c^2 = 58$

$c \approx 7.62 \, \text{cm}$

3. A

$180° - (90° + 34°) = 56°$

4. D

similar in size and shape

5. B

$\dfrac{5}{8} = \dfrac{l}{7} = \dfrac{n}{9}$

$l = 4.38$ cm, $n = 5.63$ cm

6. B

$\triangle ABE$ has the same angles as $\triangle ACD$ since they are similar triangles.

7. A

SOH CAH TOA $\rightarrow \tan = \dfrac{\text{opposite}}{\text{adjacent}}$

8. B

SOH CAH TOA $\rightarrow \sin = \dfrac{\text{opposite}}{\text{hypotenuse}}$

$\sin M = \dfrac{4}{7}$

$M = \sin^{-1}\left(\dfrac{4}{7}\right)$

$M \approx 35°$

9. B

SOH CAH TOA $\rightarrow \cos = \dfrac{\text{adjacent}}{\text{hypotenuse}}$

$\cos 17° = \dfrac{x}{11}$

$x = 11\cos 17°$

$x \approx 10.5$ cm

10. C

The result of using the 2nd function key prior to tan is the inverse of tangent.

$\boxed{2nd}\,\boxed{\tan}\,\boxed{4}\,\boxed{\div}\,\boxed{3}$

11. A

$$\text{SOH CAH TOA} \rightarrow \cos = \frac{\text{adjacent}}{\text{hypotenuse}}$$

$$\cos 84° = \frac{12}{y}$$

$$y = \frac{12}{\cos 84°}$$

$$y \approx 114.8 \text{ m}$$

12. A

$$SA = 2\left(\frac{1}{2} \times 7 \times 5\right) + (5 \times 8) + 2(\sqrt{74} + 8)$$

$$SA \approx 35 + 40 + 137.6$$

$$\approx 212.6 \text{ cm}^2$$

13. D

$$V = \frac{1}{2}(b \times h \times w)$$

$$V = \frac{1}{2}(5 \times 7 \times 8)$$

$$V = 140 \text{ cm}^3$$

14. B

$$V = \frac{1}{3}\left(\pi r^2\right)(h)$$

$$V = \frac{(2.75)^2 (\pi)(13)}{3}$$

$$V = 103 \text{ cm}^3$$

15. C

$$V = (\text{Area of Base})(\text{Height})$$

$$V = \left(\pi r^2\right)(h)$$

$$V = \pi \times (0.35)^2 \times (1.2)$$

$$V \approx 0.46 \text{ m}^3$$

16. A

$$SA = \pi r^2 + 2\pi rh$$

$$SA = (\pi)(0.35)^2 + 2\pi(0.35)(1.2)$$

$$SA \approx 3.02 \text{ m}^2$$

Note: Only the base is calculated in this surface area as there is no cover on the barrel.

17. C

$$SA = 150 \text{ cm}^2$$

$$SA = 6y^2$$

$$6y^2 = 150$$

$$y^2 = \frac{150}{6}$$

$$y^2 = 25$$

$$\sqrt{y^2} = \sqrt{25}$$

$$y = 5 \text{ cm}$$

18. C

$$V = \frac{1}{3}(\text{BaseArea})(\text{Height})$$

$$V = \frac{(7 \times 3)(12)}{3}$$

$$V = 84 \text{ cm}^3$$

19. D

$$V = l \times w \times h$$

$$V = 60 \times 30 \times 45$$

$$V = 81\,000 \text{ cm}^3 \text{ or } 81 \text{ L}$$

20. A

slide

21. C

$$[-7, 4]$$

22. C

$E'(-3, 1), F'(-1, 4), G'(-5, 4)$

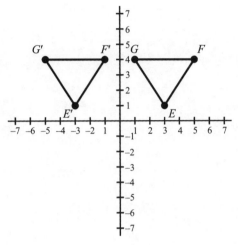

23. A

$\dfrac{3}{4}$ turn cw

24. D

Note the vertical mirror image.

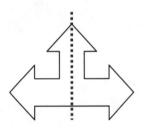

25. B

The origin is (0, 0) so that corner has to stay at the origin when rotating. 90° ccw rotation is a ¼ turn counterclockwise placing the object where the new image rests.

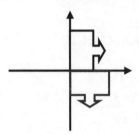

26. C

Dilatations – transformations where objects are either reduced or enlarged using a scale factor.

27. C

Each side of the second pentagon is 3 times larger than the first.

28. D

(–3, 0)
After plotting the 4 choices, it is noted that only (–3, 0) is situated within the trapezoid created by the four originally stated vertices.

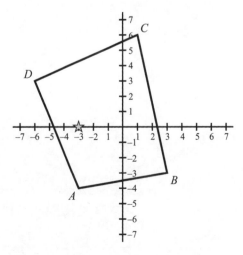

NR1. 55

$\angle Y = 180° - (90° + 35°)$

$\angle Y = 55°$

NR2. 9.0

$\angle Y = 55° \therefore \angle Y' = 55°$

$\angle Y' = 55° \therefore \angle Z' = 35°$

Using SOH CAH TOA

$\cos 35° = \dfrac{y'}{11}$

$y' = 11\cos 35°$

$y' \approx 9.0$ cm

NR3. 3

If $y = 3$ cm and $y' = 9$ cm, the scale factor is 3. You can further solve for x, z and z' to further confirm if this scale factor is accurate.

SOLUTIONS – STATISTICS AND PROBABILITY

1. B	9. A	16. A	NR3. 0.56	27. B
2. A	10. D	17. C	23. D	28. D
3. A	11. D	18. C	24. B	WR1. See Solution
4. B	12. C	19. D	NR4. 0.50	WR2. See Solution
5. D	13. D	20. B	NR5. 30	
6. C	14. A	NR2. 0.25	NR6. 1 296	
7. C	15. D	21. A	25. D	
8. C	NR1. 13.0	22. B	26. D	

1. B

Information about the origins of immigrants to Canada as of 1994–95 is given in the two pie charts.

The chart on the left gives information about persons who immigrated to Canada prior to 1985. (11+ years ago as of 1994-1995)

We can see from the chart that before 1985, the majority of immigrants (about 60%) came from Europe.

2. A

This question asks us to estimate the percentage of immigrants to Canada from Asia, prior to 1985. From the chart on the left, we can see that these people are represented by less than a quarter of the area of the circle (i.e., they represent less than 25% of the total).
Only choice **A**, 17%, is less than 25%.

3. A

By comparing the two pie charts given, we can see that immigration from Europe has decreased from about 60% (more than half the area of the circle) prior to 1985 to about 20% in more recent years. This is the largest decrease (about 40%) from any of the regions of the world.

4. B

We are given the number of dentists in Canada in the years 1980, 1985, and 1990. From this information, the question asks us to estimate the number of dentists in the year 1995.

The following table gives the change in the number of dentists in the two five year periods: 1980–85, and 1985–90.

Time Period	Change in the number of dentists
1980-85	1 750
1985-90	950

We can see that although the number of dentists is increasing, the rate of increase is decreasing. Assuming this trend continues, we can say that the number of dentists in 1995 should be more than in 1990, but by a smaller number than 950, which was the change in the period 1985–90.

Of the four choices, only choice **B**, with an increase of 525 dentists, is a reasonable choice if the past trend continued.

5. **D**

We are told that according to research, the resting heart rate of a fit individual tends to be lower than that of an unfit person. When the individuals are ranked by their resting heart rates from lowest to highest (most fit to least fit), the answer is **D**.

Vic	Gary	Liz	Reg	Renu
54	60	66	72	78

6. **C**

The best answer is **C**. A sample size of five is not enough to generalize across a population. Testing a larger sample would be in order.

The other choices may be valid objections but this would become apparent only through more testing, that is, a larger sample size.

7. **C**

Information about the percentage of fatal and injury collisions involving alcohol for five years (1991–95) is given in the chart. An analysis of the four choices follows.

A. Choice **A** states that the percentage of alcohol-related injury collisions is lower in recent years compared to previous years. Except for 1995, when there was a slight increase, this is true for the rest of the years.

B. The percentage decline in alcohol-related injury collisions in the year 1992–93 was 6.8%. This is larger than the decline in any of the other years—thus, statement **B** is supported by the information in the chart.

C. The chart does not provide evidence that the percentage of collisions involving alcohol will continue to drop, and it certainly does not justify a prediction that alcohol will be a contributing factor in less than 10% of all injury collisions in only five years. Thus, **C** is not supported by the given information.

D. The information in the chart supports the statement that the decrease in alcohol-related collisions is not steady, and from the evidence for 1994–95, it may in fact be levelling off.

8. **C**

Assuming that the types of jobs that high school students get are of comparable pay, then it follows that the more hours a student works, the more he/she would earn.

In scatter plot **A**, there is no obvious relationship between the number of hours worked and total earnings. It is not a plausible choice.

In scatter plot **B**, as the number of hours worked increases total earnings decrease—not a likely relationship.

In scatter plot **C**, there is a steady increase in earnings as the number of hours worked increases. Hence, **C** is the most likely scatter plot of Shirley's results.

In scatter plot **D**, total earnings seem to be independent of the number of hours worked—not plausible.

9. **A**

Of people aged 18–24, 82% use bank machines, which is the highest percentage of any age group, even higher than the 80% use of bank machines by the 25–34 age group. Also note that 42% of those aged 18–24 use the machines 3 or more times per week, again the highest percentage of any age group. Hence, from the information provided, the most reasonable conclusion is that the group of people aged 18–24 uses bank machines most often.

10. D

> Given that a greater percentage of people aged 18–24 use bank machines than those aged 25–34, it does not necessarily mean that a greater **number** of people aged 18–24 use bank machines than those aged 25–34.
>
> A greater percentage does not necessarily mean a greater number. Consider the following example. Let us say that within a given population, we are told that the number of people in the 18–24 age group is 50 000.
>
> Additionally, we are told that the number of people in the 25–34 age group is 100 000. It can be quite easily seen that although the percentage of people in the 18–24 age group may use bank machines more often, the total **number** of people who use bank machines is considerably larger in the 25-34 age group.
>
> Therefore, **D** cannot be inferred from the information provided in the table whereas statements **A**, **B**, and **C** can each be directly verified from the information in the table.

11. D

> The trend indicated in the scatter plot is that the number of athletes participating in the Olympics is increasing over time.
>
> This can reasonably be attributed to an increase in the number of athletes for each event, an increase in the number of participating nations, and an increase in the number of events.
>
> In 1992, the Olympic Winter Games and Summer Games were split up, but this change did not interfere with the trend that had been already established.

12. C

> The line of best fit for the given scatter plot best represents the data. A line of best fit is a line as close as possible to all the data points with about as many points above the line as below. Of the four lines given in the graph, line 3 is the line of best fit as it satisfies both criteria better than the other lines.
> Line 1 is below every data point and so would probably underestimate the data. Although about as many points appear to be above line 2 as below, the line is not as close as possible to all the points.
> Line 4 is above all the data points and so would probably overestimate the data.

13. D

> If we draw a line of best fit for the points in the given scatter plot, we can see that there is a positive correlation between attendance and grades, that is, the better the attendance the higher the grades.
>
> However, without more information, we cannot conclude whether higher grades are a result of better attendance or vice versa. Hence, the statement that best describes the relationship between attendance and a student's final marks is that there is a positive correlation between attendance and grades, but one does not imply the other.

14. A

> From the information in the question, we are told that each of 50 strings is attached to a button that determines whether a player wins a small, medium, or a large prize. Two strings are connected to a large prize, eight to a medium prize, and 40 to a small prize.
>
> As 10 of the 50 strings are attached to large or medium prizes, and each contestant pulls any one of the 50 strings, the probability of winning either a large or medium prize is
>
> $$\frac{\text{number of favorable outcomes}}{\text{total number of possible outcomes}} = \frac{10}{50} = \frac{1}{5}$$

15. D

A is incorrect. The graph represents money spent only on live sporting events so it would not be proper to conclude from the graph that, in general, males spend more than females.

B is incorrect. Again, the conclusion is too general. The data cover a much more specific area (that is, sporting events) that does not support a general conclusion. In addition, this survey does not distinguish between *single* and *married* males and females.

C is incorrect. The graph compares **percentage** of total income. The statement is comparing total money spent. Without information on the amounts spent or on incomes of males and females, we cannot determine whether males spend about 25% more on sporting events.

D is a correct statement about the data given in the graph. It refers to the **percentage** of income spent and refers specifically to the population studied.

NR1. **13.0**

A card is drawn from a deck of 52 cards, a dime is tossed, and a die is rolled. We are asked to find the combined probability of drawing a face card, flipping heads, and rolling a 3 or higher.

First, note that these are independent events as the outcome of any one of the events has no effect on the outcomes of any of the other events.

There are 12 face cards in a deck of cards. 4 jacks + 4 queens + 4 kings. Hence, the probability of drawing a face card (F) is

$$P(F) = \frac{12}{52} = \frac{3}{13}$$

The probability of flipping a head (H) is

$$P(H) = \frac{1}{2}$$

There are four chances of rolling a 3 or higher (R) on a six- sided die: 3, 4, 5, or 6. Thus $P(R) = \dfrac{4}{6} = \dfrac{2}{3}$

The probability of a set of independent events is the product of the probabilities of the individual events. Therefore, the combined probability of the three events is

$$P(F \text{ and } H \text{ and } R) = P(F) \times P(H) \times P(R)$$

$$= \frac{3}{13} \times \frac{1}{2} \times \frac{2}{3} = \frac{6}{78} = \frac{1}{13}$$

that is, 1 out of 13.

Therefore, the answer, correct to one decimal place, is 13.0

16. A

This question asks the probability that a second student chooses the same number if one student chooses a number from 1 to 40. Let Tom choose some number from 1 to 40. Since there are 40 numbers to select from, Joni's likelihood of choosing the same number as Tom is $\dfrac{1}{40}$.

Note: Read questions like this carefully and only use the relevant information to solve the problem.

17. C

A roulette wheel has 38 numbers — 2 green, 18 red, and 18 black. On any spin of the roulette wheel, the chance of obtaining any number is the same as the chance of obtaining any of the other numbers: they are all equally likely. Hence, the probability of getting a green number =

$$\frac{\text{the number of green numbers}}{\text{total numbers}}$$

$$= \frac{2}{2 + 18 + 18} = \frac{2}{38} = \frac{1}{19}$$

18. C

When two dice are rolled, any of the numbers: 1, 2, 3, 4, 5, or 6 can come up on each die. Hence, the possible outcomes in the sample space are $6 \times 6 = 36$.

The sample space, where the first number is the number on the first die and the second number is the number on the second die, is as follows.

(1, 1)	(1, 2)	(1, 3)	(1, 4)	(1, 5)	(1, 6)
(2, 1)	(2, 2)	(2, 3)	(2, 4)	(2, 5)	(2, 6)
(3, 1)	(3, 2)	(3, 3)	(3, 4)	(3, 5)	(3, 6)
(4, 1)	(4, 2)	(4, 3)	(4, 4)	(4, 5)	**(4, 6)**
(5, 1)	(5, 2)	(5, 3)	(5, 4)	**(5, 5)**	(5, 6)
(6, 1)	(6, 2)	(6, 3)	**(6, 4)**	(6, 4)	(6, 6)

To roll a 10 is to obtain a total of 10 on the two dice. Of the 36 possible outcomes; there are three favourable outcomes. (4, 6), (5, 5), and (6, 4)

Hence, the probability of obtaining a total of 10 on the two dice

$$= \frac{\text{the number of favourable outcomes}}{\text{total number of outcomes}} = \frac{3}{36} = \frac{1}{12}$$

If we roll the two dice a second time, the probability of obtaining another 10 is also equal to $\frac{1}{12}$.

The outcome of the first roll of the dice has no effect on the outcome of the second roll of the dice (i.e., they are independent).

Therefore, the probability of rolling a 10 followed by another 10 = (probability of obtaining a 10 on the first roll) × (probability of obtaining a 10 on the second roll)

$$= \frac{1}{12} \times \frac{1}{12} = \frac{1}{144}$$

19. D

The probability of a set of independent events is the product of the probabilities of the individual events. If we denote the events as E and F, then $P(E \text{ and } F) = P(E) \times P(F)$.

Let E be the first event of rolling a 5 on a die. As there are 6 possible outcomes, the probability of obtaining a 5 is

$$P(E) = \frac{1}{6}$$

We are given that the probability of the two independent events occurring is $\frac{1}{12}$

(i.e., $P(E \text{ and } F) = \frac{1}{12}$). If the second event is F, then by substitution

$P(E) = \frac{1}{6}$ and $P(E \text{ and } F) = \frac{1}{12}$, we get

$$\frac{1}{12} = \frac{1}{6} \times P(F)$$

Therefore, $P(F) = \dfrac{\frac{1}{12}}{\frac{1}{6}} = \frac{6}{12} = \frac{1}{2}$

This question asks us to find the event among the four choices that has the probability $P(F) = \frac{1}{2}$.

The probabilities for the four choices are

A. Selecting the ace of hearts $= \frac{1}{52}$
(only one ace of hearts)

B. Selecting a red ace $= \frac{2}{52}$ (two red aces)

C. Selecting a heart $= \frac{13}{52} = \frac{1}{4}$ (13 hearts)

D. selecting a red card $= \frac{26}{52} = \frac{1}{2}$
(26 red cards)

20. B

A die is rolled three times. The four choices given explain four possible events. To find the most likely event (i.e., the event with the highest probability), we have to calculate the probability of each of the four events.

A. All three rolls are the same numbers
The first roll (F) could be any number:

$$P(F) = \frac{6}{6} = 1$$

The second roll (S) must be the same number as the first: $P(S) = \frac{1}{6}$

The third roll (T) must be the same number as the first: $P(T) = \frac{1}{6}$

As the three events are independent, the $P(F \text{ and } S \text{ and } T) = P(F) \times P(S) \times P(T)$

$$= \frac{6}{6} \times \frac{1}{6} \times \frac{1}{6} = \frac{1}{36}$$

B. All three numbers are different
The first roll (F) could be any number:

$$P(F) = \frac{6}{6} = 1$$

The second roll (S) must be different from the first: $P(S) = \frac{5}{6}$, as there are 5 numbers different from the first. The third roll (T) must be different from the first and the second: $P(T) = \frac{4}{6}$, as there are 4 numbers different from the first and second rolls.

Hence, $P(F \text{ and } S \text{ and } T) = \frac{6}{6} \times \frac{5}{6} \times \frac{4}{6} = \frac{5}{9}$

C. All three numbers are odd: 1, 3, 5
The first roll (F) must be odd: $P(F) = \frac{3}{6} = \frac{1}{2}$

The second roll (S) must be odd:

$$P(S) = \frac{3}{6} = \frac{1}{2}$$

The third roll (T) must be odd:

$$P(T) = \frac{3}{6} = \frac{1}{2}$$

$P(F \text{ and } S \text{ and } T) = \frac{1}{2} \times \frac{1}{2} \times \frac{1}{2} = \frac{1}{8}$

D. The numbers 1, 2, and 3 are each rolled once:

F could be any of 1, 2, or 3: $P(F) = \frac{3}{6} = \frac{1}{2}$

S could be any of the remaining two:

$$P(S) = \frac{2}{6} = \frac{1}{3}$$

T must be the remaining number: $P(T) = \frac{1}{6}$

$P(F \text{ and } S \text{ and } T) = \frac{1}{2} \times \frac{1}{3} \times \frac{1}{6} = \frac{1}{36}.$

NR2. **0.25**

If all teams are equally rated (have the same chance of winning), then the probability that one of the top seeds wins the World Cup is

$$\frac{\text{number of top seeded teams}}{\text{total number of teams in the World Cup}}$$

$$P = \frac{8}{32} = \frac{1}{4}$$

Correct to two decimal places, the probability that a top seeded team wins is 0.25.

21. A

If 3 nickels are tossed, the sample space consists of 8 outcomes.

(H, H, H) (H, H, T) (H, T, H) (H, T, T)
(T, H, H) (T, T, H) (T, H, T) (T, T, T).

If **2** quarters are flipped, the sample space consists of four outcomes.

(H, H) (H, T)
(T, H) (T, T)

To find the event with the lowest probability among the four choices, calculate their probabilities.

A. Heads on all three nickels

$$P(H, H, H) = = \frac{1 \text{ favorable outcome}}{8 \text{ possible outcomes}} = \frac{1}{8}.$$

B. Tails on both quarters

$$P(T, T) = \frac{1 \text{ favourable outcome}}{4 \text{ possible outcomes}} = \frac{1}{4}$$

C. Two heads and one tail on 3 tosses

$$P(H, H, T) = \frac{3 \text{ favourable outcomes}}{8 \text{ possible outcomes}} = \frac{3}{8}$$

D. One head and one tail on 2 tosses

$P(H \text{ and } T)$

$$= \frac{2 \text{ favourable outcomes}}{4 \text{ possible outcomes}} = \frac{2}{4} = \frac{1}{2}$$

22. B

We are told that 6 of 8 possible results allow Jake to continue his turn, and that each roll is equally likely to occur. Therefore, the probability that Jake does not roll a 1 or an 8 on any roll is

$$\frac{6}{8} = 0.75.$$

The probability of a set of independent events is the product of the probabilities of the individual events. So, the probability that Jake does not roll a 1 or an 8 on two rolls is

$$0.75 \times 0.75 = 0.75^2,$$

and three rolls in a row would be

$$0.75 \times 0.75 \times 0.75 = 0.75^3.$$

Therefore, the probability of 30 successful rolls in a row is

$$0.75^{30} = 0.000\ 18$$

NR3. 0.56

We are asked to determine the probability that Karl Malone makes two consecutive free throws (FT) given that his FT percentage for the season is 75%. If each attempt is an independent event (as stated in the question), the probability of a set of independent events is the product of the probabilities of the individual events.

Let A represent the first free throw attempt and B represent the second free throw attempt.

The probability of A and B is:

$P(A \text{ and } B) = P(A) \times P(B)$
$\qquad = (0.75)(0.75)$
$\qquad = 0.562\ 5$

Therefore, correct to two decimal places, the probability that Karl Malone makes both attempts is 0.56.

23. D

Plot the points on a graph. There appears to be a non-linear relationship. **D** is the best answer. (Remember not all points have to lie on the line/curve of best fit).

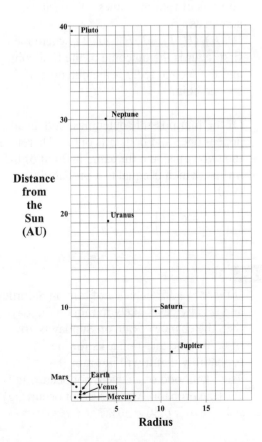

24. B

Sketch a graph. In general, as radius increases, gravity tends to increase, but the correlation is not strong, that is, there are some exceptions. The best answer is **B**.

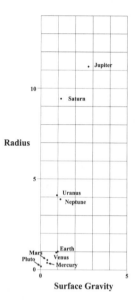

Surface Gravity

NR4. **0.50**

If two coins are flipped, the sample space consists of four outcomes. This can be shown as

$(H, H), (H, T), (T, H), (T, T)$, where the first letter is the outcome of the first coin, and the second letter is the outcome of the second coin.

Of the four possible outcomes, both heads appear once and both tails once. Therefore, the two coins land the same in 2 out of the 4 flips, which is equal to a probability of 0.50

$$\left(\frac{2}{4} = \frac{1}{2} = 0.50\right).$$

NR5. **30**

If there is a 35% chance of rain on Saturday and it is twice as likely to rain on Sunday, then the chance of rain on Sunday is 70% or 0.70. The question asks for the probability that it will **not** rain.
The likelihood of an event not occurring is
1 – (the probability of the event occurring)
= 1 – 0.70 = 0.30 = 30%

NR6. **1 296**

A table can be used to show the outcomes.

	RED	BLUE	GREEN	PURPLE
NUMBER 1	1	1	1	1
2	2	2	2	2
3	3	3	3	3
4	4	4	4	4
5	5	5	5	5
6	6	6	6	6
TOTAL	6	6	6	6

Since each die has 6 possible outcomes and there are 4 dice being rolled, the number of different outcomes are

$$6^4 = 6 \times 6 \times 6 \times 6$$

$$= 1\,296$$

25. D

When opinions are solicited, the way questions are communicated as well as the ease with which people can respond often influence the outcomes of polls. In this case, the sample space consists only of newspaper readers who, depending on the readership of the newspaper, **could** represent a large sample space. Aside from any problems associated with handling this information, a large sample space would still provide valid results. Similarly, when no limitations are placed on who from the general population can call in, the results will still be valid. The fact that people must pay to phone in would detract from the ease with which someone could respond.
This may restrict individuals who are not financially capable of responding.
Therefore, **D** is the best choice.

26. D

For each goal that Mario Lemieux scored, he took a certain number of shots that were not goals.

$171 - 35 = 136$ represents the number of shots he took in which he did not score.

We know from the information given in the question that in addition to the 136 missed shots, he scored 35 goals.

Therefore, the odds ratio is 35:136

27. B

In order to collect accurate data, we must focus on whether our sample is representative of the entire population.

Focusing on the spectators at a basketball game or the workers in a building limits our sample to people in certain positions or with certain interests, which could bias our sample. In addition, we must ensure that the participants in our survey match the question we are asking. Our survey asks for the "type of drink adults prefer," and therefore polling high school students is not appropriate.

Therefore, **B** is the best way to obtain a representative sample.

28. D

A survey may produce biased results when, through the design of the survey, certain responses become more likely or unlikely to occur. For example, the wording of the survey may make certain responses more likely or unlikely, or the sample space of the population chosen for the survey may be selected in a non-random manner.

Alternative **C** may be eliminated because the fact that people may have differing opinions would not determine whether the survey is biased or not.

Similarly, alternative **B** may be eliminated since the statement is false — there is no evidence presented to suggest that everyone would respond to the survey.

Alternative **A**, that all readers would say they are in favour speaks only of a possible result of a survey but does not give us the source of bias, if any, of the survey. In addition, there is nothing to suggest that males are the only readers, or that all males would have the same opinions.

Alternative **D** is a potential source of bias. The survey is to find out the opinions of the general population. The readers of the magazine are probably not representative of the general population because they are probably sports fans and would probably be **more likely** to give favourable opinions than the general population.

Written Response

1. a) The sample size for the civic poll is smaller, which could result in a higher variance from the true averages. This would suggest that the numbers from the Statistics Canada surveys are more reliable estimates of the true averages.

(1 mark)

The results of the poll for the small town will depend on the regional prosperity of Saskatchewan in the given years. The averages for the province might normally be higher or lower than the national average and may fluctuate significantly from year to year.

(1 mark)

b) Since Saskatchewan's economy is largely based on agriculture, seasons with good weather resulting in bumper crops could significantly increase average incomes in a given year. Conversely, poor harvests could result in an annual income below the long-term average.

(While agriculture is still a significant portion of the nation's economy, weather will likely have far less of an impact on the income averages of all Canadians because throughout the country there are a number of other industries that keep people employed.)

(1 mark)

2. a) Different sports have different scoring systems and different means of statistically evaluating the success of players. However, when you analyze the success of a player relative to other players in his sport, you can make comparisons between sports because your information does not indicate how successful a player is, but how much better or worse he is, relative to his colleagues and competitors. For any sport a similar histogram can be created to show the distribution of the top scorers. It would then be possible to determine if there are any players in other sports that are scoring leaders by as wide a margin as that of Wayne Gretzky's.

b) Complete the following line graph by plotting and connecting points for each 200-point interval, with each point representing the total number of players to have achieved that plateau.

(3 marks)

[Three marks given for a complete and correct graph. Two marks for correct points without line connections. One mark for a connected graph but with some incorrect values.]

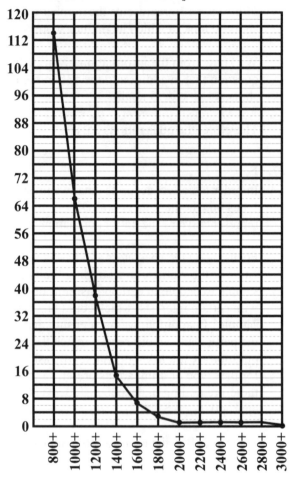

ANSWERS AND SOLUTIONS – UNIT TEST 4
STATISTICS AND PROBABILITY

1. B	5. D	9. A	13. C	NR1. 16.7
2. D	6. A	10. B	14. A	NR2. $\dfrac{1}{156}$
3. B	7. B	11. C	15. B	
4. D	8. C	12. B	16. A	NR3. 0.6

1. B

A line of best fit will run as close as possible to the majority of dots, **B** is the farthest from the line that would fit.

2. D

$$\frac{\text{number of favourable outcomes}}{\text{number of possible outcomes}} =$$

$$\frac{3}{3+6+4+2} = \frac{3}{15} = \frac{1}{5}$$

3. B

$$\frac{\text{number of favourable outcomes}}{\text{number of possible outcomes}} = \frac{1}{6}$$

4. D

These are independent events so the probabilities of each event are multiplied together.

$$\frac{1}{6} \times \frac{4}{52} = \frac{4}{312} = \frac{1}{78}$$

5. D

These are independent events so the probabilities of each event are multiplied together.

$$\frac{1}{6} \times \frac{4}{52} = \frac{4}{312}$$
$$= 0.012\,82 \times 100$$
$$= 1.282\%$$
$$\approx 1\%$$

6. A

$$\frac{\text{number of favourable outcomes}}{\text{number of possible outcomes}}$$

$$\frac{4}{52} = 0.076\,92 \times 100$$
$$= 7.692\%$$
$$\approx 7.7\%$$

7. B

The values in a graph increase going up the vertical axis and left on the horizontal axis. So if the oil price and the royalty are steadily increasing together, then the graph will rise to the right in a straight line.

8. C

$$\frac{\text{number of favourable outcomes}}{\text{number of possible outcomes}}$$

$$\frac{6}{4+8+6+2} = \frac{6}{20} = 0.3 \times 100 = 30\%$$

9. A

This can be verified by looking at the chart and the graph. **B** and **D** are wrong because they show the numbers getting smaller instead of getting larger. **C** is wrong because it uses data different than what is on the chart.

10. B

If we look at the table, only **B** is actually false, remember, roughly doubled does not mean exactly doubled.

11. C

A is incorrect, since Internet use appears to be increasing, not decreasing.

B is incorrect because nowhere in the table is the time of day and use of Internet mentioned.

There is no information in the data on the table to suggest the type of computers being used, so D is incorrect.

12. B

Each of the others can influence the outcome of the survey – volleyball players are more likely to vote for an increase in sports equipment, the wording "yet more" vs. "much needed" is used to influence where people may think the need for the money is, the survey is after the girls volleyball practice so there will be more girls than boys in the survey.

13. C

Ford, Toyota and Nissan will all present information that will try to influence you to buy one of their vehicles. Car and Driver is not a car manufacturer and so you are more likely to be able to get unbiased information.

14. A

As the number of years of education increases, the average annual income should increase. B shows decreasing education and average annual income, C shows no growth in education or income and D shows no real pattern at all.

15. B

These are independent events so the probabilities of each event are multiplied together. $\frac{1}{6} \times \frac{1}{6} = \frac{1}{36}$

16. A

Although some of the others may appear to fit, A is the best answer – remember always to give the best answer in a multiple choice.

NR1. 16.7

$$\frac{1}{6} = 0.16\overline{6} \times 100$$
$$= 16.66\overline{6}\% = 16.7\%$$

NR2. $\frac{1}{156}$

$$\frac{1}{6} \times \frac{2}{52} = \frac{2}{312} = \frac{1}{156}$$

NR3. 0.6

$$\frac{1}{6} \times \frac{2}{52} = \frac{2}{312} = 0.00641 \times 100 = 0.64\% = 0.6\%$$

KEY STRATEGIES

FOR

SUCCESS ON EXAMS

NOTES

KEY STRATEGIES FOR SUCCESS ON EXAMS

There are many different ways to assess your knowledge and understanding of course concepts. Depending on the subject, your knowledge and skills are most often assessed through a combination of methods which may include performances, demonstrations, projects, products, and oral and written tests. Written exams are one of the most common methods currently used in schools. Just as there are some study strategies that help you to improve your academic performance, there are also some test writing strategies that may help you to do better on unit test and year-end exams. To do your best on any test, you need to be well prepared. You must know the course content and be as familiar as possible with the manner in which it is usually tested. Applying test writing strategies may help you to become more successful on exams, improve your grades, and achieve your potential.

📖 STUDY OPTIONS FOR EXAM PREPARATION

Studying and preparing for exams requires a strong sense of self-discipline. Sometimes having a study buddy or joining a study group

- helps you to stick to your study schedule
- ensures you have others with whom you can practice making and answering sample questions
- clarifies information and provides peer support

It may be helpful to use a combination of individual study, working with a study buddy, or joining a study group to prepare for your unit test or year-end exam. Be sure that the study buddy or group you choose to work with is positive, knowledgeable, motivated, and supportive. Working with a study buddy or a study group usually means you have to begin your exam preparation earlier than you would if you are studying independently.

Tutorial classes are often helpful in preparing for exams. You can ask a knowledgeable student to tutor you or you can hire a private tutor. Sometimes school jurisdictions or individual schools may offer tutorials and study sessions to assist students in preparing for exams. Tutorial services are also offered by companies that specialize in preparing students for exams. Information regarding tutorial services is usually available from school counsellors, local telephone directories, and on-line search engines.

📖 EXAM QUESTION FORMATS

There is no substitute for knowing the course content. To do well in your course you need to combine your subject knowledge and understanding with effective test writing skills. Being familiar with question formats may help you in preparing for quizzes, unit tests, or year-end exams. The most typical question formats include multiple choice, numerical response, written response, and essay. The following provides a brief description of each format and suggestions for how you might consider responding to each of the formats.

MULTIPLE CHOICE

A multiple choice question provides some information for you to consider and then requires you to select a response from four choices, often referred to as distractors. The distractors may complete a statement, be a logical extension, or application of the information. When preparing for multiple choice questions, you may wish to focus on:

- studying concepts, theories, groups of facts or ideas that are similar in meaning; compare and contrast their similarities and differences; ask yourself "How do the concepts differ?", "Why is the difference important?", "What does each fact or concept mean or include?", and "What are the exceptions?"

- identifying main ideas, key information, formulas, concepts, and theories, where they apply and what the exceptions are

- memorizing important definitions, examples, and applications of key concepts

- learning to recognize **distractors** that may lead you to apply plausible but incorrect solutions, and **three and one splits** where one answer is obviously incorrect and the others are very similar in meaning or wording

- using active reading techniques such as underlining, highlighting, numbering, and circling important facts, dates, basic points

- making up your own multiple choice questions for practice

NUMERICAL RESPONSE

A numerical response question provides information and requires you to use a calculation to arrive at the response. When preparing for numerical response questions, you may wish to focus on:

- memorizing formulas and their applications
- completing chapter questions or making up your own for practice
- making a habit of **estimating the answer** prior to completing the calculation
- paying special **attention to accuracy** in computing and the use of significant digits where applicable

WRITTEN RESPONSE

A written response question requires you to respond to a question or directive such as "explain," "compare," "contrast". When preparing for written response questions, you may wish to focus on:

- ensuring your response answers the question
- recognizing directing words such as "list," "explain," and "define"
- providing concise answers within the time limit you are devoting to the written response section of the exam
- identifying subject content that lends itself to short answer questions

ESSAY

An essay is a lengthier written response requiring you to identify your position on an issue and provide logical thinking or evidence that supports the basis of your argument. When preparing for an essay, you may wish to focus on:

- examining issues that are relevant or related to the subject area or application of the concept
- comparing and contrasting two points of view, articles, or theories
- considering the merits of the opposite point of view
- identifying key concepts, principles, or ideas
- providing evidence, examples, and supporting information for your viewpoint
- preparing two or three essays on probable topics
- writing an outline and essay within the defined period of time you will have for the exam
- understanding the "marker's expectations"

📖 *KEY* TIPS FOR ANSWERING COMMON EXAM QUESTION FORMATS

Most exams use a variety of question formats to test your understanding. You must provide responses to questions ranging from lower level, information recall types to higher level, critical thinking types. The following information provides you with some suggestions on how to prepare for answering multiple choice, written response, and essay questions.

MULTIPLE CHOICE

Multiple choice questions often require you to make fine distinctions between correct and nearly correct answers so it is imperative that you:

- begin by answering only the questions for which you are certain of the correct answer

- read the question stem and formulate your own response before you read the choices available

- read the directions carefully paying close attention to words such as "mark *all* correct", "choose the *most* correct," and "choose the *one best* answer"

- use active reading techniques such as underlining, circling, or highlighting critical words and phrases

- watch for superlatives such as "all," "every," "none," "always" which indicate that the correct response must be an undisputed fact

- watch for negatives such as "none," "never," "neither," "not" which indicate that the correct response must be an undisputed fact

- examine all of the alternatives in questions which include "all of the above" or "none of the above" as responses to ensure that "all" or "none" of the statements apply *totally*

- be aware of distractors that may lead you to apply plausible but incorrect solutions, and 'three and one splits' where one answer is obviously incorrect and the others are very similar in meaning or wording

- use information from other questions to help you

- eliminate the responses you know are wrong and then assess the remaining alternatives and choose the best one

- guess if you are not certain

WRITTEN RESPONSE

Written response questions usually require a very specific answer. When answering these questions, you should:

- underline key words or phrases that indicate what is required in your answer such as "three reasons," "list," or "give an example"

- write down rough, point-form notes regarding the information you want to include in your answer

- be brief and only answer what is asked

- reread your response to ensure you have answered the question

- use the appropriate subject vocabulary and terminology in your response

- use point form to complete as many questions as possible if you are running out of time

ESSAY

Essay questions often give you the opportunity to demonstrate the breadth and depth of your learning regarding a given topic. When responding to these questions, it may be helpful to:

- read the question carefully and underline key words and phrases

- make a brief outline to organize the flow of the information and ideas you want to include in your response

- ensure you have an introduction, body, and conclusion

- begin with a clear statement of your view, position, or interpretation of the question

- address only one main point or key idea in each paragraph and include relevant supporting information and examples

- assume the reader has no prior knowledge of your topic

- conclude with a strong summary statement

- use appropriate subject vocabulary and terminology when and where it is applicable

- review your essay for clarity of thought, logic, grammar, punctuation, and spelling

- write as legibly as you can

- double space your work in case you need to edit it when you proofread your essay

- complete the essay in point form if you run short of time

📖 *KEY* TIPS FOR RESPONDING TO COMMON 'DIRECTING' WORDS

There are some commonly used words in exam questions that require you to respond in a predetermined or expected manner. The following provides you with a brief summary of how you may wish to plan your response to exam questions that contain these words.

- ◆ **EVALUATE** (to assess the worth of something)
  - ▸ Determine the use, goal, or ideal from which you can judge the worth of something
  - ▸ Make a value judgment or judgments on something
  - ▸ Make a list of reasons for the judgment
  - ▸ Develop examples, evidence, contrasts, and details to support your judgments and clarify your reasoning

- ◆ **DISCUSS** (usually to give pros and cons regarding an assertion, quotation, or policy)
  - ▸ Make a list of bases for comparing and contrasting
  - ▸ Develop details and examples to support or clarify each pro and con
  - ▸ On the basis of your lists, conclude your response by stating the extent to which you agree or disagree with what is asserted

- ◆ **COMPARE AND CONTRAST** (to give similarities and differences of two or more objects, beliefs, or positions)
  - ▸ Make a list of bases for comparing and contrasting
  - ▸ For each basis, judge similarities and differences
  - ▸ Supply details, evidence, and examples that support and clarify your judgment
  - ▸ Assess the overall similarity or difference
  - ▸ Determine the significance of similarity or difference in connection with the purpose of the comparison

- ◆ **ANALYZE** (to break into parts)
  - ▸ Break the topic, process, procedure, or object of the essay into its major parts
  - ▸ Connect and write about the parts according to the direction of the question: describe, explain, or criticize

- ◆ **CRITICIZE** (to judge strong and weak points of something)
  - ▸ Make a list of the strong points and weak points
  - ▸ Develop details, examples, and contrasts to support judgments
  - ▸ Make an overall judgment of quality

♦ **EXPLAIN** (to show causes of or reasons for something)
  ▸ In Science, usually show the process that occurs in moving from one state or phase in a process to the next, thoroughly presenting details of each step
  ▸ In Humanities and often in Social Sciences, make a list of factors that influence something, developing evidence for each factor's potential influence

♦ **DESCRIBE** (to give major features of something)
  ▸ Pick out highlights or major aspects of something
  ▸ Develop details and illustrations to give a clear picture

♦ **ARGUE** (to give reasons for one position and against another)
  ▸ Make a list of reasons for the position
  ▸ Make a list of reasons against the position
  ▸ Refute objections to your reasons for and defend against objections to your reasons opposing the position
  ▸ Fill out reasons, objections, and replies with details, examples, consequences, and logical connections

♦ **COMMENT** (to make statements about something)
  ▸ Calls for a position, discussion, explanation, judgment, or evaluation regarding a subject, idea, or situation
  ▸ Is strengthened by providing supporting evidence, information, and examples

♦ **DEMONSTRATE** (to show something)
  ▸ Depending upon the nature of the subject matter, provide evidence, clarify the logical basis of something, appeal to principles or laws as in an explanation, or supply a range of opinion and examples

♦ **SYNTHESIZE** (to invent a new or different version)
  ▸ Construct your own meaning based upon your knowledge and experiences
  ▸ Support your assertion with examples, references to literature and research studies

(Source: http://www.counc.ivic.ca/learn/program/hndouts/simple.html)

📖 TEST ANXIETY

Do you get test anxiety? Most students feel some level of stress, worry, or anxiety before an exam. Feeling a little tension or anxiety before or during an exam is normal for most students. A little stress or tension may help you rise to the challenge but too much stress or anxiety interferes with your ability to do well on the exam. Test anxiety may cause you to experience some of the following in a mild or more severe form:

- "butterflies" in your stomach, sweating, shortness of breath, or a quickened pulse
- disturbed sleep or eating patterns
- increased nervousness, fear, or irritability
- sense of hopelessness or panic
- drawing a "blank" during the exam

If you experience extreme forms of test anxiety, you need to consult your family physician.

For milder forms of anxiety, you may find some of the following strategies effective in helping you to remain calm and focused during your unit tests or year-end exams.

- Acknowledge that you are feeling some stress or test anxiety and that this is normal
- Focus upon your breathing, taking several deep breaths
- Concentrate upon a single object for a few moments
- Tense and relax the muscles in areas of your body where you feel tension
- Break your exam into smaller, manageable, and achievable parts
- Use positive self-talk to calm and motivate yourself. Tell yourself, "I can do this if I read carefully/start with the easy questions/focus on what I know/stick with it/. . ." instead of saying, "I cannot do this."
- Visualize your successful completion of your review or the exam
- Recall a time in the past when you felt calm, relaxed, and content. Replay this experience in your mind, experiencing it as fully as possible.

📖 KEY STRATEGIES FOR SUCCESS BEFORE AN EXAM – A CHECKLIST

Review, review, review. It is a huge part of your exam preparation. Here is a quick review checklist for you to see how many strategies for success you are using as you prepare to write your unit tests and year-end exams.

KEY Strategies for Success Before an Exam	Yes	No
Have you been attending classes?		
Have you determined your learning style?		
Have you organized a quiet study area for yourself?		
Have you developed a long-term study schedule?		
Have you developed a short-term study schedule?		
Are you working with a study buddy or study group?		
Is your study buddy/group positive, knowledgeable, motivated, and supportive?		
Have you registered in tutorial classes?		
Have you developed your exam study notes?		
Have you reviewed previously administered exams?		
Have you practiced answering multiple choice, numerical response, written response, and essay questions?		
Have you analyzed the most common errors students make on each subject exam?		
Have you practiced strategies for controlling your exam anxiety?		
Have you maintained a healthy diet and sleep routine?		
Have you participated in regular physical activity?		

📖 *KEY* STRATEGIES FOR SUCCESS DURING AN EXAM

Doing well on any exam requires that you prepare in advance by reviewing your subject material and then using your knowledge to respond effectively to the exam questions during the test session.
Combining subject knowledge with effective test writing skills gives you the best opportunity for success.
The following are some strategies you may find useful in writing your exam.

- Managing Test Anxiety
  - Be as prepared as possible to increase your self-confidence.
  - Arrive at the exam on time and bring whatever materials you need to complete the exam such as pens, pencils, erasers, and calculators if they are allowed.
  - Drink enough water before you begin the exam so you are hydrated.
  - Associate with positive, calm individuals until you enter the exam room.
  - Use positive self-talk to calm yourself.
  - Remind yourself that it is normal to feel anxious about the exam.
  - Visualize your successful completion of the exam.
  - Breathe deeply several times.
  - Rotate your head, shrug your shoulders, and change positions to relax.

- While the information from your crib notes is still fresh in your memory, write down the key words, concepts, definitions, theories, or formulas on the back of the test paper before you look at the exam questions.
  - Review the entire exam.
  - Budget your time.
  - Begin with the easiest question or the question that you know you can answer correctly rather than following the numerical question order of the exam.
  - Be aware of linked questions and use the clues to help you with other questions or in other parts of the exam.

If you "blank" on the exam, try repeating the deep breathing and physical relaxation activities first.
Then, move to visualization and positive self-talk to get you going. You can also try to open the "information flow" by writing down anything that you remember about the subject on the reverse side of your exam paper. This activity sometimes helps to remind you that you *do* know something and that you are capable of writing the exam.

📖 GETTING STARTED

MANAGING YOUR TIME

- Plan on staying in the exam room for the full time that is available to you.

- Review the entire exam and calculate how much time you can spend on each section. Write your time schedule on the top of your paper and stick as closely as possible to the time you have allotted for each section of the exam.

- Be strategic and use your time where you will get the most marks. Avoid spending too much time on challenging questions that are not worth more marks than other questions that may be easier.

- If you are running short of time, switch to point form and write as much as you can for written response and essay questions so you have a chance of receiving partial marks.

- Leave time to review your paper asking yourself, "Did I do all of the questions I was supposed to do?", "Can I answer any questions now that I skipped over before?", and "Are there any questions that I misinterpreted or misread?"

USING THE FIVE PASS METHOD

- **BROWSING STAGE** – Scan the entire exam noting the format, the specific instructions, marks allotted for each section, which questions you will complete, and which ones you will omit if there is a choice.

- **THE FIRST ANSWERING PASS** – To gain confidence and momentum, answer only the questions you are confident you can answer correctly and quickly. These questions are most often found in the multiple choice or numerical response sections of the exam. Maintain a brisk pace; if a question is taking too long to answer, leave it for the Second or Third Pass.

- **THE SECOND ANSWERING PASS** – This Pass addresses questions which require more effort per mark. Answer as many of the remaining questions as possible while maintaining steady progress toward a solution. As soon as it becomes evident the question is too difficult or is taking an inordinate amount of time, leave it for the Third Answering Pass.

- **THE THIRD ANSWERING PASS** – During the Third Answering Pass, you should complete all partial solutions from the first two Passes. Marks are produced at a slower rate during this stage. At the end of this stage, all questions should have full or partial answers. Guess at any multiple choice questions that you have not yet answered.

- **THE FINAL REVIEW STAGE** – Use the remaining time to review the entire exam, making sure that no questions have been overlooked. Check answers and calculations as time permits.

USING THE THREE PASS METHOD

- **OVERVIEW** – Begin with an overview of the exam to see what it contains. Look for "easy" questions and questions on topics that you know thoroughly.

- **SECOND PASS** – Answer all the questions that you can complete without too much trouble. These questions help to build your confidence and establish a positive start.

- **LAST PASS** – Now go through and answer the questions that are left. This is when you begin to try solving the questions you find particularly challenging.

📖 *KEY* EXAM TIPS FOR SELECTED SUBJECT AREAS

The following are a few additional suggestions you may wish to consider when writing exams in any of the selected subject areas.

ENGLISH LANGUAGE ARTS

Exams in English Language Arts usually have two components, writing and reading. Sometimes students are allowed to bring approved reference books such as a dictionary, thesaurus, and writing handbook into the exam. If you have not used these references on a regular basis, you may find them more of a hindrance than a help in an exam situation. When completing the written section of an English Language Arts exam:

- plan your essay

- focus on the issue presented

- establish a clear position using a thesis statement to direct and unify your writing

- organize your writing in a manner that logically presents your views

- support your viewpoint with specific examples

- edit and proofread your writing

In completing the reading section of an English Language Arts exam:

- read the entire selection before responding

- use titles, dates, footnotes, pictures, introductions, and notes on the author to assist you in developing an understanding of the piece presented

- when using line references, read a few lines before and after the identified section

MATHEMATICS

In some instances, the use of calculators is permitted (or required) to complete complex calculations, modeling, simulations, or to demonstrate your use of technology. It is imperative that you are familiar with the approved calculator and the modes you may be using during your exam. When writing exams in mathematics:

- use appropriate mathematical notation and symbols
- clearly show or explain all the steps involved in solving the problem
- check to be sure you have included the correct units of measurement and have rounded to the appropriate significant digit
- use appropriate labelling and equal increments on graphs

SCIENCES

In the sciences, written response and open-ended questions usually require a clear, organized, and detailed explanation of the science involved in the question. You may find it helpful to use the acronym **STEEPLES** to organize your response to these types of questions. STEEPLES stands for **S**cience, **T**echnological, **E**cological, **E**thical, **P**olitical, **L**egal, **E**conomical, and **S**ocial aspects of the issue presented. When writing exams in the sciences:

- use scientific vocabulary to clearly explain your understanding of the processes or issues
- state your position in an objective manner
- demonstrate your understanding of both sides of the issue
- clearly label graphs, diagrams, tables, and charts using accepted conventions
- provide all formulas and equations

SOCIAL STUDIES, HISTORY, GEOGRAPHY

Exams in these courses of study often require you to take a position on an issue and defend your point of view. Your response should demonstrate your understanding of both the positive and negative aspects of the issue and be supported by well-considered arguments and evidence. When writing exams in Social Studies, History or Geography, the following acronyms may be helpful to you in organizing your approach.

- **SEE** – stands for **S**tatement, **E**xplanation, **E**xample. This acronym reminds you to couple your statement regarding your position with an explanation and then an example.

- **PERMS** – stands for **P**olitical, **E**conomic, **R**eligious or moral, **M**ilitary, and **S**ocietal values. Your position statement may be derived from or based upon any of these points of view. Your argument is more credible if you can show that recognized authorities such as leaders, theorists, writers or scientists back your position.

📖 SUMMARY

Writing exams involves a certain amount of stress and anxiety. If you want to do your best on the exam, *there is no substitute for being well prepared.* Being well prepared helps you to feel more confident about your ability to succeed and less anxious about writing tests. When preparing for unit or year-end exams, remember to:

- use as many senses as possible in preparing for exams
- start as early as possible set realistic goals and targets
- take advantage of study buddies, study groups, and tutorials
- review previously used exams
- study with positive, knowledgeable, motivated, and supportive individuals
- practice the material in the format in which you are to be tested
- try to simulate the test situation as much as possible
- keep a positive attitude
- end your study time with a quick review and then do something different before you try to go to sleep on the night before the exam
- drink a sufficient amount of water prior to an exam
- stay in the exam room for the full amount of time available
- try to relax by focusing on your breathing

If you combine your best study habits with some of the strategies presented here, you may increase your chances of writing a strong exam and maximizing your potential to do well.

PROVINCIAL ACHIEVEMENT TEST

A GUIDE TO WRITING THE PROVINCIAL ACHIEVEMENT TEST

The *Provincial Achievement Test* section contains all of the questions from the 2000 and 2001 Provincial Achievement Tests (PATs). The questions presented here are distinct from those in the Unit Review section. It is recommended that students carefully work through these exams as they are reflective of the format and difficulty level that students are likely to encounter on the exam.

THE KEY contains detailed answers that illustrate the problem-solving process for each question in this section.

When writing practice exams, students are encouraged to simulate actual Provincial Achievement Test conditions. This will help students become:

- *aware of the mental and physical stamina required to sit through an entire exam*
- *familiar with the exam format and how the course content is tested*
- *aware of any units or concepts that are troublesome or require additional study*
- *more successful in managing their review effectively*

To simulate the exam conditions, students should:

- *use an alarm clock or other timer to monitor the time allowed for the exam*
- *select a quiet writing spot away from all distractions*
- *assemble the appropriate materials that are allowed for writing the exam such as pens, HB pencils, calculator, and a dictionary*
- *use "test wiseness" skills*
- *complete as much of the exam as possible within the allowable time*

When writing the practice exam, students should:

- *read instructions, directions, and questions carefully*
- *organize writing time according to the exam emphasis on each section*
- *highlight key words*
- *think about what is being asked*
- *plan their writing; once complete, proof for errors in content, spelling, and grammar*
- *watch for bolded words such as not, most, least, best*
- *cross out any choices students know are incorrect in multiple-choice questions*
- *review all responses upon completion of the exam, if possible*

2000 PROVINCIAL ACHIEVEMENT TEST

CONNECTIONS WITHIN MATHEMATICS

Use the following information to answer question 1.

A right-angled triangle is shown below.

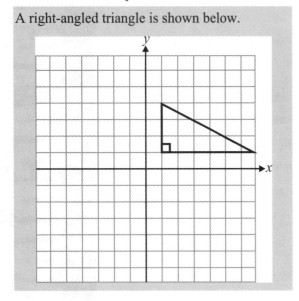

1. Which of the following diagrams represents the triangle above when it is reflected using the *x*-axis as the line of reflection?

A. 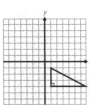 **B.**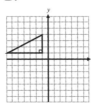

C.   **D.**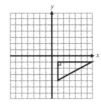

Use the following algebra-tile legend to answer questions 2 and 3.

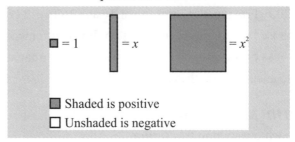

2. Which of the following area diagrams represents the product of $(x + 3)(x - 4)$?

A. 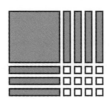 **B.**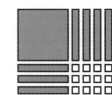

C. 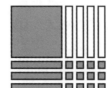 **D.**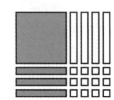

3. Kent and Larissa go to a movie. Admission is *x* dollars per person. They have a $5 discount coupon. Which of the following algebra-tile models represents a mathematical expression for what they pay?

A. 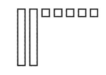 **B.**

C.  **D.**

Use the following information to answer question 4.

On the grid below, the original image is $\triangle ABC$ and the dilatation image is $\triangle A'B'C'$.

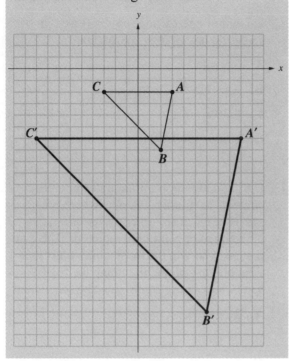

4. The scale factor of the dilatation is

A. $\dfrac{1}{4}$ B. $\dfrac{1}{3}$

C. 3 D. 4

Use the following information to answer question 5.

A home builder is installing carpet in a new home. The area, in square metres, of the living room can be expressed as $x^2 - 8x + 15$.

$$A = (x^2 - 8x + 15)\text{m}^2$$

$\longleftarrow\ (x-3)\text{m}\ \longrightarrow$

5. If the length of this room is represented by $(x - 3)$ m, then the width is represented by

A. $(x - 5)$ m

B. $(x + 5)$ m

C. $(7x - 5)$ m

D. $(-7x + 5)$ m

6. Which of the following number lines represents the solution to the inequality $x + 8 > 3x - 6;\ x \in \mathbb{R}$?

A.

B.

C.

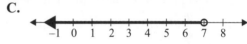

D.

7. The calculator keystroke sequence that would give the solution of $\dfrac{28 + 7}{5 \times (4 + 3)}$ is

A. $28\ \boxed{+}\ 7\ \boxed{\div}\ 5\ \boxed{\times}\ 4\ \boxed{+}\ 3\ \boxed{=}$

B. $\boxed{(}\ 28\ \boxed{+}\ 7\ \boxed{)}\ \boxed{\div}\ 5\ \boxed{\times}\ \boxed{(}\ 4$ $\boxed{+}\ 3\ \boxed{)}\ \boxed{=}$

C. $28\ \boxed{+}\ 7\ \boxed{\div}\ \boxed{(}\ 5\ \boxed{\times}\ \boxed{(}\ 4\ \boxed{+}\ 3$ $\boxed{)}\ \boxed{)}\ \boxed{=}$

D. $\boxed{(}\ 28\ \boxed{+}\ 7\ \boxed{)}\ \boxed{\div}\ \boxed{(}\ 5\ \boxed{\times}\ \boxed{(}$ $4\ \boxed{+}\ 3\ \boxed{)}\ \boxed{)}\ \boxed{=}$

8. If $2x + 23 = -7 + 8x$, then x equals

A. 5 B. 3

C. -3 D. -5

9. A square has an area of 196 cm². Given that $\pi = 3.14$, what is the area of the largest circle that can be drawn within this square?

    A. 615.44 cm²

    B. 153.86 cm²

    C. 62.42 cm²

    D. 43.96 cm²

10. You are asked to conduct a survey to determine the favourite sport of people attending a co-ed camp. Which of the following samples is **least** biased?

    A. A sample of all campers

    B. A sample of all of the boys at camp

    C. A sample of the camp football team

    D. A sample of spectators at a camp soccer game

Use the following information to answer question 11.

A square-based pyramid in northern Egypt has a base width of 31 m and a face height of 21 m.

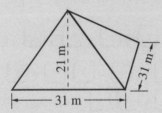

11. The total surface area of the 4 exposed faces of this pyramid is

    A. 2 604.0 m²

    B. 1 302.0 m²

    C. 651.0 m²

    D. 325.5 m²

12. Alex runs on a treadmill and consumes about 5×10^5 joules (J) of energy every 15 minutes. At this rate of energy consumption, if Alex runs for $1\frac{3}{4}$ hours, the amount of energy he uses, expressed in scientific notation, is approximately

    A. 3.5×10^6 J

    B. 35×10^5 J

    C. 8.75×10^5 J

    D. 87.5×10^4 J

13. During badminton intramurals, 5 players compete in round robin play where each player plays every other player one game. No tiebreaker games are required. The two players who win the most games meet in a final playoff game. Including the final game, how many games must be scheduled?

    A. 26 games

    B. 21 games

    C. 11 games

    D. 6 games

14. What is the value of $\dfrac{(-2)^7}{4^0}$?

    A. +128   B. −128

    C. 0   D. Undefined

Use the following scatter plot to answer question 15.

Practice Time versus Golf Scores

15. If a line of best fit were drawn on the scatter plot above, the coordinate point that would lie closest to the line of best fit would be

A. (60, 14)   B. (65, 6)

C. (73, 16)   D. (77, 8)

MATHEMATICS OF FARMING

Farmers use math everyday. The following questions show ways in which farmers may use math in their daily work.

16. A farmer and his son leave a barn at the same time and walk in opposite directions checking a fence line. The son walks at a speed of 3.5 km/h and the farmer at 4.0 km/h. How much time will have elapsed when the farmer and his son are 2.5 km apart?

A. $\frac{1}{5}$ h   B. $\frac{1}{3}$ h

C. 3 h   D. 5 h

17. On Monday, the farmer's hens laid 50 eggs. Of the 50 eggs, 35 were white and 15 were brown. When the farmer gathered the eggs, what was the probability that the first egg he randomly picked was a white egg?

A. $\frac{1}{50}$

B. $\frac{1}{35}$

C. $\frac{15}{35}$

D. $\frac{35}{50}$

Use the following information to answer question 18.

The farmer's son makes a work arrangement with his father. In return for unlimited use of a truck for one year, he agrees to pay the following estimated yearly truck expenses.

•	Insurance	$556.40
•	Gasoline	$1 040.40
•	Repairs	$800.00
•	Maintenance	$200.00

The son also wishes to earn $2 000.00 above these truck expenses.

18. The son works 8 hours a week for 52 weeks on the farm. What is the lowest hourly wage he must earn in order to pay these truck expenses for one year and also save $2 000.00?

A. $6.25/h

B. $10.50/h

C. $11.05/h

D. $12.50/h

Use the following information to answer question 19.

A conveyor belt is used to move hay bales from the ground to the top of a haystack. The loading end of the conveyor belt is 7.3 m from the haystack. Each hay bale moves 8.0 m along the conveyor belt.

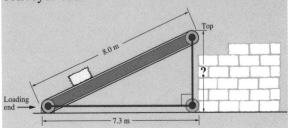

19. What is the height to the top of the conveyor belt?

A. 2.6 m

B. 3.3 m

C. 6.8 m

D. 10.7 m

Use the following picture to answer question 20.

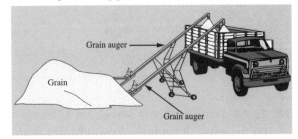

20. At the farm, two augers are being used to fill a truck with grain. One auger alone can fill the truck in 15 minutes. The other auger alone can fill the truck in 10 minutes. How long will it take the two augers together to fill the truck?

A. 5.5 min   **B.** 6.0 min

C. 12.5 min   **D.** 25.0 min

21. In the fall, the farmer sells his grain. Which of the following graphs shows the relationship between grain price and farm income?

A.
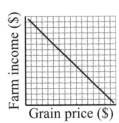

B.
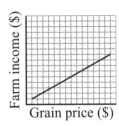

C.
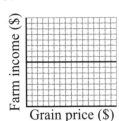

D.
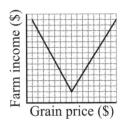

22. A surveyor's report states that a field being planted measures 302 m by 604 m. A farmer spreads seed at a rate of 2.7 kg for every 100 m^2. Given that 1 t = 1 000 kg, approximately how many tonnes (t) of seed are needed to plant the entire field?

A. 5 t

B. 25 t

C. 65 t

D. 651 t

Use the following information to answer question 23.

A farmer hires a worker. Each week, the worker works 9 h at a rate of $5.60/h. From each weekly paycheque, the worker must pay

- 1% of the total pay for disability insurance
- 2.2% of the total pay for employment insurance
- 15% of the total pay for income tax and Canada Pension

23. What are the worker's weekly earnings after these deductions are made?

    A. $50.40

    B. $41.48

    C. $41.23

    D. $32.20

Use the following diagram to answer question 24.

The farmer builds a ramp to load cattle into a truck. The truck deck is 1 m above the ground, and the base of the ramp is 5.65 m long.

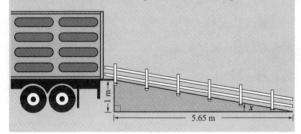

24. What is the angle of inclination (*x*) of the ramp?

    A. 10.0°

    B. 17.0°

    C. 27.0°

    D. 45.0°

MATHEMATICS AT THE CABIN

Michael and Marie are completing work on their cabin at the lake.

Use the following information to answer question 25.

Michael stacks boxes of building materials in his storage shed.

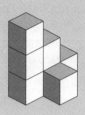

25. Which of the following sets of views represents the layout of Michael's boxes?

A.

   Plan or Top view   Front view   Side view

B.

   Plan or Top view   Front view   Side view

C.

   Plan or Top view   Front view   Side view

D.

   Plan or Top view   Front view   Side view

26. Michael is 1.7 m tall. At 2:00 P.M., he casts a shadow 90 cm long and the cabin casts a shadow 305 cm long. The height of the cabin, to the nearest tenth of a metre, is

A. 0.5 m   B. 2.0 m

C. 4.7 m   D. 5.8 m

27. Michael buys a fan for the cabin. The store purchased the fan for $60. The store then marked up the price by 20%. When the fan went on sale, it was decreased by 20%. What was the sale price of the fan that Michael bought?

A. $57.60   B. $60.00

C. $60.20   D. $72.00

28. Michael and Marie select wood to build a fence around their cabin property. Out of every 10 pieces of wood they look at, 7 of them are of a good quality and 3 of them have a defect. If Michael and Marie each select 1 piece of wood from a different pile, what is the probability that they both select a good-quality piece?

A. $\dfrac{6}{100}$ B. $\dfrac{9}{100}$

C. $\dfrac{14}{100}$ D. $\dfrac{49}{100}$

29. Michael has a cylindrical rainwater barrel that needs a lid. Which of the following equations could Michael use to determine the radius of the lid?

A. $r = \dfrac{2C}{\pi}$

B. $r = \dfrac{C}{2\pi}$

C. $r = \dfrac{\pi}{2C}$

D. $r = \dfrac{2\pi}{C}$

Use the following information to answer question 30.

Marie made an arrangement to buy a used television for a total cost of $200. She made a $50 down payment and arranged to make 6 equal payments to pay the balance.

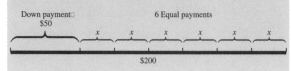

30. Which of the following formulas can Marie use to determine the amount of each of the 6 equal payments?

A. $x = 200 \div 6 + 50$

B. $x = (200 + 50) \div 6$

C. $x = 200 \div 6 - 50$

D. $x = (200 - 50) \div 6$

31. Marie wants to build a rectangular flower bed. If Marie's flower bed has the greatest possible area within a perimeter of 24 m, then the length of the longest side of her flower bed will be

A. 6 m

B. 7 m

C. 10 m

D. 11 m

Use the following information to answer question 32.

Marie is concerned about the cost of energy consumption at the cabin.

Using her neighbour's power bills for the past two years, Marie graphed the energy consumption of the neighbour's cabin, as shown below.

Energy Consumption

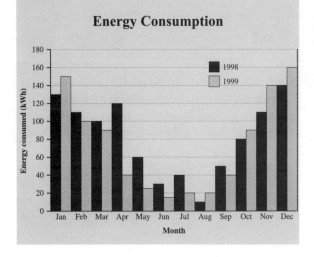

32. When Marie compares the energy consumption for the two years, she realizes that the

   A. July 1999 consumption was one-half the July 1998 consumption

   B. August 1999 consumption was one-half the August 1998 consumption

   C. April 1999 consumption was three times as great as the April 1998 consumption

   D. February 1999 consumption was the same as the February 1998 consumption

SUMMER VACATION

Summer vacation has finally arrived! Grade 9 final exams have been completed, and a great summer awaits you. You belong to a travel club, and you are on the way to the airport to fly to London, England, for a one-week holiday.

The questions in this section fall under the sub-headings

- at the airport before departure
- takeoff, flight, and landing
- on tour in London

AT THE AIRPORT BEFORE DEPARTURE

33. To enter the boarding area, each person walks through a metal detector. If 1 person out of every 10 people sets off the detector, what is the probability that 2 people selected at random will both set off the detector?

   A. $\dfrac{1}{10}$ **B.** $\dfrac{2}{10}$

   C. $\dfrac{1}{100}$ **D.** $\dfrac{81}{100}$

Use the following information to answer question 34.

In the boarding area, a vending machine attendant is servicing the machines. In one of the machines, the attendant finds that the dollar coins, quarters, and dimes have a total value of $67.40. There are 50 more dollar coins than quarters and twice as many dimes as quarters.

34. What is the total value of the dimes the attendant collected?

   A. $1.20

   B. $2.40

   C. $12.00

   D. $24.00

35. While looking out the windows in the boarding area, you notice a cargo plane being loaded. The total volume of storage space available on the cargo plane is 1.488×10^3 m³. How many crates with a volume of 1.24×10^1 m³ can fit in this storage space?

A. 1.20×10^4 crates

B. 1.20×10^3 crates

C. 1.20×10^2 crates

D. 1.20×10^1 crates

TAKEOFF, FLIGHT, AND LANDING

Use the following information to answer question 36.

Your plane requires 20 L of fuel for each kilometre travelled after it reaches cruising altitude.

To determine the total amount of fuel required for a flight (F), the pilot also needs to know:

- the amount of fuel needed to reach cruising altitude (A)

- the distance, in kilometres, travelled after the plane reaches cruising altitude (C)

- the amount of fuel needed for descent and landing (D)

36. Which of the following formulas represents the total amount of fuel required for the flight?

A. $F = C + A + 20F$

B. $F = C + D + 20A$

C. $F = A + C + 20D$

D. $F = A + D + 20C$

Use the following information to answer question 37.

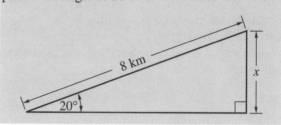

After takeoff, your plane ascends along its flight path at an angle of 20°.

37. A formula that can be used to find the plane's vertical height (x), in kilometres, above ground level after it has travelled 8 km along its flight path is

A. $\sin 20° = \dfrac{x}{8}$

B. $\sin 20° = \dfrac{8}{x}$

C. $\cos 20° = \dfrac{x}{8}$

D. $\cos 20° = \dfrac{8}{x}$

During the flight to London, you try to solve two puzzles from your Logic Puzzle Magazine.

Use the following puzzle to answer question 38.

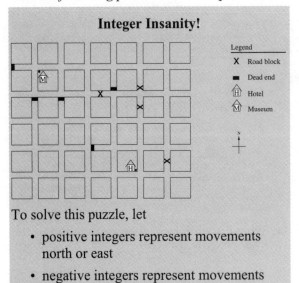

Integer Insanity!

Legend

X Road block

▬ Dead end

H Hotel

M Museum

N

To solve this puzzle, let

- positive integers represent movements north or east
- negative integers represent movements south or west
- 1 block = 1 integer value

38. In the first puzzle, which of the following sets of integers represents the shortest route, in blocks, from the hotel to the museum?

    A. +2, +1, +2, –5

    B. –5, +3, +1, +1

    C. +1, +1, +3, –5

    D. –2, +3, –2, +1

39. In the second puzzle, you have 3 consecutive odd numbers whose sum is 219. What is the value of the largest number?

    A. 77

    B. 75

    C. 73

    D. 71

Use the following information to answer question 40.

Your flight lands at Heathrow Airport in London. A sample of planes arriving at Heathrow Airport between 12:00 P.M. and 10:00 P.M. on a particular day and the number of passengers on each are plotted on the scatter plot below.

Flight Arrivals at Heathrow Airport

Number of passengers per plane

Flight arrival time (P.M.)

40. The scatter plot shows that in the

    A. afternoon, fewer planes land than in the evening

    B. evening, there are more passengers per plane than in the afternoon

    C. evening, more planes land than in the afternoon

    D. afternoon, there are more passengers per plane than in the evening

ON TOUR IN LONDON

41. While on a tour, you see a rectangular dock on the River Thames. The area of the surface of the dock can be represented by $24y^2$ square units. The length is 6 times the width. What are the dimensions of the surface of the dock?

    A. $2y$ units by $12y$ units

    B. $4y$ units by $24y$ units

    C. y units by $6y$ units

    D. y units by $24y$ units

42. The total cost of admission to an attraction in London is $240.00 Canadian for 2 adults and 3 children. An adult admission is $15 more than a child's. How much is an adult admission?

    A. $42.00   **B.** $45.00

    C. $48.00   **D.** $57.00

43. Your tour stops at a castle. You stop for a rest $\frac{1}{3}$ of the way up a stairway in the castle. If you climb 11 more steps, you will be $\frac{1}{2}$ of the way up. How many steps are there in the stairway?

    A. 33 steps   **B.** 44 steps

    C. 66 steps   **D.** 132 steps

Use the following information to answer question 44.

From the castle, your group walks to the flower gardens.

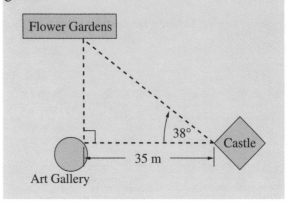

44. What is the shortest distance from the castle to the flower gardens?

    A. 57 m   C. 44 m

    B. 49 m   D. 28 m

You have now completed the multiple-choice questions.

Proceed directly to the numerical-response questions.

Numerical Response

1. If $a = 1.5$, $b = -2$, and $c = -5$, then

$\dfrac{(a-b)^2}{c^2}$ is equal to _____.

(Round your answer to the nearest hundredth.)

2. While travelling in Europe, you exchange $50.00 in Canadian money for local currency. You receive 8 identical bills and 4 identical coins. If each coin is worth $1.24 Canadian, then the value of each bill, in Canadian currency, is

$ _____.

Use the following information to answer numerical-response question 3.

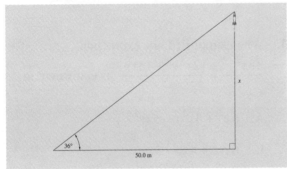

In a park, some people are launching model rockets. To find out the maximum height, x, that a rocket reaches, a person stands 50.0 m from the launch site and measures the angle from the ground to the rocket at its maximum height. If the angle is 36°, then the maximum height, x, of the rocket is _____ m.

(Round your answer to the nearest tenth of a metre.)

4. What is the value of $2^3 + 4^{-1}$ expressed as a decimal? _____.

Use the following algebra-tile legend to answer numerical-response question 5.

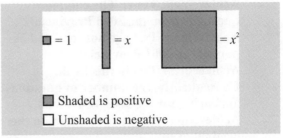

5. If $x = 4.5$, the value of the expression shown below is _____.
(Round your answer to the nearest tenth.)

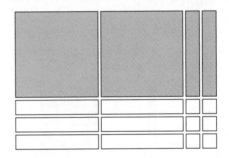

6. A foghorn sounds a blast for 2 seconds and then is silent for 8 seconds. This pattern continues for $3\frac{1}{2}$ hours. How many blasts does the foghorn make in this period of time? _____.

You have now completed the test.

If you have time, you may wish to check your answers.

2001 PROVINCIAL ACHIEVEMENT TEST

Note: Some questions are common in both the 2000 and 2001 Provincial Achievement Tests. The common questions from the 2000 Provincial Achievement Test are not repeated as part of the 2001 Provincial Achievement Test in this book. Consequently, the number of questions appearing for the 2001 Provincial Achievement Test is fewer than on the original exam.

CONNECTIONS WITHIN MATHEMATICS

Use the following algebra-tile legend to answer question 1.

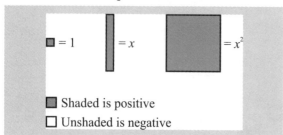

Shaded is positive
Unshaded is negative

Use the following algebra-tile model to answer question 1.

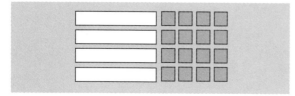

1. Which of the following products is represented by the algebra-tile model above?

   A. $4(-x + 4)$

   B. $4(x - 4)$

   C. $2(-2x + 4)$

   D. $2(2x - 4)$

Use the following diagram to answer question 2.

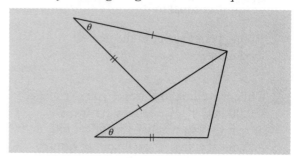

2. Which set of conditions for congruency proves that the triangles above are congruent?

   A. ASA   **B.** AAS

   C. SSA   **D.** SAS

3. When simplified, the expression $\dfrac{18x^2y^3 + 12x^4y^2 - 15xy^4}{3x^2y}$ is equivalent to

   A. $6y^2 + 4x^2y - 5xy^3$

   B. $6xy^2 + 4xy - 5xy^3$

   C. $6y^2 + 4x^2y - 5x^{-1}y^3$

   D. $6xy^2 + 4xy - 5x^{-1}y^3$

4. In a class of 27 students who are studying the history of music, there are $(3x + 2)$ students studying rock and roll, $(2x + 1)$ students studying rap, and $(7x)$ students studying jazz. The actual number of students who are studying each musical category is

   A. 8 in rock and roll, 5 in rap, and 14 in jazz

   B. 7 in rock and roll, 6 in rap, and 14 in jazz

   C. 6 in rock and roll, 7 in rap, and 14 in jazz

   D. 5 in rock and roll, 8 in rap, and 14 in jazz

5. The numbers -20, $\dfrac{5}{11}$, 0, 42, and 24 all belong to the

   A. rational number system

   B. integral number system

   C. whole number system

   D. natural number system

Use the following information to answer question 6.

On the number line below, the letters represent real numbers.

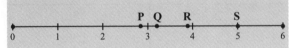

6. On the number line, the approximate value of $\sqrt{10}$ is represented by the letter

   A. P

   B. Q

   C. R

   D. S

7. The solution to $(5.2 \times 10^{-3}) \times (1.5 \times 10^2)$ is

   A. 6.7×10^{-1}

   B. 7.8×10^{-1}

   C. 6.7×10^{-6}

   D. 7.8×10^{-6}

8. A paper bag contains 20 green, 15 blue, 15 white, 8 pink, and 2 orange bubble gums. What is the probability that a person will randomly draw a blue or a green bubble gum out of the bag on the first try?

   A. $\dfrac{2}{35}$

   B. $\dfrac{7}{12}$

   C. $\dfrac{1}{3}$

   D. $\dfrac{1}{4}$

9. A car travelling at a speed of 105 km/h uses 8.2 L of gas per 100 km. If the vehicle travels for 72 min, how many litres of gas does it use?

   A. 10.33 L

   B. 12.20 L

   C. 12.80 L

   D. 14.63 L

10. Ms. Carlson put $3.75 into a parking meter. She used twice as many nickels as quarters, and three fewer dimes than quarters. How many dimes did she use?

    A. 3

    B. 6

    C. 9

    D. 18

Use the following information to answer question 11.

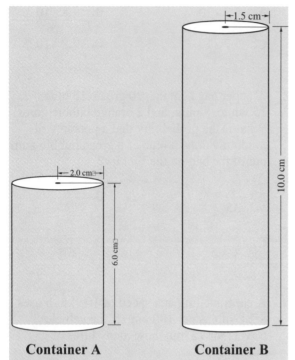

Container A   **Container B**

The formula for the volume of a cylinder is
$V = \pi r^2 h$.

11. The volume of container A is how much greater than the volume of container B?

A. 4.71 cm^3 B. 9.42 cm^3

C. 70.65 cm^3 D. 75.36 cm^3

MATHEMATICS OF FARMING

Farmers use math everyday. The following questions show ways in which farmers may use math in their daily work.

12. Some of the hens became sick. At 9:00 A.M. on Saturday, 3 hens were sick. Every half hour, 2 more hens got sick. If this pattern were to continue, the number of hens that would be sick at 2:00 P.M. can be represented by the expression

A. 3×2^9

B. 3×2^{10}

C. $3 + (2 \times 10)$

D. $3 + (3 \times 10)$

Use the following information to answer question 13.

The farmer bought some new hens. The following table shows the number of eggs laid (*E*) by some of these hens in one week and the number of hens (*H*) that laid them.

Number of hens (*H*)	Number of eggs laid (*E*)
2	12
3	19
4	26

13. Which of the following equations represents the relationship between the number of eggs laid in one week and the number of hens that laid them?

A. $E = 6H$

B. $E = 6H + 1$

C. $E = 7H - 2$

D. $E = 7H - 7$

MATHEMATICS AT THE CABIN

Michael and Marie are completing work on their cabin at the lake.

Use the following information to answer question 14.

One wall of the cabin needs to be painted. The wall is 8.5 m long and 2.5 m high, and it has two windows that each measure 0.9 m by 0.7 m.

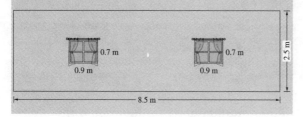

14. The area of the wall that needs to be painted, to the nearest tenth, is

A. 20.0 m^2 **B.** 20.6 m^2

C. 21.3 m^2 **D.** 22.5 m^2

Use the following information to answer question 15.

Marie wants to buy a used canoe. She found the advertisement shown below; however, the last two digits of the phone number were missing.

For Sale
Canoe
• like new •
• dark green •
• 2 passenger •
Asking $350
Phone: Joanne
283-49

15. What is the maximum number of calls that Marie will have to make to be certain of reaching the person who placed the advertisement?

A. 100   **B.** 90

C. 81   **D.** 72

MATHEMATICS AND SPORTS

People involved in sports use mathematical concepts everyday.

16. A parachutist jumps out of a plane that is flying at an altitude of 3 km, and she immediately opens her parachute. If she falls at an average rate of 24 m/s, she will reach the ground in

A. 1.25 s   **B.** 12.5 s

C. 125 s   **D.** 1 250 s

17. If it takes one snowmaking machine 6 h to cover a portion of a ski hill with snow and another snowmaking machine 4 h to cover the same area, how long will it take to cover the same area if both machines are working at the same time?

A. 0.42 h   **B.** 2.4 h

C. 5 h   **D.** 10 h

Use the following information to answer questions 18 and 19.

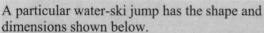

A particular water-ski jump has the shape and dimensions shown below.

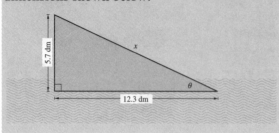

18. What is the length of side *x* of the ramp?

    A. 183.87 dm

    B. 18.0 dm

    C. 13.56 dm

    D. 6.6 dm

19. What is the angle of elevation, (θ), to the nearest degree, of the ramp?

    A. 25°

    B. 28°

    C. 62°

    D. 65°

Use the following information to answer question 20.

The sails of two sailboards are similar triangles, as shown below.

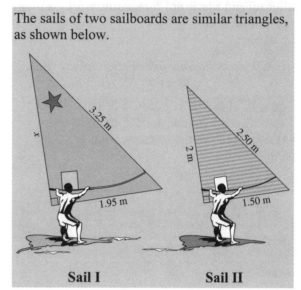

Sail I   **Sail II**

20. What is the length of side *x* of sail I?

    A. 2.45 m

    B. 2.6 m

    C. 2.75 m

    D. 3.8 m

MATHEMATICS AND CAMPING

The Smith family is going camping during their summer vacation.

Use the following information to answer question 21.

The Smiths need to purchase a tent. A sporting goods store has a tent set up in a display area. The tent has rectangular walls, a covered door, and a square-based pyramidal roof, as shown below.

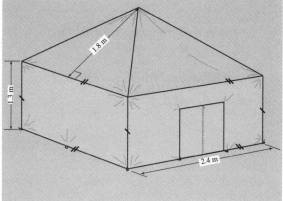

21. Excluding the floor and seams, the amount of material that was used to make this tent was

A. 16.32 m²   **B.** 17.16 m²

C. 21.12 m²   **D.** 26.88 m²

Use the following information to answer question 22.

For a five-night camping trip, the Smith family had budgeted to spend an average of $80 per night for campground fees, food, and entertainment. Their actual costs for the first four nights are recorded below.

	1st Night	2nd Night	3rd Night	4th Night	5th Night
Amount Spent	$130	$95	$45	$70	x

22. In order to remain within their total budget, the maximum amount that the Smith family can spend on the fifth night is

A. $85   **B.** $80

C. $68   **D.** $60

23. The campground owner surveys the number of campers that arrive at different times of the day. He finds that, generally, more campers arrive later in the day. Which of the following scatter plots best represents the campground owner's findings?

A.   **B.**

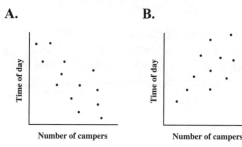

C.   **D.**

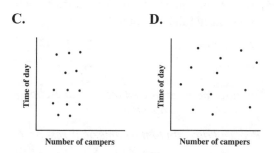

Use the following information to answer question 24.

At a campground, an outdoor stage is directly north of a small store, and the shower building is directly east of the store, as shown below.

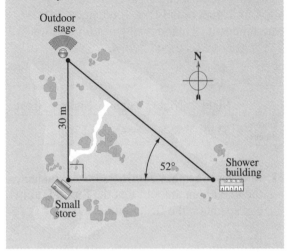

24. The distance from the outdoor stage to the shower building, to the nearest metre, is

A. 18 m   **B.** 24 m

C. 38 m   **D.** 49 m

Use the following information to answer question 25.

The Smiths think of a plan to save spending money for next year's trip. They will save 2 quarters the first month and then double the number of quarters each month thereafter.

Month	1	2	3	4	
Quarters	2	4	8	16	

25. How many quarters will the Smiths have to save during the 12th month?

A. 4 096   **B.** 2 048

C. 144   **D.** 24

You have now completed the multiple-choice questions.

Proceed directly to the numerical-response questions.

Numerical Response

Use the following information to answer numerical response question 1.

Two companies advertise the following labour costs for car repair.

A-1 Car Repair

Cost = $31.60 per hour plus a $45 service charge

Classix Car Repair

Cost = $41.70 per hour plus a $30 service charge

1. If a particular repair takes 6 hours at A-1, but only 5 hours at Classix, how much money would a customer save by going to A-1 Car Repair? _____

2. A rectangle has the dimensions $(5x + 6)$ by $(2x + 1)$. If $x = 4$ m, then the area of the rectangle is _____ m^2.

You have now completed the test.

If you have time, you may wish to check your answers.

ANSWERS AND SOLUTIONS
2000 PROVINCIAL ACHIEVEMENT TEST

1. D	11. B	21. B	31. A	41. A
2. D	12. A	22. A	32. A	42. D
3. D	13. C	23. C	33. C	43. C
4. C	14. B	24. A	34. B	44. C
5. A	15. D	25. B	35. C	NR1. 0.49
6. C	16. B	26. D	36. D	NR2. 5.63
7. D	17. D	27. A	37. A	NR3. 36.3
8. A	18. C	28. D	38. D	NR4. 8.25
9. B	19. B	29. B	39. B	NR5. 16.5
10. A	20. B	30. D	40. B	NR6. 1 260

1. D

The right angle is at (1, 1); its image should be 1 unit from the reflection line.

The image in diagram **A** is in quadrant 4, but is a translation.

The image in diagram **B** is a reflection, but using the *y*-axis as the reflection line.

The image in diagram **C** is in quadrant 3 and is a translation.

Figure **D** is correct. The image is in quadrant 4, and the corresponding vertices are the same number of units from the reflection line.

2. D

An approach to solving this problem is to identify the side measure of each rectangle.

A. 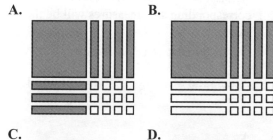 **B.**

C. 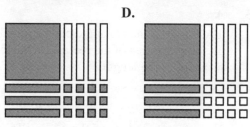 **D.**

Diagrams **A** and **B** are incorrect because one side measure is $x + 4$; it should be $x - 4$.

This leaves **C** and **D** as possible solutions. **C** is incorrect because if $(x + 3)(x - 4)$ is expanded using FOIL, we get $x^2 - x - 12$. This means there should be 12 unshaded (negative) 1 tiles.

3. **D**

Kent and Larissa each have to pay x dollars. The admission for both can be represented with 2 x-tiles:

Having a \$5 coupon means \$5 will be deducted from the admission cost.

Subtracting \$5 can be represented with

5 unshaded tiles: ☐ ☐ ☐ ☐ ☐
Therefore, the total cost would be

 ☐ ☐ ☐ ☐ ☐

4. **C**

The dilatation image and the original image are similar triangles. The ratio of corresponding side measures will be the same.
$\overline{AC}$ is 6 units; $\overline{A'C'}$ is 18 units.

∴ the ratio of $\dfrac{\overline{A'C'}}{\overline{AC}}$ is 18 to 6 or 3 to 1.

5. **A**

The width of the rectangle can be found by dividing the area of the rectangle by the measure of the length.

$$\text{Width} = \frac{x^2 - 8x + 15}{x - 3}$$

Now, factor the trinomial $x^2 - 8x + 15$ by using the sum and product method.

$x^2 - 8x + 15$
sum = –8 ⎫ Find 2 factors which will
product = 15 ⎭ satisfy these two conditions.
These 2 factors are –3 and –5.
Check : $\quad -3 + -5 = -8$
$\qquad\qquad -3 \times -5 = +15$
Therefore, $x^2 - 8x + 15 = (x - 3)(x - 5)$
Now, we can divide:

$$\frac{x^2 - 8x + 15}{x - 3} = \frac{(x - 3)(x - 5)}{x - 3}$$

Eliminate the common factor $x - 3$ from the numerator and denominator, leaving $x - 5$.

6. **C**

To choose the correct number line, solve for x first.

$x + 8 > 3x - 6$

$x + 8 - 8 > 3x - 6 - 8$ (Subtract 8 from both sides)

$x > 3x - 14$

$x - 3x > 3x - 3x - 14$ (Subtract $3x$ from both sides)

$-2x > -14$

$\dfrac{-2x}{-2} < \dfrac{-14}{-2}$ (Divide both sides by –2, ∴ reverse inequality sign)

$x < 7$

C is correct since $(\circ)$ indicates the values are less than 7, whereas, $(\bullet)$ in **D** indicates less than or **equal** to.

7. **D**

The calculator sequence must take into account that the sum of 28 and 7 will be divided by the value of the denominator. Parentheses are to be used to separate the numerator and denominator.
The problem could be expressed as
$(28 + 7) \div [5 \times (4 + 3)]$.

8. A

To solve for x in the expression
$2x + 23 = -7 + 8x$, combine like terms

$2x - 8x + 23 = -7 + 8x - 8x$ (Subtract $8x$ from both sides)

$-6x + 23 = -7$

$-6x + 23 - 23 = -7 - 23$ (Subtract 23 from both sides)

$-6x = -30$

$\dfrac{-6x}{-6} = \dfrac{-30}{-6}$ (Divide both sides by –6)

$x = 5$

9. B

The first step is to calculate the side measure of the square.

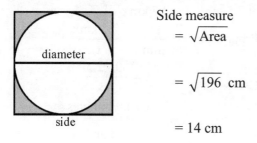

Side measure
$= \sqrt{\text{Area}}$

$= \sqrt{196}$ cm

$= 14$ cm

The side measure of the square is equal to the diameter of the largest possible circle.
Diameter = 14 cm ∴ radius = 7 cm
To find the area of the circle, use the formula

$A = \pi r^2$

$A \approx 3.14(7)^2$

$A = 153.86$ cm^2

10. A

The least biased sample should include members from all groups.
Statement **B** is incorrect because there would be a strong bias toward male-dominated sports.
Statement **C** is incorrect because of a bias toward football.
Statement **D** is incorrect because of a bias toward soccer.
Statement **A** would be the **least** biased because all campers would include boys and girls, who could be fans of any sport.

11. B

The four exposed faces of the pyramid are congruent. Therefore, find the area of one triangular face and multiply by 4.

$SA = 4\left(\dfrac{b \times h}{2}\right)$

$SA = 4\left(\dfrac{31 \times 21}{2}\right)$

$SA = 1\,302.0$ m^2

12. A

Alex consumes 5×10^5 joules of energy every 15 minutes. In $1\dfrac{3}{4}$ hours, there are seven 15-minute intervals.

∴ $7 \times 5 \times 10^5 = 35 \times 10^5$

For the amount of energy to be expressed in scientific notation, the decimal needs to be placed between the 3 and 5; therefore, the exponent will increase by 1.

∴ $35 \times 10^5 = 3.5 \times 10^{5+1}$

$= 3.5 \times 10^6$

13. C

Identify the 5 players as *A*, *B*, *C*, *D,* and *E*. Each player will play every other player only once.

Players: *A B C D E*

Games:

A vs. *B*	*B* vs. *C*	*C* vs. *D*	*D* vs. *E*
A vs. *C*	*B* vs. *D*	*C* vs. *E*	
A vs. *D*	*B* vs. *E*		
A vs. *E*			
4 games	3 games	2 games	1 game

The top 2 players will play 1 game to determine the winner. The total number of games that need to be scheduled is
$4 + 3 + 2 + 1 + 1 = 11$ games.

14. B

To find the value of $\dfrac{(-2)^7}{4^0}$, we need to review the zero exponent rule, which states that any non-zero base with an exponent of 0 is equal to 1.

This means we have

$$\frac{(-2)(-2)(-2)(-2)(-2)(-2)(-2)}{1} = -128$$

15. D

Draw a line of best fit for the scatter plot. A line of best fit should be drawn as close as possible to all the points and should have an equal number of points above and below the line.

The scatter plot has 11 points; therefore, sketch a line of best fit with 6 points above the line and 5 points below the line.

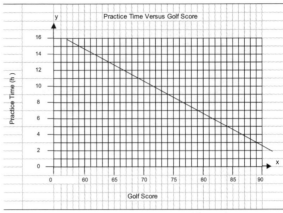

From the line of best fit, the point closest to the line is $(77, 8)$.

16. B

Sketch a diagram.

Father		Son
← 4.0 km/hr	Barn	3.5 km/hr →

2.5 km

Both farmer and son start walking at the same time and stop when they are 2.5 km apart.

Combine the farmer's speed with his son's speed:

4.0 + 3.5 = 7.5 km/h

Think of this problem as 1 person travelling at 7.5 km/h for 2.5 km.

Proportion : $\dfrac{7.5 \text{ km}}{60 \text{ min}} = \dfrac{2.5 \text{ km}}{x}$

Cross-multiply: $x = \dfrac{60 \times 2.5}{7.5}$

$x = 20$ minutes

$\therefore \dfrac{20 \text{ minutes}}{60 \text{ minutes}} = \dfrac{1}{3}$ of an hour

17. D

Probability of an event $= \dfrac{\text{number of favourable outcomes}}{\text{total number of outcomes}}$

The number of favourable outcomes (white eggs) is 35; the total number of outcomes is 50.

$$P(\text{white egg}) = \frac{35}{50}$$

18. C

First, we need to find the total truck expenses:
$556.40 + $1 040.40 + $800.00 + $200.00
= $2 596.80

He wishes to earn $2 000 above the truck expenses, therefore; his total earnings must be
$2 596.80 + $2 000.00 = $4 596.80

The total number of hours worked during the year is

$52 \text{ weeks} \times 8\, \dfrac{\text{hours}}{\text{week}}$, which is 416 hours.

His hourly wage would need to be
$4 596.80 ÷ 416 hours = $11.05/hour

19. B

The diagram shows a right triangle. Finding a missing side measure of a right triangle requires the Pythagorean Theorem:
$c^2 = a^2 + b^2$
Keep in mind that c, the hypotenuse, is always the longest side measure and opposite the right angle. The variables a and b represent the other two sides of the triangle (often called the legs).
Therefore,

$$c^2 = a^2 + b^2$$
$$8^2 = a^2 + (7.3)^2$$
$$64 = a^2 + 53.29$$

(Subtract 53.29 from both sides)

$$64 - 53.29 = a^2 + 53.29 - 53.29$$
$$10.71 = a^2$$
$$\sqrt{10.71} = \sqrt{a^2}$$
$$3.3\ m = a$$

20. B

This is a rate of work problem. We can use the formula:

$$\frac{x}{a} + \frac{x}{b} = 1$$

Let x = number of minutes needed if both augers work together
a = minutes first auger can do the job (15)
b = minutes other auger can do the job (10)

$$\therefore\ \frac{x}{15} + \frac{x}{10} = 1$$

Multiply each term by the lowest common denominator (LCD), which is 30.

$$30\left(\frac{x}{15}\right) + 30\left(\frac{x}{10}\right) = 30(1)$$
$$2x + 3x = 30$$
$$5x = 30$$
$$x = 6 \text{ minutes}$$

21. B

As the price of grain increases, the farm income would increase as well.

Graph **A** indicates farm income would decrease as the grain price increases. This is false.

Graph **C** shows farm income remaining the same even when grain prices increases. False.

Graph **D** shows that farm income decreases as grain prices increases (false); then farm incomes sharply increase for some unknown reason.

Graph B clearly shows that farm income will increase when grain prices increase, which is correct.

22. A

The field being planted is a rectangle with dimensions 302 m by 604 m.

We need to find the area of the rectangle $(A = l \times w)$.

Area $= 302 \text{ m} \times 604 \text{ m}$
$= 182\ 408 \text{ m}^2$

The farmer spreads seed at a rate of 2.7 kg for every 100 m². To find how many kg of seed are needed, we set up a proportion:

$$\frac{2.7 \text{ kg}}{100 \text{ m}^2} = \frac{x}{182\ 408 \text{ m}^2}$$

Solve for x:

$$x = \frac{2.7 \times 182\ 408}{100}$$

$x = 4\ 925.016 \text{ kg}$

Given that 1 t = 1 000 kg, set up another proportion.

$$\frac{1 \text{ t}}{1\ 000 \text{ kg}} = \frac{x}{4\ 925.016 \text{ kg}}$$

Solve for x:

$$x = \frac{1 \times 4\ 925.016}{1\ 000}$$

$x = 4.925$ tonnes

Approximately 5 tonnes of seed will be needed.

23. C

The worker's weekly earnings, before deductions, are
$5.60/h × 9 h/week = $50.40

Each deduction is based on a percentage of his earnings. Convert each percent to a decimal and multiply by his earnings.

Disability insurance
$= 1\%$ of 50.40
$= 0.01 \times 50.40 = 0.50$

Employment insurance
$= 2.2\%$ of 50.40
$= 0.022 \times 50.40 = 1.11$

Income tax and Canada Pension
$= 15\%$ of 50.40
$= 0.15 \times 50.40 = 7.56$

Total deductions
$= 0.50 + 1.11 + 7.56$
$= \$9.17$

His weekly earnings, after deductions, are
$50.40 – $9.17 = $41.23

24. A

From the angle of inclination, $x°$, we are given the side measure adjacent (5.65 m) to angle x and the side measure opposite (1 m) angle $x°$.

To solve for x, use of tangent ratio.

$$\text{Tangent } x = \frac{\text{opposite}}{\text{adjacent}}$$

$$\text{Tan } x = \frac{1 \text{ m}}{565 \text{ m}}$$

$Tan\ x = 0.1770$

$$\angle x° = \tan^{-1} 0.1770$$

$$\angle x° = 10°$$

25. B

Examine each of the 4 sets.
A is incorrect. The front view should be

C is incorrect. The top view should be

D is incorrect. The top view should be

and the front view should be

26. D

Draw a diagram from the information presented.

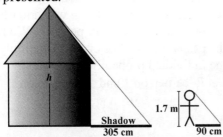

We have two similar triangles, which means the ratio of corresponding sides will be equal.

Setting a proportion, we get

$$\frac{\text{height of cabin}}{\text{height of man}} = \frac{\text{shadow of cabin}}{\text{shadow of man}}$$

$$\frac{h}{1.7 \text{ m}} = \frac{3.05 \text{ m}}{0.90 \text{ m}}$$

$$h = \frac{(1.7)(3.05)}{(0.90)} \quad \text{(Cross multiply)}$$

$$h = 5.8 \text{ m}$$

27. A

The mark-up is 20% of the purchase price.

20% of $60 = 0.2 × 60.00

   = 12.00

Store plans to sell the fan for

$60 + 12 = \$72.00$

When the fan was on sale, the price was reduced by 20%. This means 20% of $72.00.

$0.20 \times \$72.00 = \$14.40$

Hence, the sale price is

$\$72.00 - \$14.40 = \$57.60$

28. D

Michael and Marie will each be selecting 1 piece of wood from different piles. The outcome for one person has no effect on the outcome for the other person. These are independent events.

The probability of selecting 1 good quality piece of wood for each person is $\frac{7}{10}$

Hence,

$$P(\text{Michael, Marie}) = P(\text{Michael}) \times P(\text{Marie})$$

$$= \frac{7}{10} \times \frac{7}{10}$$

$$= \frac{49}{100}$$

29. B

The rainwater barrel is a cylinder, which means the lid is a circle.

The circumference of a circle is calculated by using the formula $C = 2\pi r$

To determine the radius, we need to isolate the variable r in the equation $C = 2\pi r$

$$C = 2\pi r$$

Divide both sides by 2π.

$$\frac{C}{2\pi} = \frac{2\pi r}{2\pi}$$

$$\frac{C}{2\pi} = r$$

30. D

The total cost of the television set is $200.00. The $50 down payment is to be subtracted from the cost of the television set.

The amount of each of the 6 equal payments is determined by the balance divided by 6.

$$\therefore \text{ balance} = 200 - 50$$

$$= 150$$

$$\therefore \text{ each equal payment is } \frac{(200-50)}{6}$$

31. A

Creating a chart may be helpful in solving this question.

Length (m)	Width (m)	Perimeter $(P = 2l + 2w)$	Area $(A = l \times w)$
1	11	$P = 2(1) + 2(11)$ $= 24$ m	$A = (1)(11)$ $= 11$ m^2
2	10	$P = 2(2) + 2(10)$ $= 24$ m	$A = (2)(10)$ $= 20$ m^2
3	9	$P = 2(3) + 2(9)$ $= 24$ m	$A = (3)(9)$ $= 27$ m^2
4	8	$P = 2(4) + 2(8)$ $= 24$ m	$A = (4)(8)$ $= 32$ m^2
5	7	$P = 2(5) + 2(7)$ $= 24$ m	$A = (5)(7)$ $= 35$ m^2
6	6	$P = 2(6) + 2(6)$ $= 24$ m	$A = (6)(6)$ $= 36$ m^2
7	5	$P = 2(7) + 2(5)$ $= 24$ m	$A = (7)(5)$ $= 35$ m^2

Repetition of side measures begins, so there is no need to continue.

From the chart, the greatest area is 36 m^2. The flower bed would have side measures of 6 m each. Keep in mind, a square is a rectangle. (opposite side measures are congruent).

32. A

Statement **B** is incorrect. The August 1999 consumption is 20 KWh. The August 1998 consumption is about 10 KWh.
The number 20 is twice 10, not half as much.
Statement **C** is incorrect. The April 1999 consumption is 40 KWh. The April 1998 consumption is 120 KWh. The number 40 is one-third of 120, not three times as much.
Statement **D** is incorrect. The February 1999 consumption is 100 KWh.
The February 1998 is about 110 KWh.
The number 110 is not equal to 100.
Statement **A** is correct. The July 1999 consumption is 20 KWh. The July 1998 consumption is 40 KWh. The number 20 is half of 40.

33. C

This problem involves finding the probability of two independent events if (the outcome of one person will not affect the outcome of the other person). We find the probability of this event by multiplying the individual probabilities.
Let P_1 be person 1 and P_2 be person 2.
$$\therefore\ P(P_1, P_2) = P(P_1) \times P(P_2)$$
$$= \frac{1}{10} \times \frac{1}{10} = \frac{1}{100}$$

34. B

Set up a chart to show the number of each different type of coin, and their total value.

	Quarters	Dollar Coins	Dimes
Number	x	$x + 50$	$2x$
Value	$0.25(x)$	$1.00(x + 50)$	$0.10(2x)$

Now, set up an equation using the above information.
$$0.25x + 1.00(x + 50) + 0.10(2x) = 67.40$$
$$0.25x + 1.00x + 50 + 0.20x = 67.40$$

$$1.45x + 50 = 67.40 \qquad \text{(Simplify)}$$

$$1.45x + 50 - 50 = 67.40 - 50 \qquad \text{(Subtract 50 from both sides)}$$

$$1.45x = 17.40$$

$$\frac{1.45x}{1.45} = \frac{17.40}{1.45} \qquad \text{(Divide both sides by 1.45)}$$

$$x = 12$$

The number of dimes is $2x$.
Therefore, $2(12) = 24$ dimes.
The total value of dimes is
$24(0.10) = \$2.40$

35. C

To find the number of crates that can fit in the storage space, divide the volume of the storage space by the volume of one crate.

Number of crates $= \dfrac{1.488 \times 10^3}{1.24 \times 10^1}$

$= \dfrac{1.488}{1.24} \times \dfrac{10^3}{10^1}$

$= 1.20 \times 10^2$

36. D

The amount of fuel required for a flight (F) can be broken down to 3 phases: the amount of fuel needed to reach cruising altitude (A), plus the fuel needed to travel after reaching cruising altitude, plus the fuel needed for descent and landing (D).

The plane requires 20 litres of fuel per kilometre after reaching "cruising altitude". If C is the distance travelled after reaching cruising altitude, then 20 times C would be total fuel needed to travel this distance.

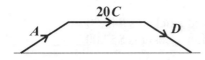

$\therefore F = A + 20C + D$

37. A

From the diagram, we see that the hypotenuse is 8 km, and the unknown side measure, x, is opposite the 20° angle. Given this information, the sine ratio would be best to use.

$\sin 20° = \dfrac{\text{opposite}}{\text{hypotenuse}}$

$\sin 20° = \dfrac{x}{8}$

38. D

The shortest route from the hotel to the museum would be the fewest number of blocks travelled.
Examine each of the 4 routes.
Route **A**: Total of 10 blocks would be travelled.
Route **B**: Total of 10 blocks would be travelled.
Route **C**: Total of 10 blocks would be travelled.
Route **D**: Total of 8 blocks would be travelled.
The shortest route is 8 blocks; **D**.

39. B

It is important to note that we are looking for 3 consecutive **odd** numbers.
Consecutive odd numbers have a difference of 2. (5, 7, 9, . . .).
Let x = the first odd number
$x + 2$ = the second odd number
$x + 4$ = the third odd number
Set up an equation: $x + x + 2 + x + 4 = 219$

$3x + 6 = 219$ (Collect like terms)

$3x + 6 - 6 = 219 - 6$ (Subtract 6 from both sides)

$3x = 213$

$\dfrac{3x}{3} = \dfrac{213}{3}$ (Divide both sides by 3)

$x = 71$

$x + 2 = 73$

$x + 4 = 75$

The largest number is 75.

40. B

From 12:00 to 6:00 would be considered afternoon, and from 6:00 to 10:00 is evening. Examine each statement.
Statement **A** is incorrect.
More planes land in the afternoon (22) than in the evening (10).
Statement **C** is incorrect.
More planes land in the afternoon (22) than in the evening (10).
Statement **D** is incorrect.
The 10 planes that land in the evening carry more than 250 passengers per plane.
There are only 3 planes that land in the afternoon that carry more than 250 passengers per plane.
Statement **B** is correct, for the same reason as stated above regarding **D**.

41. A

The solution to this problem must satisfy two conditions:
1. length is 6 times the width, and
2. length times width equals $24y^2$ units

Statement **A**: $(12y) \div (2y) = 6$
$A = (12y)(2y) = 24y^2$ units

Statement **B**: $(24y) \div (4y) = 6$
$A = (24y)(4y) = 96y^2$ units — (wrong)

Statement **C**: $(6y) \div (y) = 6$
$A = (6y)(y) = 6y^2$ units — (wrong)

Statement **D**: $(24y) \div (y) = 24$ — (wrong)
$A = (24y)(y) = 24y^2$

The only statement that satisfies both conditions is **A**.

42. D

Algebraically represent the cost of each different type of ticket.
Let x = the cost of a child's ticket
Then $x + 15$ = the cost of an adult's ticket
3 children tickets = $3(x)$ and
2 adult tickets = $2(x + 15)$
If the total spent was $240.00, then set up an equation and solve for x.
$$2(x+15)+3(x)=240$$

$2x + 30 + 3x = 240$	(Distributive Property)
$5x + 30 = 240$	(Simplify)
$5x + 30 - 30 = 240 - 30$	(Subtract 30 from both sides)
$5x = 210$	
$\dfrac{5x}{5} = \dfrac{210}{5}$	(Divide both sides by 5)

$x = 42$; then $x + 15 = 57$
Child's ticket is $42.00
Adult's ticket is $57.00

43. C

The 11 steps taken represent the difference between $\dfrac{1}{2}$ of the way up the stairway and $\dfrac{1}{3}$ of the way up the stairway.

$$\therefore \quad \frac{1}{2} - \frac{1}{3} = \frac{3}{6} - \frac{2}{6}$$

This means the 11 steps is $\dfrac{1}{6}$ of the entire stairway.

$$\frac{1}{6}x = 11$$
$$\frac{x}{6} = 11$$
$$x = (11)(6)$$
$$x = 66$$

44. C

The unknown side measure from the castle to the flower garden is the hypotenuse of the right triangle. The 35 m side measure is adjacent to the 38° angle. This means that the cosine ratio would be the best to use.

$$\cos 38° = \frac{\text{adjacent}}{\text{hypotenuse}}$$

$$\cos 38° = \frac{35}{x}$$

$$(x)(\cos 38°) = \frac{35}{x} \times x \qquad \text{(Multiply both sides by } x\text{)}$$

$$(x)(\cos 38°) = 35$$

$$\frac{(x)(\cos 38°)}{\cos 38°} = \frac{35}{\cos 38°} \qquad \text{(Divide both sides by cos 38°)}$$

$$x = \frac{35}{\cos 38°}$$

$$x = 44.42 \text{ m or } 44 \text{ m}$$

NR1. 0.49

To evaluate the expression, we must substitute the given values for the variables.

We get $\dfrac{(a-b)^2}{c^2} = \dfrac{\left[(1.5)-(-2)\right]^2}{(-5)^2}$

Perform operations within parenthesis first (BEDMAS)

$$(1.5)-(-2) = (1.5)+(+2) \qquad \text{(Add the opposite)}$$

$$= 3.5$$

The result is now $\dfrac{(3.5)^2}{(-5)^2} = \dfrac{12.25}{25}$

The last step is to find the quotient of 12.25 and 25, which is 0.49.

NR2. 5.63

If each coin is worth $1.24 Canadian, then 4 coins equals $1.24 × 4 = $4.96 Canadian. The total value of the 8 bills would then be $50.00 – $4.96, which is $45.04.
To find the value of each bill, in Canadian currency, we divide the total value by the number of bills.

That is, $\dfrac{\$45.04}{8 \text{ bills}} = \$5.63$

NR3. 36.3

The unknown side, x, is opposite the 36° angle. The side measuring 50 m is adjacent to the 36° angle. Given this information, we should use the tangent ratio.

$$\text{Tangent } 36° = \frac{\text{opposite}}{\text{adjacent}}$$

$$0.727 \approx \frac{x}{50}$$

Multiplying both sides by 50, we get
$$(0.727)(50) = x$$
$$36.3 \text{ m} = x$$

NR4. **8.25**

A negative exponent indicates the reciprocal of the power with a positive exponent.

Therefore, $4^{-1} = \dfrac{1}{4^1} = \dfrac{1}{4}$

We know 2^3 is $2 \times 2 \times 2$, which is equal to 8.

Therefore, $8 + \dfrac{1}{4} = 8 + 0.25$

$\qquad\qquad = 8.25$

NR5. **16.5**

The diagram shows:

2	x^2 tiles	(shaded is positive)
2	x tiles	(shaded is positive)
6	$-x$ tiles	(unshaded is negative)
6	-1 tiles	(unshaded is negative)

The expression represented by the tiles is $2x^2 + 2x - 6x - 6$

Combining the like terms $2x$ and $-6x$, we get $2x^2 - 4x - 6$.

Now, substitute 4.5 for the variable x.

$2(4.5)^2 - 4(4.5) - 6$

Following the order of operations (BEDMAS), we get:

$2(4.5 \times 4.5) - 4(4.5) - 6$

$2(20.25) - 4(4.5) - 6$

$40.5 - 18 - 6 = 16.5$

NR6. **1 260**

From the information, we see that there will be 1 blast and silence every 10 seconds. In 1 minute, there will be 6×1 or 6, and in 30 minutes (half-hour), there will be 6×30 or 180 blasts.

During $3\dfrac{1}{2}$ hours, there will be 7 half-hour intervals; therefore, 7×180 is 1 260 blasts.

ANSWERS AND SOLUTIONS
2001 PROVINCIAL ACHIEVEMENT TEST

1. A	7. B	13.C	19.A	25. A
2. D	8. B	14.A	20.B	NR1. 3.90
3. C	9. A	15.A	21.C	NR2. 234
4. A	10.B	16.C	22.D	
5. A	11.A	17.B	23.B	
6. B	12.C	18.C	24.C	

1.   A

From the diagram, notice that there are 4
identical rows of algebra tiles.
Each row has an unshaded x-tile and 4
shaded 1-tiles. That means 4 times $(-x + 4)$
or $4(-x + 4)$
The correct answer is **A**.

2.   D

The corresponding two side measures of the
two triangles are congruent.
The corresponding angles between the two
corresponding congruent side measures are
congruent as well.
The case that proves the two triangles are
congruent is SAS.

3.   C

To simplify the expression, we divide the
numerical coefficients in the numerator by
the numerical coefficient in the
denominator.

Recall the quotient property: When
dividing powers with the same base,
subtract the exponents.

$$\frac{18x^2 y^3 + 12x^4 y^2 - 15xy^4}{3x^2 y}$$
$$= (18 \div 3)x^{2-2} y^{3-1} + (12 \div 3)x^{4-2} y^{2-1}$$
$$\qquad\qquad\qquad - (15 \div 3)x^{1-2} y^{4-1}$$
$$= 6y^2 + 4x^2 y - 5x^{-1} y^3$$

4.   A

The first step is to set up an equation to find
the value of x.
Equation: $(3x + 2) + (2x + 1) + (7x) = 27$
$12x + 3 = 27$ (Collect like terms)
$12x + 3 - 3 = 27 - 3$ (Subtract 3 from
both sides)

$12x = 24$
$$\frac{12x}{12} = \frac{24}{12}$$ (Divide both sides by 12)
$x = 2$

Now, substitute 2 for x for each music type.
Rock and roll: $3(2) + 2 = 6 + 2 = 8$
Rap: $2(2) + 1 = 4 + 1 = 5$
Jazz: $7(2) = 14$

5.   A

Recall the definitions of the following
number systems.
Natural Numbers:
 $\{1, 2, 3, 4,\dots\}$
Whole Numbers:
 $\{0, 1, 2, 3, 4,\dots\}$
Integers:
 $\{\dots, -3, -2, -1, 0, 1, 2, 3 \dots\}$
Rational Numbers: any number that can be
written in the form $\dfrac{a}{b}$, where "a" and "b"
are integers and $b \neq 0$.

Given the information above:

Statement **B** is incorrect: $\dfrac{5}{11}$ does not belong to the set of integral numbers (integers).

Statement **C** is incorrect: -20 and $\dfrac{5}{11}$ do not belong to the set of whole numbers.

Statement **D** is incorrect: -20, $\dfrac{5}{11}$, and 0 do not belong to the set of natural numbers. Statement **A** is correct; rational numbers include natural numbers, whole numbers, and integral numbers. All the numbers in the list given can be written as fractions.

$-20 = \dfrac{-20}{1}$; $\dfrac{5}{11}$; $0 = \dfrac{0}{1}$; $42 = \dfrac{42}{1}$; $24 = \dfrac{24}{1}$

6. **B**

We know that $3^2 = 9$ and $4^2 = 16$, and since 10 is between 9 and 16, the square root of 10 is between the whole numbers 3 and 4.
Therefore, the square root of 10 is either Q or R. Since 10 is closer to 9 than 16, then $\sqrt{10}$ is closer to 3 than it is 4.
Q is the best approximation.

7. **B**

To find the solution to $(5.2 \times 10^{-3}) \times (1.5 \times 10^{2})$, we can apply the commutative property of multiplication.
$5.2 \times 10^{-3} \times 1.5 \times 10^{2}$
$5.2 \times 1.5 \times 10^{-3} \times 10^{2}$ (Rearrange the order)
$\quad 5.2 \times 1.5 = 7.8$
$10^{-3} \times 10^{2} = 10^{-3+2}$
$\qquad\qquad = 10^{-1}$

The solution is 7.8×10^{-1}

8. **B**

Recall the probability formula:

$\text{Probability} = \dfrac{\text{number of favourable outcomes}}{\text{total number of outcomes}}$

The total number of outcomes is:
$20 + 15 + 15 + 8 + 2 = 60$
To find out the number of favourable outcomes, add the total number of blue bubble gums to the total number of green bubble gums; that is $15 + 20 = 35$.

Therefore, $P(\text{blue or green}) = \dfrac{35}{60}$
$\qquad\qquad\qquad\qquad\qquad = \dfrac{7}{12}$

9. **A**

The first step is to find the distance travelled during the 72 minutes of travel. To do this, set up a proportion:

$\dfrac{105 \text{ km}}{60 \text{ minutes}} = \dfrac{x}{72 \text{ minutes}}$

$\qquad x = \dfrac{105 \times 72}{60}$ (Cross multiply)

$\qquad x = 10.33 \text{ liters}$

$x = 126 \text{ km}$
Then, set up a proportion to find how many litres of gas used:

$\dfrac{8.2 \text{ litres}}{100 \text{ km}} = \dfrac{x}{126 \text{ km}}$

$\qquad x = \dfrac{8.2 \times 126}{100}$ (Cross multiply)

$\qquad x = 10.33 \text{ litres}$

10. **B**

We have to determine the number of different coins to solve this problem. The total value of all the coins is $3.75. Algebraically represent the number of different coins as:

$\qquad\qquad\qquad x = \text{number of quarters}$
then $\qquad\qquad 2x = \text{number of nickels}$
and $\qquad\qquad x - 3 = \text{number of dimes}$
The value of each coin is:
quarter $= 0.25$, nickel $= 0.05$, dime $= 0.10$

The total value of all:
   quarters = 0.25(x)
   nickels = 0.05($2x$)
   dimes = 0.10($x - 3$)
Now, set up an equation and solve for x.
$0.25(x) + 0.05(2x) + 0.10(x - 3) = 3.75$
$0.25x + 0.10x + 0.10x - 0.3 = 3.75$
$0.45x - 0.3 = 3.75$ (Simplify)
$0.45x - 0.3 + 0.3 = 3.75 + 0.3$ (Add 0.3 to
                                       both sides)

$$\frac{0.45x}{0.45} = \frac{4.05}{0.45}$$

$0.45x = 4.05$ (Divide both sides by 0.45)
      $x = 9$

The number of quarters is 9.
The number of nickels is $9 \times 2 = 18$.
The number of dimes is $9 - 3 = 6$.

11. A

Use the volume formula given.
Volume of container A:
$V = \pi r^2 h = (3.14)(2)^2(6)$
$V = 75.36$ cm^3
Volume of container B:
$V = \pi r^2 h = (3.14)(1.5)^2(10.0)$
$V = 70.65$ cm^3
Volume of container A minus volume of
container B is $75.36 - 70.65 = 4.71$ cm^3.

12. C

Examine the pattern more closely:

TIME	Number of chickens sick
9:00	3
9:30	5
10:00	7
10:30	9
11:00	11
11:30	13
12:00	15
12:30	17
1:00	19
1:30	21
2:00	23

There are 10 half-hour intervals and 2
chickens sick for each half-hour interval.
This results in 10×2 chickens sick.
Now, add the 3 chickens sick at 9:00 and
we have $3 + (2 \times 10)$, which equals 23.

13. C

Substituting value(s) of H in each equation
will lead us to the correct equation.
Recall that all values of H must satisfy the
equation.
Equation **A** is incorrect.
If $H = 3$, then $E = 18$.
Equation **B** is incorrect.
If $H = 4$, then $E = 25$.
Equation **D** is incorrect.
If $H = 2$, then $E = 7$
Equation **C** is correct for all values of H.
$E = 7(2) - 2 = 12$
$E = 7(3) - 2 = 19$
$E = 7(4) - 2 = 26$

14. A

The area of the wall that needs to be
painted is the area of the entire wall minus
the area of two windows.
Painting area
= Area of wall – area of the two windows
        $= (b \times h) - 2(b - h)$
        $= 8.5 \times 2.5 - 2(0.9 \times 0.7)$
        $= 21.25 - 1.26$
        $= 19.99$ m^2,
          which rounds to 20.0 m^2

15. A

Each of the last 2 digits can be
0, 1, 2, 3, 4, 5, 6, 7, 8, or 9
If the sixth digit is 0, then the seventh digit
can be any one of the 10 digits.
If the sixth digit is 1, the seventh digit can
be any one of the 10 digits.
Continue the process for each possible sixth
digit, then add the results together. You
will end up with

$$10 + 10 + 10 + 10 + 10 + 10$$
$$+ 10 + 10 + 10 + 10 = 100$$

Or
There are 10 possible sixth digits and 10
possible seventh digits. To find the total
number of possible arrangements of the
sixth and seventh digits, multiply.
$10 \times 10 = 100$

16. C

Given the information, set up a proportion.
(Remember to convert the altitude to
metres.)
$$\frac{24 \text{ m}}{1 \text{ s}} = \frac{3\,000 \text{ m}}{x}$$
$$x = \frac{1 \text{ s} \times 3\,000 \text{ m}}{24 \text{ m}}$$
$$x = 125 \text{ s}$$

17. B

To solve rate of work problems, we use the
formula:
$$\frac{x}{a} + \frac{x}{b} = 1$$
Let x = time needed if both machines work
together.
a and b are the two individual machine
times.

Therefore, $\left(\dfrac{x}{6}\right) + \left(\dfrac{x}{4}\right) = 1$

$$12\left(\frac{x}{6}\right) + 12\left(\frac{x}{4}\right) = 12(1) \quad \text{(Multiply each}$$
$$\text{term by LCD)}$$
$$\frac{12x}{6} + \frac{12x}{4} = 12$$
$$2x + 3x = 12$$
$$5x = 12 \quad \text{(Simplify)}$$
$$\frac{5x}{5} = \frac{12}{5} \quad \text{(Divide both sides by 5)}$$
$$x = 2.4 \text{ hours}$$

18. C

The diagram illustrates a right triangle.
We can use Pythagorean Theorem to find
the measure of the missing side of a right
triangle.
$c^2 = a^2 + b^2$
x is the hypotenuse, which is the unknown.
$x2 = (5.7)2 + (12.3)2$
$x2 = 32.49 + 151.29$
$x2 = 183.78$
$x = \sqrt{183.78}$
$x = 13.56 \text{ dm}$

19. A

From the angle of elevation (θ), we know
the opposite side (5.7 dm) and an adjacent
side (12.3 dm).
The trigonometric ratio involving the
opposite and adjacent is the tangent ratio.
$$\text{Tang} = \frac{\text{opposite}}{\text{adjacent}}$$
$$= \frac{5.7}{12.3}$$
$$= .463$$
Tang $\theta = 0.463$, then using $\tan^{-1}$, we get
$\theta \approx 24.9°$, or 25° to the nearest degree.

20. B

The sails of the two sailboards are similar,
which means that the ratio of corresponding
sides will be equal.

For sail I, the ratio of $\dfrac{3.25}{1.95}$ is $1.\overline{6}$.

The ratio of the corresponding sides of sail II is $\dfrac{2.50}{1.50}$, which is also $1.\overline{6}$.

Given this information, we can set up a proportion to solve for x.

$$\frac{x}{3.25} = \frac{2.0}{2.50}$$

$$x = \frac{(3.25)(2.0)}{2.50} \qquad \text{(Cross multiply)}$$

$$x = 2.6 \text{ m}$$

21. C

If we exclude the floor and the seams, we need to find the combined surface area of the walls and the roof.

From the diagram, we notice that there are four congruent rectangular walls with a base of 2.4 m and a height of 1.3 m.

Hence, area of the walls
$$\begin{aligned}
&= 4(2.4 \times 1.3) \\
&= 4 \,(3.12) \\
&= 12.48 \text{ m}^2
\end{aligned}$$

Since the roof is a square-based pyramid, this means we have four congruent triangular faces. The slant height of the triangular face is 1.8 m and the base of the triangular face is 2.4 m.

Hence, the area of the roof

$$= 4 \times \left(\frac{2.4 \times 1.8}{2} \right)$$

$$= 8.64 \text{ m}^2$$

$\therefore$ the total surface area
$$\begin{aligned}
&= 12.48 \text{ m}^2 + 8.64 \text{ m}^2 \\
&= 21.12 \text{ m}^2
\end{aligned}$$

22. D

The Smith family had budgeted to spend $80 per night for 5 nights. Their total budget for this camping trip is
$80 × 5 = $400.00.
The amount spent for the first four nights is
$30 + $95 + $45 + $70, which is $340.00.
To remain within budget, the family can only spend
$400 – $340 = $60 on their last night.

23. B

Examine the trend in each of the scatter plots.

Scatter plot **A** is incorrect because it shows more campers arrive earlier in the day. This is the reverse of what the owner observed.

Scatter plot **C** is incorrect. It displays approximately the same number of campers arriving throughout the day.

Scatter plot **D** shows no relationship between time of day and number of campers, so it is incorrect.

Scatter plot **B** is correct: The later the time of day, the more campers arrive.

24. C

The distance from the outdoor stage to the shower building is the hypotenuse of the right triangle. The 30 m distance from the small store to the outdoor stage is opposite the 52° angle.

The trigonometric ratio that involves the opposite side and the hypotenuse is the sine ratio.

Therefore, $\sin 52° = \dfrac{\text{opposite}}{\text{hypotenuse}}$

$$0.788 \approx \frac{30 \text{ m}}{x}$$

Multiplying both sides by x, we get
$$0.788x \approx 30$$
Dividing both sides by 0.788, we get
$$x = 38 \text{ m}$$

25. A

Complete the pattern that has been started.

Month	Quarters
1	2
2	4
3	8
4	16
5	32
6	64
7	128
8	256
9	512
10	1 024
11	2 048
12	4 096

× 2 (between each row)

The 12th month shows 4 096 quarters.

NR1. To determine the savings, we need to calculate the total car repair costs of each company.

A-1 Car Repair:
$$\text{Cost} = \$31.60 \ (6 \text{ hours}) + \$45$$
$$= \$189.60 + \$45$$
$$= \$234.60$$

Classix Car Repair:
$$\text{Cost} = \$41.70 \ (5 \text{ hours}) + \$30$$
$$= \$208.50 + \$30$$
$$= \$238.50$$
$$\text{Savings} = \$238.50 - \$234.60$$
$$= \$3.90$$

NR2. To find the area of a rectangle, we multiply the length by the width.

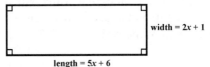

Substitute the value 4 m for x to determine the length and width.

$$\text{length} = 5x + 6$$
$$= 5(4) + 6$$
$$= 20 + 6$$
$$= 26 \text{ m}$$

$$\text{width} = 2x + 1$$
$$= 2(4) + 1$$
$$= 8 + 1$$
$$= 9 \text{ m}$$

$$\text{Area} = \text{length} \times \text{width}$$
$$= (26 \text{ m}) \times (9 \text{ m})$$
$$= 234 \text{ m}^2$$

Or
$$A = (5x + 6)(2x + 1)$$
$$= 10x^2 + 5x + 12x + 6 \quad \text{(FOIL)}$$
$$A = 10x^2 + 17x + 6$$

If $x = 4$ m, then we have

$$A = 10(4)^2 + 17(4) + 6$$
$$= 10(16) + 17(4) + 6$$
$$A = 160 + 68 + 6 = 234 \text{ m}^2$$

GLOSSARY OF TERMS

acute angle: an angle measuring less than 90°

acute triangle: a triangle with three angles measuring less than 90°

additive inverse: the number that is added to an original number to yield a sum of 0. (–2) is the additive inverse of (2) : (-2) + (2) = 0

algebraic expression: an expression containing a variable or variables (*a*, *b*, *c*...) and/or numbers (-1, 3, 14...), and/or operational symbols (+, ×...).
Example: $3x + 5y^2$

altitude: a line segment perpendicular to the base of a figure to the opposite side or vertex

angle: the point of intersection of two rays or line segments

angle of depression: the angle formed by the horizontal and the line of sight to something below the horizontal

angle of elevation: the angle formed by the horizontal and the line of sight to something above the horizontal

angle of rotation: the degrees and direction that a figure rotates

area: the space within a region measured in square units

average: the mean of a set of numbers, found by summing all numbers in the group and dividing by the number of members in the group

axis: either of the number lines on a graph that intersect at the origin

bar notation: a horizontal bar over a decimal digit or digits to signify repetition

base: the side or face of a polygon or solid from which an altitude rises

base (of a power): the number in a power used as a factor for multiplication (see exponent). In the power 9^3, the base is 9.

BEDMAS or PEDMAS: an acronym for Brackets or Parentheses, Exponents, Division, Multiplication, Addition, Subtraction, designating the order of operations

binomial: a polynomial with exactly two terms

bisector: a ray or line segment that divides an angle or line into two equal parts

box-and-whisker plot: organization of data within a horizontal plot showing distribution of values in each quartile

capacity: the greatest volume a container can hold

centre of rotation: the point around which a figure rotates

chord: a line segment connecting two points on the circumference of a circle

circle: a collection of points in a plane that are an equal distance from a fixed point (centre).

circle or pie graph: a circular diagram used to display data

circumference: the measure of the distance around a circle (the perimeter of a circle)

clockwise: rotating in the same direction as the hands of a clock

coefficient (numerical): the numerical part of a term that determines the factor by which the variable is multiplied. In $13x$, the numerical coefficient is 13.

coefficient (variable): the variable part of a term that determines the factor by which the numerical portion is multiplied. In $13x$, the variable coefficient is x.

common denominator: a number that is a multiple of all of the denominators of a set of fractions

common factor: a number that can be evenly divided into each number within a set of given numbers

common multiple: a number that is a multiple of two or more numbers

complementary angles: two angles whose sum is exactly 90°

composite number: a number with a minimum of three factors including 1 and itself

cone: a solid formed by the convergence of points from a circular base to a single point

congruent: figures having the same shape and size

constant or constant term: a number by itself

coordinate plane: a two-dimensional surface across which a number line extends horizontally (the x-axis) and is intersected by a number line extending vertically (the y-axis)

coordinates: the numbers on a coordinate plane that signify the value of x and the value of y for a given point on the plane

corresponding angles/sides: angles and sides that have the same relative positions in two or more geometric figures

cosine: a measure in a right triangle that is the ratio of the side adjacent to the hypotenuse, for either of the acute angles in the triangle

counterclockwise: rotating in the direction opposite to that of the hands of a clock

cube: a solid with six square faces

cylinder: a solid with two parallel, congruent, circular bases

data: facts, statistics, or bits of information

database: an organized collection of data

degree (of an angle): the unit (°) for measuring angles with 1° equal to $\dfrac{1}{360}$ of a circle

degree of a monomial: the exponent of the variable or the sum of all exponents

degree of a polynomial: the highest sum of the exponents of the variables in any one term of the polynomial

denominator: the term below the line in a fraction by which the numerator is divided (see numerator)

density: the mass per unit volume of a substance

diagonal: a line connecting two non-adjacent vertices of a figure

diameter: the longest distance connecting two points on a circle and passing through the centre

dilatation: a transformation in which the image is either enlarged or reduced but maintains the same shape

elevation: a two-dimensional view of a figure from either of six perspectives (top, bottom, left, right, front, or back)

enlargement: a dilatation where the resulting image is larger than the original figure

equation: an arrangement of two expressions so that one side is equal to the other

equidistant: points that are the same distance apart

equilateral triangle: a triangle with three equal sides

estimate: an approximate judgment, opinion, or answer

evaluate: to find the value of an expression by substituting values for variables

experimental probability: the probability of an outcome based on experimental results

exponent: a number, shown in a smaller size and raised, that tells how many times the number before it (the base) is used as a factor; for example, 2 is the exponent in 6^2 (see base (of a power)).

face: any surface of a solid

factoring: to write as a product of two or more factors

factor: numbers or expressions that are multiplied to form another number or expression

flow chart: a diagram depicting the steps involved in solving a problem

FOIL: an acronym for First terms, Outside terms, Inside terms, and Last terms, which relates to one sequence for multiplying the terms of one binomial by a second binomial

formula: an equation that shows a general relationship

fraction: an indicated quotient of two quantities that represents part of a whole or a group

frequency: the number of times a particular number or event occurs

Greatest Common Factor (GCF): the largest factor common to two or more numbers

hectare: a unit of area equal to 10 000 m^2

histogram: a graph that uses bars representing continuous displays of data

hypotenuse: the side of a right triangle that is opposite to the right angle

image: the resulting figure from a transformation

independent events: two or more events that are not influenced by each other

inequality: an arrangement of two expressions so that one side is greater than the other

integers: the set of numbers... –3, –2, –1, 0, +1, +2, +3,...

interest: the amount earned on investments, usually at a predetermined percentage rate

intersecting lines: lines with one point in common; the point of intersection

interval: a distance or space between values

irrational number: a number that cannot be written in the form $\frac{m}{n}$, where m and n are integers (n is not equal to 0)

isometric view: an object represented three-dimensionally

isosceles triangle: a triangle with two equal sides

light-year: the distance light travels in one year, used for measuring astronomical distances

like terms: terms having the same variables

line of best fit: a line that passes as close as possible to points plotted on a graph

line segment: the part of a line between two points

lowest common denominator (LCD): the lowest of all multiples shared by two or more numbers

mapping: a correspondence of points or figures that has undergone a transformation

mass: the amount of matter in an object

mean: the sum of all numbers in a group divided by the number of members in the group

median: in a set of data arranged in numerical order, the value that has an equal number of values above it as it has below it

median of a triangle: a line from the vertex to the midpoint of the opposite side

midpoint: a point that divides a line segment into two equal parts

mode: the value that occurs most frequently in a set of data

monomial: a polynomial with only one term

multiples: the product of two or more numbers

multiplicative inverses: the number that is multiplied to an original number to yield a product of 1, also called the reciprocal

natural numbers: the set of numbers 1, 2, 3, 4, 5,...

negative number: any number less than 0

net: a pattern that, when folded, makes a three-dimensional object

non-repeating decimal: a decimal representation without repetition

non-terminating decimal: a decimal representation that continues without end

numerator: the term above the line in a fraction into which the denominator is divided (see denominator)

obtuse angle: an angle measuring more than 90° and less than 180°

obtuse triangle: a triangle containing one angle greater than 90°

operation: any mathematical process or action such as addition, subtraction, multiplication, or division

order of magnitude: a quantity expressed as a power of 10

order of operations: the sequence of operations that are followed when simplifying or evaluating an expression (see BEDMAS)

ordered pair: a pair of numbers, (x, y), showing the coordinates of a point on a graph

origin: the point of intersection of the horizontal and vertical axes on a graph, defined as (0, 0)

outcome: a possible result of an experiment

parallel lines: lines in the same plane that are an equal distant apart

percent (%): a fraction or ratio with a denominator of 100

perimeter: the measure of the distance around a closed figure

perpendicular: intersecting at a 90° angle

perpendicular bisector: a line perpendicular to a line segment that divides it in two equal parts

perspective: the different views of an object (see elevation)

pi (π): the ratio of the circumference of a circle to its diameter, 3.14...

pictograph: a graph in which data is represented by a symbol or picture

plane geometry: the study of figures drawn on a coordinate plane.

polygon: a closed two-dimensional figure of three or more line segments

polynomial: a mathematical expression with one or more terms, integral exponents, and coefficients that are real numbers

population: the entire set of objects or people from which data can be taken

positive number: a number greater than 0

power: notation of a number with a base and an exponent (see base, exponent) such as a^n where a is called the base and n is called the exponent

prime number: a whole number with only two factors, itself and 1

prism: a solid formed by two congruent and parallel sides and other faces that are parallelograms (see face)

probability: the ratio of the number of favourable outcomes to the event to the total number of outcomes, where all outcomes are equally likely (see outcome)

proportion: two equal ratios

pyramid: a solid that has one face that is a polygon (the base) and triangular faces that have a common vertex

Pythagorean Theorem: in a right triangle, the square of the hypotenuse is equal to the sum of the squares of the other two sides

quadrant: any of the four regions of the coordinate plane formed by the two axes

quadrilateral: any polygon with four sides

radius (plural, radii): the distance from the centre of a circle to any point lying on the circumference of the circle (see diameter)

random number: any number selected by chance such as rolling a die or using the random function of a calculator or computer

random sample: a sample or survey in which all members of the population have an equal chance of being selected

range: the highest and lowest values in a set of data

rate: a certain quantity or amount relative to a different quantity or amount

ratio: a comparison of two or more quantities having similar units

rational number: a number that can be expressed as the quotient of two integers where the denominator is not 0

real numbers: the set of all rational and irrational numbers

reciprocals: two numbers whose product is 1

reduction: a dilatation where the resulting image is smaller than the original figure

reflection: a flip transformation in which all the points of the figure and the corresponding points of its image are an equal distance from the line across which it is reflected

reflex angle: an angle whose measure is between $180°$ and $360°$

regular polygon: a polygon with equal sides and angles

relative frequency: the number of times a particular outcome occurs related to the number of times the experiment is conducted

restriction: a condition or limitation placed on a variable

right angle: an angle measuring $90°$

right triangle: a triangle containing one angle that is $90°$

rotation: a transformation in which a figure is turned relative to a fixed point

sample: a representative portion of a given population

sample size: the number of items selected as a sample from the entire population

scalene triangle: a triangle without any equal sides

scatter plot: a collection of points on a graph that represents the data

scientific notation: a number expressed as the product n and a power of 10, where $-1 \le n \le 1$

similar figures: figures with the same shape, but not necessarily the same size or orientation

sine: the measure in a right triangle that is the ratio of the side opposite to the hypotenuse for either of the acute angles in the triangle

square of a number: any number multiplied by itself

square root: for any product, the factor which is multiplied by itself to get the product. For the product 16, the one factor that is multiplied by itself is +4 or −4, so ±4 are the square roots of 16

statistics: the study of mathematics related to the collection, organization, and interpretation of data

substitution: When a specific value is used in place of a variable in an algebraic expression

supplementary angles: two angles whose sum is $180°$

tangent: the measure in a right triangle that is the ratio of the side opposite to the side adjacent, for either of the acute angles in the triangle

term: each individual expression in a polynomial or equation

terminating decimal: any decimal whose digits terminate

theoretical probability: an outcome determined mathematically without conducting an experiment

three-dimensional: having length, width, and depth or height

transformation: any mapping of a figure that results in a change in position, shape, size, or appearance of the figure. Translations, rotations, reflections, and dilatations are transformations

translation: a transformation that moves a point or a figure to another position in the same plane

trigonometry: the study of the relationships among the sides and angles of triangles

trinomial: any polynomial with exactly three terms; for example, $4x^2 + 14x + 259$ is a trinomial

two-dimensional: having length and width

unit price: the price for a single unit or item

unlike terms: terms that have either different variables or exponents

variable: a letter or symbol that represents a changing quantity

vertex (plural, vertices): the point of convergence of two or more lines or sides in a figure or a solid

volume: the amount of space occupied by an object measured in cubic units

whole numbers: the set of numbers 0, 1, 2, 3...

x-axis: the horizontal number line on a coordinate plane

y-axis: the vertical number line on a coordinate plane

Formula Sheet

Laws of Exponents

$$x^a \times x^b = x^{a+b}$$

$$x^a \div x^b = x^{a-b}, \ x \neq 0$$

$$x^0 = 1, \ x \neq 0$$

$$x^{-a} = \frac{1}{x^a}, \ x \neq 0$$

$$(xy)^a = x^a y^a \ \text{(where } a \text{ is an integer)}$$

$$\left(\frac{x}{y}\right)^a = \left(\frac{x^a}{y^a}\right) \ (a \text{ is an integer}, \ y \neq 0)$$

$$(x^a)^b = x^{ab} \ (a \text{ and } b \text{ are integers})$$

Trigonometric Ratios

$$\text{Sine} = \frac{\text{Opposite}}{\text{Hypotenuse}}$$

$$\text{Cosine} = \frac{\text{Adjacent}}{\text{Hypotenuse}}$$

$$\text{Tangent} = \frac{\text{Opposite}}{\text{Adjacent}}$$

Probability of Event "A" =

$$\frac{\textit{Number of outcomes favourable to A}}{\textit{Total number of outcomes}}$$

Perimeter

Square = $4s$

Rectangle = $2l + 2w$

Circle = πd or $2\pi r$

Area

Square = s^2

Rectangle = lw

Triangle = $\frac{1}{2}bh$

Circle = πr^2

Trapezoid = $\frac{1}{2}(a+b)h$

Volume

Sphere = $\frac{4}{3}\pi r^3$

Cylinder = $\pi r^2 h$

Cone = $\frac{1}{3}\pi r^2 h$

Pyramid = $\frac{1}{3}abh$, (where a and b are the length and width of the rectangular base)

Rectangular Prism = lwh

Acceleration =

$$\frac{(\text{Final Velocity}) - (\text{Initial Velocity})}{\text{Time}}$$

Average Velocity =

$$\frac{\text{Distance Travelled}}{\text{Time}}$$

Acknowledgements

Photo Credits

page 25:   NASA

page 99:   NBA Enterprises

page 101: Pittsburgh Penguins

ORDERING INFORMATION

All School Orders

School Authorities are eligible to purchase these resources by applying the Learning Resource Credit Allocation (LRCA – 25% school discount) on their purchase through the Learning Resources Centre (LRC). Call LRC for details.

THE KEY Study Guides are specifically designed to assist students in preparing for unit tests, final exams, and provincial examinations.

KEY Study Guides – $29.95 each plus G.S.T.

SENIOR HIGH		JUNIOR HIGH	ELEMENTARY
Biology 30 Chemistry 30 English 30-1 English 30-2 Math 30 (Pure) Math 30 (Applied) Physics 30 Social Studies 30 Social Studies 33	Biology 20 Chemistry 20 English 20-1 Math 20 (Pure) Physics 20 Social Studies 20 English 10-1 Math 10 (Pure) Science 10 Social Studies 10	Language Arts 9 Math 9 Science 9 Social Studies 9 Math 8 Math 7	Language Arts 6 Math 6 Science 6 Social Studies 6 Math 4 Language Arts 3 Math 3

Student Notes and Problems (SNAP) Workbooks contain complete explanations of curriculum concepts, examples, and exercise questions.

SNAP Workbooks – $29.95 each plus G.S.T.

SENIOR HIGH		JUNIOR HIGH	ELEMENTARY
Chemistry 30 Math 30 Pure Math 30 Applied Math 31 Physics 30	Chemistry 20 Math 20 Pure Math 20 Applied Physics 20 Math 10 Pure Math 10 Applied Science 10	Math 9 Science 9 Math 8 Math 7	Math 6 Math 5 Math 4 Math 3

Visit our website for a "tour" of resource content and features at
www.castlerockresearch.com

Castle Rock Research Corp

#2340, 10180 – 101 Street
Edmonton, AB Canada T5J 3S4
e-mail: learn@castlerockresearch.com

Phone: 780.448.9619
Toll-free: 1.800.840.6224
Fax: 780.426.3917

2006 (3)

SCHOOL ORDER FORM

Castle Rock Research Corp

THE KEY	QUANTITY
Biology 30	
Chemistry 30	
English 30-1	
English 30-2	
Math30 (Pure)	
Math 30 (Applied)	
Physics 30	
Social Studies 30	
Social Studies 33	
Biology 20	
Chemistry 20	
English 20-1	
Math 20 (Pure)	
Physics 20	
Social Studies 20	
English 10-1	
Math 10 (Pure)	
Science 10	
Social Studies 10	
Language Arts 9	
Math 9	
Science 9	
Social Studies 9	
Math 8	
Math 7	
Language Arts 6	
Math 6	
Science 6	
Social Studies 6	
Math 4	
Math 3	
Language Arts 3	

SNAP WORKBOOKS
Notes and Problems/
Student Notes and Problems

	QUANTITY	
	Workbooks	Solutions Manuals
Chemistry 30		
Chemistry 20		
Physics 30		
Physics 20		
Math 30 Pure		
Math 30 Applied		
Math 31		
Math 20 Pure		
Math 20 Applied		
Math 10 Pure		
Math 10 Applied		
Science 10		
Science 9		
Math 9		
Math 8		
Math 7		
Math 6		
Math 5		
Math 4		
Math 3		

TOTALS

KEYS	
WORKBOOKS	
SOLUTION MANUALS	

Learning Resources Centre

Castle Rock Research is pleased to announce an exclusive distribution arrangement with the Learning Resources Centre (LRC). Under this agreement, schools can now place all their orders with LRC for order fulfillment. As well, these resources are eligible for applying the Learning Resource Credit Allocation (LRCA), which gives schools a 25% discount off LRC's selling price. Call LRC for details.

Orders may be placed with LRC by
telephone: (780) 427-5775
fax: (780) 422-9750
internet: www.lrc.learning.gov.ab.ca
or mail: 12360 - 142 Street NW
Edmonton, AB T5L 4X9

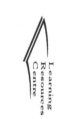
Learning Resources Centre

PAYMENT AND SHIPPING INFORMATION

Name: _____

School Telephone: _____

SHIP TO
School: _____
Address: _____
City: _____ Postal Code: _____

PAYMENT
☐ by credit card
VISA/MC Number: _____
Name on Card: _____ Expiry Date: _____
☐ enclosed cheque
☐ invoice school P.O. number: _____

#2340, 10180 – 101 Street, Edmonton, AB T5J 3S4   Tel: 780.448.9619   Fax: 780.426.3917
email: learn@castlerockresearch.com   Toll-free: 1.800.840.6224

www.castlerockresearch.com